CHILD LAW
FOR SOCIAL WORK

CHILD LAW
FOR SOCIAL WORK

JANE WILLIAMS

Los Angeles • London • New Delhi • Singapore

SAGE Publications Ltd
1 Oliver's Yard
55 City Road
London EC1Y 1SP

SAGE Publications Inc.
2455 Teller Road
Thousand Oaks, California 91320

SAGE Publications India Pvt Ltd
B 1/I 1 Mohan Cooperative Industrial Area
Mathura Road
New Delhi 110 044

SAGE Publications Asia-Pacific Pte Ltd
33 Pekin Street #02-01
Far East Square
Singapore 048763

Library of Congress Control Number: 2007939013

British Library Cataloguing in Publication data

A catalogue record for this book is available from the British
Library

ISBN 978-1-4129-0803-0
ISBN 978-1-4129-0804-7 (pbk)

Typeset by Cepha Imaging Pvt Ltd, Bangalore, India
Printed in Great Britain by The Cromwell Press Ltd,
Trowbridge, Wiltshire
Printed on paper from sustainable resources

CONTENTS

ALPHABETICAL LIST OF CASES

ALPHABETICAL LIST OF INTERNATIONAL INSTRUMENTS

ALPHABETICAL LIST OF STATUTES

ACTS OF PARLIAMENT

Adoption Act 1976   36, 51, 56, 197
Adoption and Children Act 2002   36, 39, 56, 80, 87, 98, 117, 119, 156,
    165, 180, 196, 198, 200, 202, 204, 206, 207, 208, 209, 212, 214, 215,
    216, 217, 218
Adoption (Inter Country Aspects) Act 1999   56
Anti-social Behaviour Act 2003   232, 233, 234, 240
Care Standards Act 2000   13, 36, 51, 81, 82, 109, 204
Carers and Disabled Children Act 2000   115, 125
Child Abduction and Custody Act 1985   53, 56
Childcare Act 2006   36, 70
Children Act 1948   35, 36
Children Act 1989   22, 25, 26, 27, 32, 35, 36, 37, 51,57, 70, 71, 72, 85, 87,
    92, 93, 97, 98, 108, 115, 116, 117, 121, 124, 128, 132, 133, 141, 142,
    143, 146, 148, 149, 152, 153, 168, 170, 183, 185, 202, 204, 213, 214,
    228, 234, 239, 242, 253; s. 1: 90, 147, 165, 168, 170, 179, 206, 213;
    s. 2: 117; s. 3: 116; s. 10: 207; s. 4: 117; s. 8: 117, 206, 207, 209, 211, 217;
    s. 14A–14G: 208, 209, 218; s. 17: 39, 60, 74, 76, 92, 94, 125, 126, 128,
    129, 130, 133–42, 144, 145, 227, 241, 243; s. 17A: 137; s. 20: 76, 139–40,
    142, 144, 157, 194, 206; s. 21: 194; s. 22: 27, 197, 198, 199, 204, 205,
    206, 242, 256; s. 23: 144, 205; s. 23A–E: 218; s. 24A–D: 218; s. 25: 18,
    199, 202; s. 26: 76, 80, 125, 164, 196, 199, 209, 255; s. 26A: 80, 196,
    199; s. 27: 93, 133; s. 33: 202, 207, 209; s. 31: 117, 118, 152, 154, 156,
    167, 173–5, 178–82, 189, 191, 193, 232, 234; s. 34: 149, 198, 205, 215,
    217, 218; s. 36: 155; s. 37: 174; s. 38: 155, 157, 174, 193; s. 38A: 157;
    s. 39: 211; s. 41: 148, 174; s. 43: 118, 154, 157, 161; s. 44: 118, 154, 157,
    161, 193; s. 44A: 157; s. 46: 117, 118, 151, 154, 159; s. 47: 93, 133, 151,
    153, 156, 157, 162, 164, 227, 233; s. 48: 93; s. 50: 118, 154; s. 67: 205;
    s. 83: 194; s. 86: 103; s. 91: 209; s. 92: 86; s. 98: 190, 191; Sched. 2: 129,
    130, 134, 137, 211, 242
Children Act 2004   22, 25, 26, 36, 45, 51, 56, 57, 61, 63, 64, 65, 67, 69,
    71, 77, 82, 84, 86, 90, 95, 106, 108, 109, 110, 120, 121, 123, 124, 128, 129,
    133, 143, 145, 149, 151, 152, 189, 193; s. 2: 83; s. 3: 96; s. 10: 96;

SECONDARY LEGISLATION

ACKNOWLEDGEMENTS

I would like to express my thanks to all the participants in the Swansea Family Court Inter Disciplinary Forum, from whom I have learned much over the last six years, and my colleagues on the Wales UNCRC monitoring group, especially its co-ordinator Rhian Croke. I am indebted to Professor Mary Hayes for invaluable encouragement and for comments on early drafts. Most of all I would like to thank my husband, Mike, without whose encouragement and support I would not have started, carried on or finished this book.

INTRODUCTION: HOW TO USE THIS BOOK

The mission of this book is to promote the practical implementation of rights-based social work policy and practice. It seeks to encourage a rights-based focus on the way in which the legal framework is understood and employed and to explain why this approach is wholly consistent with – indeed, required by – social work values and legal imperatives.

Part One of the book discusses contextual matters and themes of general application in social work with children. This includes the relationship between social work values and law, and the role and significance of the Human Rights Act 1998 (HRA 1998), the European Convention on Human Rights (ECHR) and the United Nations Convention on the Rights of the Child (UNCRC). It also includes structural and organisational issues, mechanisms for accountability, inter-agency working and confidentiality. Part Two employs the preceding discussion to inform and explain how law, interpreted through a rights-based focus, must inform social work practice in particular areas of intervention.

Since Part Two builds on Part One in this way, the reader will gain greater benefit if the book is read in the sequence in which it is presented, that is, Part One first. If time prevents this, however, the reader will find ample cross-referencing to relevant Part One discussion when dealing with the case-work issues in Part Two.

A brief Introduction to Part Two explains the key legal concept of parental responsibility and the terms 'voluntary engagement' and 'compulsory measures' which are used in Part Two to distinguish social work involvement which depends on the consent of the child and/or persons with parental responsibility from that which does not. It is explained that these terms are more accurate to describe what is being done in law, as well as in practice, than the now outmoded distinction between 'support for children and families' and 'child protection'. The Introduction to Part Two concludes by spelling out how a rights-based focus can be integrated into the social work process by adopting a particular approach to decision-making in individual cases.

The End Note to the book returns to its overarching mission. Drawing on an argument presented at greater length elsewhere (Williams, 2007), it asserts the critical significance of the approach taken by social workers in the daily exercise of their functions in relation to children and families. It points out that the decisions and actions taken in daily social work practice affect far more people than even the totality of court decisions, administrative appeals, complaints processes and other mechanisms for accountability. Whilst acknowledging the constraints imposed by resource, organisational and policy issues, it concludes with an exhortation to practitioners actively to engage, through local, sub-national activity, in the supra-national reporting and monitoring process of the UNCRC. It suggests this as a means of looking beyond current barriers to implementation, contributing their professional experience to the pool of evidence on which further necessary policy changes may be made, whether at local, national or even international levels of governance.

The law is stated as at September 2007, and is the law applying in England and Wales. Wherever relevant, attention is drawn to differences in law and policy between Wales and England, the majority of central government responsibilities relevant to social work having transferred to the Welsh Assembly under the Government of Wales Act 1998. At the time of writing, a new phase in Welsh devolution, pursuant to the Government of Wales Act 2006, is set to facilitate further differentiation in the legal and policy framework for social work with children and families. Practitioners on either side of the border will ignore this at their peril!

Part One

Context and Themes

1

Law, Social Work and Children

- **Introduction: legal values and social work values in child care practice**
  Common values of law and social work
  Values for child care social work practice
  *Where the tensions arise: interpretation of values and principles, and
  functional differences*
- **The functions of law and the functions of social work**
  A definition of social work
  A definition of law?
  *Duty and discretion: the role of the law and the role of the child and family
  social worker*
  Exercise of discretion: legal principles and requirements
  The welfare principle
  Standard-setting
  Human rights
  Law's functions and social work's values
- **Law and the principles of human rights**
  Where does human rights law come from?
  The ECHR
  The UNCRC
  Impact on social work
- **Law and the principles of social justice**
  What is social justice?
  Social justice and human rights
  Using human rights law to promote social justice
- **Law, professional integrity and accountability**
  How does law support these values?
  The rule of law
  The meaning of 'accountability'
  Openness and impartiality
- **Lawyers and social workers**
  Inter-disciplinary working: from good practice to good law?
  Child and family social workers: law enforcers or human rights campaigners?
- **Law, social work and the child**
  Theorising children and childhood
  The child and family social worker's dilemma
- **Conclusion**

Introduction: legal values and social work values in child care practice

The purposes of this chapter are to describe the respective functions of law and social work with children, to identify common values underlying the two disciplines and to introduce some concepts and themes that run throughout the book. Some of these concepts and themes are illustrated by examples drawn from case-law and legislation that will be explained in more detail in later chapters.

Law both enables and constrains the practice of social work with children and families. Law provides:

- authority: law confers on social workers authority to take action which would otherwise, in many situations, constitute an unlawful interference in private and family life; and
- principles: law imports principles, rooted in legal values, which are applied in interpreting rules and in assessing the legality of social work decisions.

Common values of law and social work

There is substantial commonality between the underlying values of the disciplines of law and social work. In particular, law provides a set of rules of obvious relevance to the social work value of human dignity and worth, by providing a code of internationally recognised human rights. Less obviously, the same set of rules may help promote the rather more uncertain value of social justice. Legal values such as the rule of law, equality under the law, accountability and fairness/due process can also be seen as supportive of the social work values of integrity and competence. Box 1.1 illustrates this.

Values for child care social work practice

The National Occupational Standards for Child Care at Post Qualifying Level (NOSCCPQ) contain a statement of 'child care values for social work practice' which makes explicit links with some of the legal values and legal rules shown in Box 1.1. The child care values are stated to be 'drawn from the UN Convention on the Rights of the Child and human rights legislation' (Sector Skills Council, 2005: 8). Box 1.2 notes the relevant UNCRC articles in relation to the list of values in the NOSCCPQ.

As the NOSCCPQ state, 'values are integral to rather than separate from good practice' (Sector Skills Council, 2005: 8). This link between social work standards and legal values and rules makes effective and proactive promotion of the rights of children and families, understood in terms of the UNCRC and ECHR, a measure of professional competence as well as a legal obligation. At the level of values and principles, this suggests a close affinity between the two disciplines.

Box 1.1   VALUES AND RULES

Social work value (from the British Association of Social Workers Code of Ethics)	Legal values	Legal rules
Human dignity and worth	Protection of individual liberty	The common law (trespass, false imprisonment, etc.)
	Respect for fundamental human rights	Human Rights Act 1998 European Convention on Human Rights, United Nations Convention on the Rights of the Child
	Equality	Anti-discrimination, equality and human rights legislation
Social justice	Respect for fundamental human rights	Interpretation of international human rights and children's rights obligations, imposing a positive duty on the State to provide for and protect the exercise of rights by all persons
Integrity and competence	Rule of law	Social work interventions require lawful authority, especially where they involve compulsion. Authority is provided by legislation, for example the Children Act 1989
	Equality under the law	Social workers must comply with the law and have no special immunity from legal action
	Accountability	Social work actions may be challenged in the courts or may be the subject of complaints under statutory procedures

(Continued)

Social work value (from the British Association of Social Workers Code of Ethics)	Legal values	Legal rules
	Fairness/ due process	Social workers must act fairly and transparently: those whose rights and interests are at stake have a right to participate effectively in decision-making processes

---

Box 1.2   VALUES FOR CHILD CARE SOCIAL WORK PRACTICE: NATIONAL OCCUPATIONAL STANDARDS FOR CHILD CARE AT POST QUALIFYING LEVEL

- children's and young people's best interests shall be of primary consideration in all actions affecting them (Article 3 UNCRC);
- children and young people are enabled to develop and achieve their full potential (Articles 6, 24–29 UNCRC);
- children and young people have the right to express their views and have them taken into account in all matters affecting them (Article 12 UNCRC);
- children and young people should remain, wherever possible, within their family and community networks (Articles 9, 18 UNCRC);
- children and young people are to be protected from and empowered to address all forms of discrimination (Article 2 UNCRC);
- children and young people are to be protected from and empowered to address all forms of abuse (Article 19 UNCRC);
- children and young people have the right to be given proper care by those looking after them (Articles 18, 20 UNCRC);
- children and young people with disabilities must be helped to be as independent as possible and to be able to play a full and active part in everyday life (Article 23 UNCRC);
- children and young people should have their identity affirmed through the promotion of their religious, cultural, racial and linguistic background (Articles 8, 20, 30 UNCRC);
- children and young people in Wales have the right to receive services in the Welsh language (Article 30 UNCRC);
- children and young people have the right to services which are free from prejudice (Article 2 UNCRC).

In practice, despite this commonality of underlying values, there can be tension between lawyers and social workers. This flows in part from functional, structural and organisational differences. It also flows from traditional and counter-traditional views of children and childhood, which play differently into different areas of law and practice: for example, when dealing with child protection or youth justice. Lawyers and social workers alike are influenced by their own personal experiences and perspectives as well as the professional culture in which they work. Mutual, enhanced understanding of the roles, functions, views and traditions of practitioners in the different disciplines is important if inter-disciplinary working, which is a statutory requirement under the Children Act 1989 and Children Act 2004 as well as a professional objective, is to deliver the hoped-for benefits.

The functions of law and the functions of social work

A definition of social work

Despite the common ground between social work values and legal values, the two disciplines clearly have different functions and the focus of professional practice in each is, necessarily, different. The definition of social work agreed by the International Federation of Social Workers and adopted by the British Association of Social Workers (BASW) says that it is:

> a profession which promotes social change, problem solving in human relationships and the empowerment and liberation of people to enhance well-being. Utilising theories of human behaviour and social systems, social work intervenes at the points where people interact with their environments. Principles of human rights and social justice are fundamental to social work. (BASW, 2003)

It is clear from this that social work is concerned with outcomes: with effecting change in people's lives, improving their well-being, enabling them to 'interact with their environments' more successfully. This may mean being able to improve their family relationships, the material condition of their lives, their physical and emotional health and so on.

A definition of law?

There is no generally accepted definition of 'law'. The question 'What is law?' has been addressed by many legal philosophers, sometimes by avoiding the question or transforming it into a description of legal rules and activities that can be contrasted with other forms of obligations and activities. However, law is often seen as being concerned pre-eminently with authority and process rather than outcomes. In the field of public law, where the interaction between law and social work with children and families is for the most part situated, law confers authority for social work action (by means of statutory powers and duties) and provides supervision over the process of its exercise (by means of mechanisms such as statutory complaints procedures, statutory appeals or judicial review). The law is generally constructed and applied in a way which confers discretion on those empowered to act (social workers or, formally, local authorities carrying out social services functions), reserving to the legal system the role of ensuring, in the event of challenge, that this discretion is properly interpreted and applied.

Duty and discretion: the role of the law and the role of the child and family social worker

The general principle is that the courts should not trespass into the area of discretion which Parliament has conferred on local authority social work teams. This is in part because of the constitutional concept of the separation of powers which holds that the legislative, executive and judicial functions of the State must each be confined to their proper role. Thus, once Parliament (the 'legislative' function) has created a system whereby discretion is conferred on local authorities (the 'executive' function), the courts (the 'judicial' function) should not interfere in a way that undermines the legislative intention or substitutes the court's own judgment for that of the local authority. The quotation from Lord Nicholls in *Re S, Re W* [2002] in Box 1.3 neatly demonstrates this principle. The case concerned the court's role in keeping under review the implementation of care plans. The judgment contributed to legislative changes, dealt with in Chapter 8. Here, the case is used simply to demonstrate the careful demarcation of functions between the courts and local authorities, in this case under the Children Act 1989.

Exercise of discretion: legal principles and requirements

This neat division between authority, process and outcomes is, however, over-simplistic as a description of the way in which law impacts on social work. In the same speech in *Re S, Re W*, Lord Nicholls went on to point out that the Children Act 1989 confers certain key outcome-oriented decisions on the court rather than on the local authority, notably the decision whether a care order should be made. Furthermore, law enshrines principles and sets standards which must be adhered to in the course of social work interventions in the lives of children and their families. Such principles and standards help to resolve the tensions inherent in social work practice with children, in the sense that the application of the relevant principle or adherence to the relevant standard will provide direction and enable a decision to be made.

Box 1.3 *RE S, RE W* [2002], EXTRACT FROM THE JUDGMENT OF LORD NICHOLLS

... the 1989 Act gave effect to a policy decision on the appropriate division of responsibilities between the courts and local authorities ... The particular strength of the court lies in the resolution of disputes: its ability to hear all sides of a case, to decide issues of fact and law, and to make a firm decision on a particular issue at a particular time. But a court cannot have day-to-day responsibility for a child. The court cannot deliver the services which may best serve a child's needs. Unlike a local authority, a court does not have close, personal and continuing knowledge of the child. The court cannot respond with immediacy and informality to practical problems and changed circumstances as they arise. Supervision by the court would encourage 'drift' in decision-making, a perennial problem in children cases. Nor does a court have the task of managing the financial and human resources available to a local authority for dealing with all children in need in its area. The authority must manage these resources in the best interests of all the children for whom it is responsible.

These tensions are somewhat glossed over in the language of empowerment and individual liberty in the definition of social work cited above. There is often a tension between empowering and enabling one person and protecting another person. For example, the aim of empowering a parent to overcome various forms of disadvantage may come into conflict with the aim of protecting her child from the risk of significant harm as a result of her inadequate parenting, itself a consequence of those disadvantages. Equally, there may be a tension between empowering and protecting the same person, for example where that person is a teenager whose views as to his own best interests are in conflict with those of his social worker.

The welfare principle

The longest-serving example of a legal principle which is designed to resolve such tensions is the welfare principle enshrined in s. 1 Children Act 1989. This has the effect that in many cases falling to be decided by the courts, conflicts between competing interests will be resolved in favour of the solution that best serves the welfare of the child. Although this 'paramountcy' of welfare is confined to court decisions, the 1989 Act also imposes on local authorities duties to safeguard and promote the welfare of children: for example, s. 17(1) (general duty to provide services for children in need), s. 22(3) (general duty in relation to looked after children) and s. 47(1) (duty to investigate).

The welfare principle thus provides a criterion for taking action (or for doing nothing). So here, law is determining a particular outcome, not just providing authority and process. There is still scope for the exercise of discretion and judgement by the individual social worker and social work teams, especially in relation to a decision to instigate any legal process and in relation to the kind of support to be given or other action to be taken, but closer examination of the statutory provisions reveals that here too the law provides both direction and constraint as to how this discretion is to be exercised. Box 1.4 illustrates this in relation to the duty of a local authority to provide services for children in their area who are in need, under s. 17 Children Act 1989. The general duty is triggered by the principle that children's welfare should be protected. In carrying out that duty, the local authority is given discretion to act, the exercise of which is itself governed by specific statutory requirements or limitations.

Box 1.4 DUTY/DISCRETION

Statutory provision	Duty	Discretion	Qualifications on discretion
Section 17(1)(a) Children Act 1989	Local authority must provide a range and level of services to safeguard and promote the welfare of children in need	What services to provide	The Children Act 1989, Sched. 2, sets out certain services to be provided and other steps to be taken by local authority
		How to assess need	Local authorities must act in accordance with statutory guidance unless they can show good reason to depart from it
		How to apply in an individual case	The Children Act 1989, s.17(8), requires means testing before giving assistance in kind or in cash

While some criteria prescribed by law are general principles, like the welfare principle, others are highly specific, leaving less discretion to the person charged with making decisions or taking action. Prescription of standards, accompanied by inspection and enforcement mechanisms, is something of a growth industry. There is a raft of statutory regulation imposing detailed standards on child care practice across all kinds of children's services, with associated machinery for investigation and complaint. The Care Standards Act 2000 added substantially to legal regulation of this kind, as illustrated in Box 1.5.

Human rights

On top of all of this, or rather, integrated throughout, is the legal requirement to act in a way which is compatible with human rights principles. This has been a legal requirement since the coming into force of the Human Rights Act 1998, which impacts on all acts and decisions of public bodies. 'Human rights' in this context means the rights and freedoms guaranteed by the European Convention on Human Rights, to which the 1998 Act was designed to give further effect.

Box 1.5   CHILDREN'S HOMES

A children's home is a home that provides accommodation wholly or mainly for children. Children may be placed in a children's home either under a voluntary arrangement or in the exercise of authority conferred by a court order. All children's homes must be registered. Arrangements for registration are governed by the Care Standards Act 2000 and are administered in England by the National Care Standards Commission and in Wales by the Care Standards Inspectorate for Wales. National Minimum Standards are prescribed for the purposes of registration and inspection by these bodies. They run to some 36 standards, ranging from management and staffing, physical design and environment and quality of care to procedures for complaints, protection and representation. Failure to meet these standards may result in refusal or revocation of registration. In addition, the Children's Homes Regulations 2001 (for England) and the Children's Homes Regulations (Wales) 2002, made under the Care Standards Act 2000 by the Secretary of State and the Welsh Assembly respectively, lay down detailed requirements about the running of children's homes and the treatment of children therein. Contravention of these Regulations may result in criminal prosecution.

Law's functions and social work values

Thus the law works in various ways to direct, constrain, influence and review social work with children. Law impacts on substantive decisions directed at outcomes as well as on process, so that the role and functions of social work with children are to a large extent defined by law. Yet the law can equally be seen as an instrument to be used by social workers to promote social work values in general and child care values in particular. To demonstrate this, we need to return to these social work values and consider further how they are supported by law.

Law and the principles of human rights

The influence of human rights law on social work with children is evident in case-law, legislation, policy and practice. As already observed, there is an explicit link between child care values for social work, the UNCRC and human rights legislation. The potential impact of international human rights law on the legal framework for social work with children in England and Wales is hard to overstate, although it should immediately be added that this potential has not yet been fully realised nor is it adequately reflected in relevant legislation and guidance. It is essential that social workers acquire a familiarity with the way human rights law operates, not only to ensure that their actions are lawful, but also to be able to deploy it in pursuance of their professional duties: to develop and maintain practice which is 'founded on, informed by and capable of being judged against a clear value base' (Sector Skills Council, 2005: 8), rooted in the promotion of human rights and children's rights in particular.

Where does human rights law come from?

The main source of human rights law is international law. It is the result of agreements (normally called treaties or conventions) entered into after negotiation and agreement between national governments, national and international organisations. These agreements are binding in international law (that is, the law which governs relations between nation States) once they are 'ratified' by a State Party. Their provisions may also be integrated into national, or 'domestic', law, so as to become part of the law regulating the conduct of individuals within the State and the relationship between the State and the individual. This happens if the national law of the State concerned so provides. The Human Rights Act 1998, which integrated into UK law most of the ECHR rights, is an example of this. When in 1997 the newly elected Labour Government chose the slogan 'Bringing Rights Home' to introduce its plans for what eventually became the 1998 Act, it was reflecting the dynamic relationship between international and domestic law. The ECHR was drafted by a process of negotiation and discussion in which the legal traditions and principles of the UK, as well as other States, played a part. Thus, for example, the concept of natural justice as developed in the UK courts contributed to the key 'due process' provision in Article 6 ECHR. In allowing the Convention rights so created to be enforced by courts within the UK, the Human Rights Act 1998 did, in this sense, 'bring rights home'.

Not only governments, but individuals and organisations providing front-line services, can and do feed into the process by which international legal standards are drawn up. The Convention which has the most obvious significance in relation to children – the UNCRC – is a good example of this. It originated in a proposal of the Polish Government in 1979, and was drawn up over the next decade, through a process of consensus-building at meetings of experts, legal advisers and drafters representing governments and non-governmental organisations. The UNCRC has become the most ratified international human rights convention ever: the only State in the world not to have signed up to it is the USA. As yet, the UK Government has not 'brought home' the rights contained in the UNCRC by passing a law integrating the UNCRC into domestic law but, as will be seen below and throughout this book, the UNCRC nonetheless has an increasing impact on domestic law and practice.

There are other international agreements relevant to social work practice with children, some of which are referred to in later chapters, but the ECHR and the UNCRC are the most important as sources of general human rights principles applicable to children. Reference to them will suffice for the present purpose of demonstrating the way in which the law can promote social work values in child care practice. Taken together, these two Conventions also introduce an important point about different enforcement mechanisms for international human rights law.

The ECHR

The ECHR was negotiated as the cornerstone human rights treaty of the Council of Europe following the Second World War. Its prime aim was to provide entrenched, constitutional protection for civil and political rights, on the premise that this would help prevent any future rise within Europe of terrible totalitarian regimes such as had been experienced in Nazi Germany. To that end, the Convention set out a code of individual rights and fundamental freedoms, applying to all persons from birth, and – this was and remains most unusual in an international treaty – established a right of individual petition to an international court, the European Court of Human Rights (ECtHR). This enabled a person in a member State who claimed to be a victim of a violation by a public authority of his or her Convention rights to bring the government of that member State to account and, if successful, to obtain a remedy. The number of cases brought before the ECtHR has grown enormously, especially since the Court's procedures were revised in 1998.

At first sight, the protection of individuals from totalitarian forms of government may seem rather remote from social work practice with children. Yet every social work intervention, be it in the course of providing support for families and children in need, producing sentencing reports or supporting a child in criminal proceedings, taking emergency action to remove a child from danger or applying for a care or supervision order, engages the 'Convention rights' of the child, usually engages the Convention rights of members of the child's family and may also engage the Convention rights of other members of the wider community. Even doing nothing may engage these rights, as seen in the case of *Z v United Kingdom* [2001] (Box 1.6).

Box 1.6   DUTY TO SAFEGUARD HUMAN RIGHTS

As seen in Box 1.4 above, the Children Act 1989 confers discretion on the local authority, and in exercising that discretion the local authority must comply with supplementary provisions in the 1989 Act itself and with statutory guidance. In addition, the local authority, and any social worker acting on its behalf, is under a legal duty to act in a way which is compatible with Convention rights: s. 6 Human Rights Act 1998. This may mean that, in some circumstances, a 'mere' discretion is effectively converted into a duty to take a particular course. *Z v United Kingdom* [2001] concerned the availability of a legal remedy where a local authority was alleged to have violated the right of a child to be protected from inhuman or degrading treatment under Article 3 ECHR. The ECtHR accepted that this right could be violated where a local authority failed to exercise its discretion under the Children Act 1989 to apply for a care order so that the children could be removed from the family home where they were, to the knowledge of the local authority, suffering extreme domestic abuse. The statutory discretion, when read in conjunction with the relevant human rights obligations, could in this situation become, in effect, a duty to act.

The significance of this has been magnified many times over since the coming into force of the Human Rights Act 1998. Before then, there was always the possibility that a challenge based on breach of a person's Convention rights could be made, but recourse had first to be made to domestic legal procedures, including any possible appeals. Thereafter the route to the ECtHR in Strasbourg was notoriously long, expensive and slow. Furthermore, the domestic courts were not obliged to give effect to the Convention rights. The Convention could be brought into a legal argument before the courts in England and Wales only where some ambiguity existed in domestic law: then, the courts would apply a long-established interpretive rule favouring consistency with the UK's international obligations. Nor were public authorities such as local authorities and those acting on their behalf, like social workers, under any direct duty to act compatibly with Convention rights. The law did not therefore impose a duty on social workers to respect human rights as such. The Human Rights Act 1998 changed all of this.

Most significant in terms of the legal framework for social work practice with children is the deceptively simple provision in s. 6(1) of the 1998 Act:

> It is unlawful for a public authority to act in a way which is incompatible with a Convention right.

The effect of this on social work practice with children is to require social workers to act in a way which is compatible with the Convention rights not only of the child with whom they are working but also others whose Convention rights are affected. Consequently, when considering what powers they have, and how they should set about exercising them, social workers need to refer to two sources of law: the domestic provision which confers authority to take specific steps, and the ECHR. Box 1.6 above provided one illustration of how this works in practice. The position is complicated by the fact that there may not be an obvious match between the domestic legislation and the provisions of the ECHR. In such a case, the courts will strive to interpret the domestic legislation in a way which is compatible with the ECHR, as illustrated in Box 1.7.

This example illustrates the need for intervention to be lawful under both domestic and ECHR law, and the importance of the courts' interpretation of both where there is not an obvious match between these two sources of law. It also demonstrates the way the courts strive to find a compatible interpretation, even when this is not immediately obvious when comparing the texts of domestic legislation and the Convention. As explained further in Chapter 2, this approach is expressly required by s. 3 of the Human Rights Act 1998.

The UNCRC

The antecedents of the UNCRC are different from those of the ECHR. The UNCRC is one of a number of human rights instruments negotiated and agreed within the United Nations, dealing with a particular category of persons deemed to be especially vulnerable or to have special needs. The idea of having an international agreement about children was first mooted by Eglantyne Jebb, the remarkable woman who went on to co-found Save the Children. Horrified by her experience of the condition of many displaced and deprived children in Europe in the aftermath of the First World War, she campaigned within the newly established League of Nations (the forerunner to the United Nations) for an international declaration of children's rights. Her idea, simply, was that certain rights should be claimed for children and that these rights should be given universal recognition. The resultant 'Geneva' Declaration of the Rights of the Child, adopted by the League of Nations

Box 1.7   SECURE ACCOMMODATION

Where a child is being looked after by a local authority, the Children Act 1989 places constraints on placing her in secure accommodation: this can only be done where the criteria set out in s. 25 of the 1989 Act apply. These are that the child has a history of absconding, is likely to abscond again unless placed in secure accommodation, and is likely to suffer significant harm if she does so, or is likely, if not placed in secure accommodation, to injure herself or other persons. These are the criteria laid down in domestic legislation. However, placing a child in secure accommodation also engages the child's 'Convention right', under Article 5 ECHR, not to be deprived of her liberty except in specified circumstances. The specified circumstances do not include the criteria set out in s. 25, but do include 'the detention of a minor by lawful order for the purpose of educational supervision'. In *Re K (Secure Accommodation: right to liberty)* [2001], an 11-year-old boy in the care of a local authority, described as presenting a 'serious risk to himself and others', was placed in secure accommodation. The placement was clearly authorised by the criteria in s. 25 of the 1989 Act, but could it be justified under Article 5 ECHR? The Court of Appeal said it could, because in the care context 'educational supervision' should not be equated rigidly with the notion of classroom teaching, but could embrace many aspects of the exercise by the local authority of parental responsibility for the benefit of the child. Provided some educational provision was being made, the use of secure accommodation pursuant to s. 25 would not in itself violate Article 5 ECHR.

in 1924, was not, despite its title, expressed in terms of the rights of children but rather of adults' obligations towards children – to feed, clothe, protect, nurture, educate and so on. The Declaration was not an enforceable agreement neither in international law nor in the domestic law of member States, but merely a statement of principle. Its importance was largely symbolic, but as the subsequent history shows, it was ultimately highly influential.

The idea was revisited a quarter of a century later by the United Nations. The creation of the United Nations marked the beginning of a new era in international law, in which protection of human rights was a key aim of the new international order. The Geneva Declaration was replaced in 1959 by a new Declaration of the Rights of the Child, which expanded on the substantive 'rights' identified in the 1924 version and, significantly, was framed in a way which treated the child as a legal subject rather than object: 'The child shall enjoy the rights set forth in this Declaration'. But it remained a statement of principle only, non-binding on the member States.

The preparation of the UNCRC took 10 years from the original proposal by Poland to its conclusion and opening for signature in 1989. When compared to the earlier texts, the UNCRC suggests a sea change in thinking about the human rights of children. First, the UNCRC is not merely declaratory – it has binding effect on the national governments that sign up to it. Second, the rights contained in it go far beyond either the 1924 or the 1959 Declarations and include 'participation' rights as well as rights to provision and protection.

The UK ratified the UNCRC in 1991. As a result the UK is under an international obligation to implement its provisions in law, policy and practice in relation to children. This obligation is 'policed' by a monitoring and reporting system established under the UNCRC itself, but there is no right of individual petition and no court comparable to the ECtHR. The rights contained in the UNCRC have not been integrated into UK domestic law by a measure comparable to the Human Rights Act 1998. Public bodies and their officials, including social workers, are not under a statutory duty to act compatibly with its provisions. Nonetheless, the UNCRC has an important impact on policy and practice, on decisions made by the courts in the UK when interpreting and applying domestic law and on decisions of the ECtHR when interpreting the ECHR.

Athough not formally integrated either into the ECHR or into UK domestic law, the UNCRC influences the way in which ECHR Convention rights are interpreted by the courts. This is true both of the ECtHR and the domestic courts in England and Wales. One senior judge has gone so far as to say that this means that human rights law imposes enforceable obligations on a public body to have regard to the principles of the UNCRC (Munby J. in *R (Howard League for Penal Reform) v Secretary of State for the Home Department and Dept of Health* [2002]). The UNCRC, he said, could and should be consulted by the courts in England and Wales, insofar as it proclaims, reaffirms or elucidates the contents of human rights, in particular the nature and scope of Convention rights under the Human Rights Act 1998.

Impact on social work

This brief account of the impact of the ECHR and UNCRC is enough to demonstrate that a child care social worker seeking to develop and maintain practice which is 'founded on, informed by and capable of being judged against a clear value base' (Sector Skills Council, 2005: 8), needs to be aware of the relevant requirements of international human rights law. For guidance as to what, in a particular situation, adherence to the 'principles of human rights' requires her to do (or refrain from doing), she must look to legal sources, in particular the Human Rights Act 1998 and associated case-law. There are both positive and negative aspects to this. On the negative side, a social worker is prohibited by law from acting incompatibly with the ECHR. On the positive side, she may find that her knowledge of the way in which human rights law operates may be deployed on behalf of her client towards achieving the objectives of 'empowerment and liberation' to which she is professionally committed.

Law and the principles of social justice

What is social justice?

The law does not provide the same kind of clarification in relation to 'the principles of social justice', at least not nearly so clearly. There is no legal definition of social justice, no catalogue of provisions comparable to the ECHR and UNCRC which codify the 'principles of human rights'. However, on any understanding of social justice, respect for individual human rights forms an important part of it. In its Code of Ethics, the British Association of Social Workers uses the term in an all-embracing way to encompass aspects of individual rights, equal treatment and protection as well as fair and equitable distribution of resources and environmental matters (BASW, 2003: 3). 'Social justice', and associated concepts such as 'social exclusion' or 'social inclusion', feature in numerous official policy documents, so that the notion has acquired a familiarity across different fields of public service, including but not limited to social work and social care, without as yet finding clear expression in law.

A consistent theme of the concept is the need to alleviate poverty and the multiple problems of impoverished communities. The UK Government's Social Exclusion Taskforce (the successor to the Social Exclusion Unit established in 1997) employs a broad explanation of 'social exclusion', making it clear that its effect is to create injustice from birth. Thus

social exclusion happens when people and places suffer from a series of problems such as unemployment, discrimination, poor skills, low incomes, poor housing, high crime, ill health and family breakdown, and it is recognised that being born into poverty or to parents with low skills has a major influence on future life chances. (Levitas, Pantazis, Fahmy et al., 2007)

Social justice and human rights

This description has obvious resonances for social work with children and families. It is notable that although the concept has not been translated as such into a legal principle, there are indications that human rights law can, in some circumstances, be applied to support it since there is an inextricable link between the principles of social justice and the principles of human rights. As Reichert (2003) argues, social exclusion violates human rights by depriving people of the social and economic conditions for the exercise of their rights. Accordingly, in some cases at least, manifestations of social exclusion will be capable of forming the basis of a legal human rights claim. Some decisions of the courts in England and Wales and the ECtHR in Strasbourg suggest that the law is indeed moving in this direction, and this is a development of significance for the practice of social work with children. Broadly, the argument, demonstrated in Box 1.8 is that the State's duty to take positive steps to ensure respect for ECHR rights may in practice require the direction of resources to ensure that an individual has access to such facilities as are necessary for the development of social relations and of an individual's personality. *Botta v Italy* [1998] illustrates that at least in 'extreme' circumstances (which, on the facts, did not include Signor Botta's complaint) this may mean that action must be taken to facilitate the inclusion of disadvantaged people (such as a disabled child) in the life of the community and to ensure a minimum respect for their 'human dignity'. The 'crucial factor', according to Judge Bratza in *Botta*, is 'the extent to which a particular individual is so circumscribed and so isolated as to be deprived of the possibility of developing his personality'. If this is shown to be the case, the ECHR may require the State to make appropriate provision.

Box 1.8   BOTTA V ITALY

A physically disabled man complained that he was unable to access a beach in Italy because of the lack of disabled ramps, toilet and changing facilities. He claimed that the State had failed to ensure respect for his right to a 'private life' under Article 8 ECHR, by failing properly to monitor compliance with domestic legislation requiring such facilities to be provided (the relevant Italian law contained a provision comparable to the requirement for 'reasonable adjustment' under the UK's Disability Discrimination Act 1995). The ECtHR held that Article 8 could indeed give rise to a positive obligation on a local authority to provide facilities of this kind, if the lack of them could be shown to have a direct and immediate effect on the individual's ability to enjoy his family or private life.

Using human rights law to promote social justice

An important question is how far this notion may be developed to cover not only cases of individuals having special need because of a personal factor such as disability, but also cases where the need arises due to social and economic factors: poverty, homelessness, etc. In case-work with children and their families, this development in legal reasoning may impact on real decisions about whether and how to intervene. In particular, recognition that the ECHR guarantees a right to develop an individual's personality through social and family relationships, and that in a case where a person is prevented from doing this, the State may be obliged to provide appropriate facilities and resources, has obvious implications for social workers when assessing need and considering what sort of support should be provided to children and their families. The fact that the subject-specific legislation and government guidance (e.g. the Children Act 1989, the Children Act 2004 and the *Framework for Assessment of Children in Need and their Families* (DoH, 2000/NAW, 2001)) does not alert practitioners to this point does not detract from its validity. A social worker who is aware of the relevance of Article 8 ECHR can use the knowledge to inform her recommendations and negotiations on behalf of service users: to do so is wholly consistent with her professional and legal responsibilities.

Law, professional integrity and accountability

Codes of Practice require social care workers to 'strive to establish and maintain the trust and confidence of service users and carers', to 'uphold public trust and confidence in social care services' and to 'be accountable for the quality of their work' (Care Council for Wales, 2002: 1; General Social Care Council, 2002: 3). The British Association of Social Workers' Code of Ethics states that 'integrity', comprising 'honesty, reliability, openness and impartiality', is 'an essential value in the practice of social work' (BASW, 2003: 5).

How does law support these values?

The law which governs social work practice is, in the main, public law – that is, the law which regulates the relationship between the individual and the State (as opposed to private law which regulates relations between private individuals). This is because social work is in general concerned with State intervention in people's lives, whether by providing support of some kind or taking protective measures. Any student of public law learns about constitutional values. An important constitutional value is the rule of law, and this has obvious relevance to the social work values of integrity and accountability.

The rule of law

The rule of law requires:

- lawful authority for any action which interferes with individual liberty;
- equal treatment under the law for anyone who interferes with individual liberty without such authority, whether acting in a private capacity or on behalf of the government;
- equal protection from such interference for all people, whatever their social status or other individual characteristics.

This means, for example, that a social worker has no special immunity from legal action if, even for good reasons, she acts outside the parameters of the statutory authority conferred on her or if, despite her best endeavours, a child with whom she is working suffers foreseeable injury in consequence of her failure to maintain the standards of a reasonably competent practitioner.

It also means that there should be no discrimination between individuals in the application of the law: the concept of non-discrimination in Article 14 ECHR, imported into domestic law by the Human Rights Act 1998, can be seen as supportive of this, in addition to domestic legislation dealing with discrimination on grounds of sex, race, disability, religion or sexual orientation. Such legal provisions are designed to afford disadvantaged groups of people access to facilities and opportunities that they might otherwise be denied. Social work services are such facilities, and services must be carried out in a non-discriminatory manner as well as being directed at helping children overcome disadvantage in accessing other facilities and opportunities.

The meaning of 'accountability'

Accountability, to a lawyer, means something slightly different from the notion suggested in the social work Codes. The latter emphasise professional competence and continuous updating of knowledge (Care Council for Wales, 2002: 9; General Social Care Council, 2002: 6), whereas to a lawyer the notion is one of a system or systems for holding a person exercising official authority to account for decisions made and actions taken. This may take the form of statutory complaints procedures, inspection, ombudspersons' powers of investigation and report, monitoring and whistle-blowing procedures, judicial review and actions for damages. Of course, there is a link between the two notions in that failure to meet professional standards or exercise judgement in a manner reflective of current professional practice may contribute to a basis for a formal complaint or legal action.

Openness and impartiality

A connection can be made between the social work professional value of openness and impartiality and the lawyer's notion of fairness or due process. The law of England and Wales recognised the concept of natural justice (which incorporates the requirements of a fair hearing, impartiality and lack of bias) long before any international human rights instruments were drawn up. However, the incorporation of Convention rights under the ECHR into domestic law by the Human Rights Act 1998 has reinforced and extended due process requirements, necessitating a rethinking of aspects of social work practice with children and families. In particular it has produced an imperative to provide information and to facilitate representation of all those whose rights are affected by social work decisions. This is the aspect of social work child care practice that has attracted the most consistent criticism since the Human Rights Act 1998 came into force, typically in cases where parents are insufficiently included in planning and decision making.

Increasingly, children's rights to be consulted and make their views known in processes concerning them are also being recognised. These rights are supported by the ECHR just as much as the rights of parents and are given greater force by Article 12 UNCRC. Children must be treated as legal subjects, not mere objects of concern. Even before they are mature enough to form views on the matters to be decided, children have separate interests that need to be properly investigated and represented: in child care practice there can be a danger that social workers focus too much on the needs of adult members of the family. Open, impartial practice means seeing children as well as adults as bearers of procedural rights.

Lawyers and social workers

If, as is suggested above, there is substantial common ground between the values of law and social work, it might be expected that this would be reflected in broadly compatible and complementary working practices and attitudes on the part of lawyers and social workers, and that conflicts between them should be rare. This is not necessarily the case! The reasons for conflict appear to be multi-faceted: commonality of values is clearly not the end of the story. Dickens has noted that:

there has been relatively little research ... into the working relationship between child care social workers and their own legal advisers, and how the nature of this relationship might affect outcomes for children. The research that has been done, however ... has shown that it is a relationship that can be fraught with tension and misunderstanding, role conflict and role confusion. (2004: 17)

On the basis of his own study, undertaken in England in 2001–02, and drawing on what older research was available, Dickens found that in practice, there was overlap between the tasks carried out by lawyers and social workers, especially in relation to the preparation of statements for court proceedings and their contribution to decisions whether to start legal proceedings. This overlap not infrequently gave rise to tension, resentment or conflict, although there was evidence too of good relationships and mutual understanding of the respective roles. Dickens suggests that the starting point for resolving the problems is for 'both groups to recognise that lawyers and social workers alike have multiple responsibilities' (2004: 25). Social workers' responsibilities included professional responsibilities to the individual child, to the child's parents, all the other children and families on their caseload, to their department and to the court, and on a day-to-day level these had to be prioritised according to their own decisions on the apportionment of their time and other resources. Lawyers saw their responsibilities as being to the social worker (their 'client'), to the social services department, the local authority as a whole, to the court and to the child. These multiple responsibilities, the different priorities attached to them by lawyers and social workers (both in general and in individual cases) and the overlap in their roles, coupled with organisational issues and pressure on staffing and other resources, rendered the 'mantra' of 'lawyers advise, social workers instruct' unhelpful as a way of describing their relationship in practice. In practice, the better way to perceive lawyers and social workers in relation to child care practice is surely as members of a team, recognising their different contributions and responsibilities which spring from the functional differences between the disciplines of law and social work and from their defined roles within their organisation.

Inter-disciplinary working: from good practice to good law?

Legislation and guidance emphasises the need for inter-disciplinary and multi-disciplinary working in planning and delivering children's services. Partnership working was one of the main themes of the Children Act 1989, and the key guidance document on child protection, *Working Together to Safeguard Children* (DfES, 2006/WAG, 2006), repeatedly underlines the importance of inter-professional working in ensuring the protection of children who are at risk of significant harm. The Children Act 2004 promotes this inter-disciplinary agenda further, requiring local authorities in England and Wales to promote co-operation between agencies to improve the well-being of children in relation to five 'aspects of well-being': physical health and emotional well-being, protection from harm and neglect, education, training and recreation, the contribution made by them to society, and social and economic well-being. The 2004 Act requires local authorities in England and Wales to produce children and young people's plans which include action towards this end. In England this responsibility must be carried out by a director of children's services appointed by the authority. A team approach both within the local authority and with external partners has thus become a legal as well as professional imperative.

Achieving such an approach, within the complex legal and policy framework of child care, is a challenging task. Statutory and policy aims flow from numerous sources, as illustrated in Box 1.9. The detail is explored in Chapter 2.

Child and family social workers: law enforcers or human rights campaigners?

Against this background, and in the context of a consideration of social work and legal values, it is pertinent to consider a question which has attracted the attention of commentators on the role of social workers: in their case-work and in exercising their collective professional voice, should they regard themselves as law enforcers or campaigners for human rights and social justice? A secondary question is whether law and lawyers tend to serve one end more than the other.

Some national professional social work associations, in their Code of Ethics, make a very clear connection between social work values and the enforcement

Box 1.9   THE STATUTORY AND POLICY FRAMEWORK FOR SOCIAL WORK PRACTICE WITH CHILDREN

- specific statutory powers and duties concerning the welfare of children: Children Act 1989;
- statutory guidance such as *Working Together* and the *Framework for the Assessment of Children in Need and Their Families*;
- wider statutory duties of local authorities as children's services providers: Children Act 2004;
- wider statutory duties of local authorities under general local government legislation, including responsibilities for other vulnerable groups, community safety, public health, etc.;
- cross-cutting themes enshrined in local government and other legislation: for example the duty to promote well-being (Local Government Act 2000) and, in Wales, the statutory equality duty imposed on the Welsh Assembly (Government of Wales Act 2006);
- financial constraints and organisational issues (also flowing to a large extent from statute, including the Children Act 2004);
- human rights legislation;
- children's rights, in particular the UNCRC.

of human rights. Australia and France are examples of this (AASW, 2002; ANAS, 1994). In England and Wales, as mentioned above, the connection is made at the level of values which are stated to be drawn from international human rights obligations (Sector Skills Council, 2005: 8). Williams (2004) argues that a view of social workers as human rights workers can be supported by aspects of the domestic legal powers and duties that fall in England and Wales to be exercised by social workers, while arguably being undermined by others.

In practice, however, there may be frequent tensions between these aims and the daily reality of implementing strategies for 'risk assessment, rationing and enforcement' (Jordan, 2004: 6). Litigation may expose contradictions in policies, without providing the means to resolve those contradictions. Sometimes guidance may be given by the courts which can help to avoid pitfalls that could give rise to future legal challenges, as illustrated in Box 1.10. Whether this is ever likely to be enough to resolve in *practice* the tensions that must be negotiated by social workers is doubtful.

Perhaps the answer to the question about social workers as 'law enforcers or campaigners for human rights and social justice' is that this is not really the right question! Indeed, both aims can be seen as law enforcement since the law requires compliance with human rights principles which, in practice, serve at least some aspects of social justice. The problems arise in part because the

Box 1.10   ASBOS AND CHILDREN IN CARE: *R (M (A CHILD)) V SHEFFIELD MAGISTRATES COURT* [2004]

As a result of a care order, a local authority had shared parental responsibility for a child, M. The same local authority applied for an anti-social behaviour order (ASBO) in respect of M. The housing department was the lead department in the ASBO application, whereas the social services department had responsibility for the care of M. In law, there is no distinction between these departments: the statutory powers and duties are those of 'the local authority', both under the Children Act 1989 and under the Crime and Disorder Act 1998. Could the local authority's two functions – its duties to safeguard the welfare of the child under the care order and its duties to protect the public by seeking ASBOs - be reconciled? The court found an answer in s. 22(6) Children Act 1989, which allows a local authority to take steps to protect the public, even if that means not putting the child's welfare first. Nonetheless, the difficulties for social workers employed by a local authority in this situation are not hard to imagine. The court attempted to address some of the difficulties by giving guidance as to the way in which such a situation should be handled within the local authority with a view to keeping separate the functions under the two Acts.

statutory powers and duties of social workers are generated from different strands of public policy. In these different strands, children and childhood are not always regarded in the same way. The tensions identified by Jordan (2004) therefore arise, for example, when 'family support' meets 'child protection', 'child welfare' meets 'youth justice' (as in Box 1.10) or 'parental responsibility' meets 'children's rights'. To illustrate the point, it is useful to refer to these different views of childhood and children and how they have found expression in law and policy governing social work practice with children.

Law, social work and the child

The concepts of 'children' and 'childhood' are socially constructed: they are differently understood in different places, societies and times. They are affected by moral, religious, philosophical, scientific, social and cultural influences.

This can be discerned in academic and popular literature, in everyday reporting, conversation and thinking about children and, inevitably, in policy-making and law.

Theorising children and childhood

These different views have been theorised, and the theoretical models can help us to understand approaches to children and childhood, including approaches taken in the law and legal system. Perhaps the best known work in this field is that of James, Jenks and Prout (1998), who identified five 'pre-sociological' and five 'sociological' models, the 'pre-sociological' models seeing the child variously as 'evil', 'innocent', 'immanent', 'naturally developing' or, retrospectively, as the 'unconscious' adult; and the 'sociological' models seeing the child as 'socially developing', 'socially constructed', 'tribal', a 'minority group' or simply a 'social structural' phenomenon. It is noteworthy that all of these, with the exception of the idea of the 'tribal' child (which is rooted in an attempt to apply anthropological methods to see children and childhood through the eyes of children themselves, as persons in their own right) are constructions made from the standpoint of adults, in which children are the objects of observation rather than active agents capable of bearing their own views and messages. No wonder, then, that the idea of children as legal subjects, with rights going beyond protection and provision and including a right to a voice in decisions affecting them, provoked controversy (see, for example, Alston, Parker and Seymour, 1992). Despite some landmark judicial decisions (such as that of the House of Lords in *Gillick v West Norfolk and Wisbech Area Health Authority and the DHSS [1985]*) and despite the UK's accession to the UNCRC, the consequences of the recognition of children's rights have yet to be fully worked through in child law and practice.

The different conceptual models are useful when considering legal or policy texts relating to social work with children, whether statute, case-law or guidance, as well as when reading secondary sources. Analysis of what view (or views) of children they reflect can help to make sense of the consequences that follow in law, policy and practice. The treatment of children under the law is different according to the purpose of the process in question. For example, greater direct participation in legal proceedings is allowed (and required) for a child accused of a criminal offence than for a child who is the subject of a residence dispute between his parents or even an application by a local authority for a care order. Greater prominence, even paramountcy, will be given to the welfare of the child in certain legal proceedings, and not in others. It is not fanciful to suggest that one factor contributing to these differences is the predominance of different child views in different policy contexts.

The child and family social worker's dilemma

This inevitably presents challenges for child and family social workers, who, when exercising statutory functions, cannot avoid being seen as the personification of a multi-faceted State, representing variously the role of protector, regulator, prosecutor and even gaoler of the legal subject. In particular, in child care social work practice, the law and the legal process sometimes seems to exacerbate the tension between on the one hand establishing and maintaining relationships conducive to family support work, on the other exercising child protection powers effectively and, further, taking into account the rights of members of the wider community. It is suggested throughout this book that the rights-based approach supported by the international texts, especially the UNCRC, offers the best chance of cutting through the inconsistencies and confusion created by the disparate sources of powers and duties relating to social work with children and their families.

Conclusion

We need to recognise the commonality at the root of social work values and legal values as well as to understand the differences in interpretation and in expression. We also need to recognise the functions of law in relation to social work practice with children and families. In summary, law:

- delineates the relationship between the individual and the State, prescribing the criteria for intervention by a public body in the private sphere;
- enshrines important traditions as legal principles: for example, the welfare principle, respect for private and family life;
- prescribes powers and responsibilities – of parents, local authorities, children themselves, and others;
- determines social workers' powers and duties in specific fields – directing and constraining what can or must be done in providing support for children and families, protecting children from abuse, ensuring care for looked after children and in the field of youth justice;
- provides mechanisms for policing the boundaries of power and responsibility: enabling disputes to be resolved as to who has authority to do what, when, to whom and how;
- enables principles, which must be applied in individual cases, to be properly interpreted and applied;
- prescribes the players: who can take part in the arguments – who has a voice.

In the exercise of the functions of both law and social work, dialogue between the professions is vital. Social workers need to understand not only the scope of their specific statutory functions in relation to children but also the wider legal context – to develop a critique of the legal criteria for intervention and of the decision-making processes of the law, to acquire an awareness of where the law is developing and how the developments may impact on the children and families with whom they work. In short, they need to be equipped both to serve the law and to use the law to serve the interests of their clients. The relationship between social work and law, and relationships between social workers and their legal advisers, are critical to effective practice in both disciplines.

Further Reading

Two articles referred to in this chapter are especially worth reading in full: they concern respectively the relationship between lawyers and social workers and the relationship between law and social work.

The first is Jonathan Dickens' 'Risks and responsibilities – the role of the local authority lawyer in child care cases', *Child and Family Law Quarterly*, 16 (2004), pp. 17–30. A further article by this same author, drawing on the same research project, examines the way in which lawyers and social workers respectively tend to approach decision-making in child care cases: 'Being the epitome of reason: The challenges for lawyers and social workers in child care cases', *International Journal of Law, Policy and the Family*, 19 (2004), pp. 1–29.

The second article is John Williams' 'Social work, liberty and law', *British Journal of Social Work*, 34 (2004), pp. 37–52.

The seminal examination of the socially constructed child and the way this conception influences and is reflected in law is M. King and C. Piper, *How the Law Thinks About Children*, 2nd edition Aldershot, Arena (1995).

2

Sources of Law for Child Care Social Work

- **Introduction: incorporating 'rights' in the law of England and Wales**
  How far has social work with children and families absorbed the culture of human rights?
- **Overview of the law relating to social work with children and families**
  'Child law': domestic and international agendas
  England and Wales: child protection and child welfare law
  England and Wales: local authorities' powers to promote well-being
  United Kingdom: anti-discrimination law
  United Kingdom: the law on information
  International law: the development of children's rights
  Children's rights and the United Nations
  Other UN texts
  Children's rights and the Council of Europe
  Children's rights and the European Union
  International law: mutual assistance
  International law: harmonisation of laws
- **Authority of the sources of law**
  Legislation
  Primary and subordinate legislation
  Territorial extent of legislation
  Guidance
  Case-law
  International law
  The authority of EU law
  The authority of the law of the ECHR: the Human Rights Act 1998
  Interpretative obligation, declarations of incompatibility and remedial action: ss. 3, 4 and 10 Human Rights Act 1998
  Duty of public authorities to act compatibly: s. 6
  Enforcement by individual claim against a public authority: s. 7
  Authority of other international law
- **Conclusion**

Introduction: incorporating 'rights' in the law of England and Wales

Social workers working with children need to act in a way which is conducive to respect for and promotion of human rights and, in particular, the rights of the child. As seen in Chapter 1, this is both a professional requirement and a legal requirement. Yet the various laws that frame social work practice with children have developed from different conceptual bases. The objective of this chapter is to explain the main sources of international, national and sub-national law relevant to social work with children and families, the relative authority of those sources and the way in which they interact. International sources are emphasised here because their actual impact in law is often not apparent on the face of national and sub-national legislation and guidance.

The legal framework for social work practice with children in England and Wales is rooted in ideas about child welfare, child development and the prevention of juvenile delinquency. In this framework, the State is required or enabled to step in where the private sphere of the family cannot or will not supply the necessary support, protection or control. Put another way, the general rule is non-interference by the State in the private sphere, but the State can and sometimes must intervene where a specified threshold of need or risk can be demonstrated. The core statute is the Children Act 1989 which lays down the parameters for the provision of support for children and families and for compulsory measures where necessary to protect children from significant harm.

Human rights law, on the other hand, is predicated on the idea that all persons have inalienable rights and that governments not only must not violate those rights but must take positive action to ensure they are respected by everybody, whether State officials or private individuals. One formulation of these fundamental human rights, the ECHR, has been given direct effect in UK law by means of the Human Rights Act 1998, and one of the mechanisms employed by the HRA 1998 to do this is the imposition, by s. 6, of a duty on all public authorities to act compatibly with the ECHR. This duty applies to social workers exercising statutory functions in relation to children and families. No such provision as yet exists in relation to the leading text on children's rights, the UNCRC, but in England and Wales the UNCRC is gaining prominence in case-law in the courts and, to a greater extent in Wales than in England, in broad statements of government policy. As explained later in this chapter, there are other international texts which also impact on social work practice with children and families.

Accordingly, social workers need to be able to negotiate a legally sound path, complying with both the requirements laid down in subject-specific legislation like the Children Act 1989 and with relevant provisions laid down in international law. Often this can be achieved by ensuring that the requirements of human rights law inform the way in which a specific statutory power or duty is exercised, as illustrated in Box 2.1. This is an example of a judge saying that although the specific power in the law of England and Wales has not been changed, the way in which the power is used needs to change in order to ensure compliance with international law, in this instance the UNCRC.

Box 2.1   SEPARATE REPRESENTATION OF CHILDREN IN FAMILY PROCEEDINGS: *MABON V MABON* [2005]

In divorce or separation proceedings the child is not automatically a party and is not normally represented. Where separate representation is allowed, usually a children's guardian is appointed to assist both the child and the court in the same way as in care proceedings. However, the court may permit a child who has sufficient understanding to participate in the proceedings independently. Traditionally, the courts have been very reluctant to allow this on account of concern for the child's emotional health if exposed to the court process and the material involved. However, in *Mabon v Mabon* [2005] the Court of Appeal held that this approach must change: the relevant rule (Rule 9.2A Family Proceedings Rules 1991) must be applied in the light of the requirements of Article 8 ECHR and Article 12 UNCRC. Thorpe L J said, 'Unless we in this jurisdiction are to fall out of step with other societies as they safeguard Article 12 rights, we must, in the case of articulate teenagers, accept that the right to freedom of expression and participation outweighs the paternalistic judgment of welfare.'

The case was about a judicial power, but the same could be said for the exercise of powers by social workers: specific powers in England and Wales legislation must be exercised compatibly with relevant international law. This is only possible where the professionals involved have a sufficient understanding of both sources of law. It must be said that the task of interweaving the two sources is made harder because of the different concepts and language used in the domestic legislation when compared to the international texts.

How far has social work with children and families absorbed the culture of human rights?

The legal position is that none of the specific provisions about social work powers and duties relating to children can be read in isolation from applicable human rights law. This can be seen in court judgments in children's cases, as the example in **Box 2.1** illustrates. But how far is it reflected in the day-to-day practice of child and family social workers and others carrying out their functions within local authorities, health bodies or other public bodies? In their report *Human Rights: Improving Public Service Delivery* (2003), the Audit Commission found that local authorities and other public bodies had not sufficiently absorbed into their practice the way in which international obligations and domestic provisions interact. This continues to be borne out in reported legal cases. Munby J, speaking three years after the Human Rights Act 1998 came into force, commented:

Too often still ... one is left with the feeling that local authority social workers and team managers do not appreciate the vital impact of the Human Rights Act 1998, and that in significant measure this is because the right message is not coming down from the top. Local authorities need to ensure that they have in place policies and procedures that recognise and give effect in practical ways to both the substantive and the procedural rights guaranteed to parents and children ... (2004: 432)

Social workers need to adopt rights-based thinking, seeking to ensure respect for the human rights of all those affected, including the child. In particular, practitioners need to recognise and find ways of facilitating the agency of the child in relation to any decision affecting her or, where a child lacks sufficient understanding to form or communicate a view, to ensure that the child's standpoint is adequately represented. One of the cases referred to by Munby J, **CF v Secretary of State for the Home Department [2004]**, concerned a decision whether to permit a young mother detained in a prison to continue to have her baby with her. The decision fell to be made by the Prison Service, which recognised the need for both the mother's and the baby's interests to be represented, and turned to the local authority social services department to supply a social worker to represent the baby. Unfortunately, the social worker came to the crucial meeting 'woefully unprepared', having not previously seen relevant papers nor become familiar with the case. The process was held to be flawed as it was incompatible with the procedural safeguards implied by Article 8 ECHR (explained later in this chapter, and see Box 2.6). If the rights of persons affected by decisions are the starting point in the consideration of any case, rather than coming lower down or even falling off the end of a checklist of powers and duties set out in subject-specific legislation and guidance, such avoidable errors are less likely to occur.

Overview of the law relating to social work with children and families

'Child law': domestic and international agendas

The law relating to social work with children and families can be regarded as a sub-set of the wider subject of child law. This wider subject would include special adaptations made for children in the application of the general law, for example:

- the exclusion of criminal liability for persons under 10;
- the lower standard of care expected of children in civil cases where a child is alleged to have been negligent;

- the requirement for children who are parties to civil actions to conduct their cases through a 'litigation friend'; and
- special rules for children giving evidence in court.

Some of these matters have an important bearing on the practice of social work, and Chapter 9 deals with some aspects where children come into contact with the criminal justice system. For the most part, however, this book is concerned with those laws which frame the bulk of social work child care practice, that is, laws aimed at protecting and supporting the development of children by means of imposing duties or conferring powers on local authorities. These specific powers and duties are set out mainly in legislation applying to England and Wales, like the Children Act 1989. The historical development of these powers and duties is closely associated with the development and maintenance of the social care workforce itself, within the wider context of the public policy agendas of successive UK governments and, since 1999, the Welsh Assembly Government.

In international law, provisions about children have been developed within different agendas, of which human rights is the most important but is not the only one. Others include the development of mutual assistance between countries in legal and administrative matters and harmonisation of the laws of different countries. There is cross-fertilisation between all of these international and domestic agendas.

England and Wales: child protection and child welfare law

Influences on the early development of child protection and child welfare law included lobbying from the social and philanthropic movements such as the NSPCC and Dr Barnardo's and the development from the late nineteenth century of the scientific study of children in the disciplines of educational psychology and child development. The social and legal history is analysed elsewhere (Hendrick, 2003; O'Halloran, 1999). For our purposes it is enough to note that these factors, coupled with a sense of alarm at the potential for damage to the social and economic fabric of the nation, contributed to public and political acceptance of the State's responsibility to provide for deprived children. Over time, the result was a raft of legislation dealing with provision and protection for, and control of, children, building on and eventually supplanting the Poor Law provision which dated back to the sixteenth century.

The Children Act 1948 was a landmark in the development of child protection and child welfare law and the associated development of social work with children and families. The 1948 Act implemented many of the recommendations of the *Report of the Care of Children Committee*, 1946 (the Curtis Report). The Curtis Report and the 1948 Act laid a foundation for social work with children in England and Wales by providing for the establishment of local authority children's departments, children's committees and children's officers and setting out two basic principles for provision of services. These principles have endured into the current legal framework. They are:

- the principle that local authorities must exercise their powers in such a way as to further the best interests and development of the child; and
- the principle of support for family unity: that use should be made of what the 1948 Act described as the 'facilities and services' of the child's own family wherever possible.

With the Children Act 1989, enacted in the same year as the adoption of the UNCRC, a third principle emerged: the principle that the agency of the child must be respected. This means that children's standpoint must be properly represented and they must be enabled to express and have taken into account their views on matters affecting them.

The Children Act 1989 remains the statutory basis for much of the work of a child and family social worker. Its structure and scope is shown in Box 2.2.

Subsequent legislation has added to this statutory scheme, without undermining its basic principles and structure. The Care Standards Act 2000 extended the reach of the regulatory framework for child care settings and for the social care workforce generally. The Children (Leaving Care) Act 2000 extended local authorities' duties to children and young people leaving public care. The Adoption and Children Act 2002 made some significant changes to the provisions on review of cases and complaints relating to local authority care. The Children Act 2004 added a layer of detailed provision about the aims of children's services, their structures within local authorities and arrangements with other agencies for service delivery and safeguarding children. The Childcare Act 2006 made further provision aimed at improving local early years services. In addition, there is separate legislation governing adoption in the Adoption and Children Act 2002 (which replaces the Adoption Act 1976), and separate legislation dealing with youth offending and anti-social behaviour.

With the exception of the last mentioned (youth offending and anti-social behaviour), it is uncontroversial to state that the three principles of the best interests and development of the child, support for family unity and the agency of the child permeate the whole of this legislative code. Certainly they should underpin all social work interventions in the lives of children. Equally clear is that nowhere in legislation for England and Wales are these principles articulated as children's rights.

In contrast, in the main international texts, the language of rights is prominent, and ever more so since the UNCRC was concluded in 1989. The UK Government took a deliberate decision not to adopt the language of children's rights when further articulating the purposes of children's services in the Children Act 2004. During the parliamentary passage of that Act, the Government rejected amendments that would have brought references to the UNCRC and to children's rights into the statutory framework. This decision

Box 2.2   OUTLINE OF THE CHILDREN ACT 1989

Part I: Introductory	The 'welfare', 'no order' and 'no delay' principles to be applied by courts. Meaning and acquisition of parental responsibility
Part II: Orders with respect to children in family proceedings	'Section 8' orders: residence, contact, specific issue and prohibited steps, and associated provisions
Part III: Local authority support for children and families	Provision of services and accommodation on the basis of need. Provision of advice and assistance. Duties to looked after children and young people who were looked after. Reviews, complaints and advocacy procedures
Part IV: Care and supervision	Criteria and procedures for care and supervision orders
Part V: Protection of children	Emergency protection, investigative powers and protective powers
Part VI: Community homes	Provision and regulation of residential care
Part VII: Voluntary homes and Voluntary organisations	Provision and regulation of residential care
Part VIII: Registered children's homes	Provision and regulation of residential care
Part IX: Private arrangements for fostering children	Registration and regulation of private fostering arrangements
Part XA: Child minding and day care for children in England and Wales	Registration, regulation and inspection of child minding and day care
Part XI: Functions and responsibilities of Secretary of State (England) and Welsh Assembly (Wales)	Includes a default power where a local authority has failed to carry out a duty under the Act
Part XII: Miscellaneous and general	Includes procedural and evidential provisions
Schedules 1–14	Provide detail to supplement provisions in some of the sections of the Act

37

is regrettable, since it leaves the main children's legislation for England and Wales out of tune with the UK's international obligations and provides no clear signposts for practitioners as to the relevance of the UNCRC for social work practice.

England and Wales: local authorities' power to promote well-being

The Local Government Act 2000 introduced an important new power for local authorities to do anything to promote or improve the economic, social and environmental well-being of their area. This enables local authorities to undertake activities for which they may lack clear specific authority and is intended to encourage them to be more innovative and creative in pursuing their aims. There is an obvious general connection with the aims of social work with children, but the 2000 Act power of well-being is also capable of producing sharp-edge legal arguments in individual cases, as illustrated in relation to provision of accommodation in Box 2.3. Chapter 5 provides more detail about the way in which families of children in need can be supported where their principal need is for accommodation yet they do not qualify for housing assistance: the position is not straightforward. For present purposes, the point is that the case demonstrates that although s. 2 Local Government Act 2000 confers a mere power, there may be a duty to use the power in an individual case if this is the only means of avoiding a breach of Article 8 ECHR.

United Kingdom: anti-discrimination law

For social work practice with children, anti-discrimination law performs several functions:

- it makes it unlawful for a social worker to discriminate against a child or any other person on any of the prohibited grounds;
- it provides a framework within which equality and diversity policies must be established, implemented and kept under review as an integral part of the social worker's operational environment;
- it provides mechanisms that may be deployed by social workers working with children and families to help combat unlawful discrimination.

Anti-discrimination law derives from a number of sources: UK legislation, human rights law and EU provisions. The main UK legislation is set out in Box 2.4.

There are more broadly based anti-discrimination provisions in Article 14 ECHR, Article 2 UNCRC and Article 13 of the European Union (EU) Treaty of Amsterdam. In relation to employment, occupation and access to vocational training, services and facilities, there are EU directives on equal treatment (EU, 1976; EU, 2000a) and race (EU, 2000b).

Box 2.3   PROMOTION OF WELL-BEING: POWER OR DUTY?

In *R (J) v London Borough of Enfield and Secretary of State for Health* **[2002]**, an HIV-positive Ghanaian citizen had applied for leave to remain in the UK but was at the time of the case disqualified from a range of publicly funded support, including housing. Nonetheless, she sought assistance from the local authority to obtain suitable accommodation for herself and her daughter, relying in part on s. 17 Children Act 1989 (assistance for children in need and their families). The court held that neither accommodation nor financial assistance towards the cost of accommodation could be provided under s. 17. However, the court accepted that the power in s. 2 Local Government Act 2000 was wide enough to allow the local authority to provide financial assistance in such a case, unless there was some specific statutory constraint. The judge considered that if using s. 2 of the 2000 Act was the only way to prevent mother and daughter from being separated in breach of their rights under Article 8 ECHR, the local authority was effectively under a duty to provide the assistance.

Note: On the actual issues, things have moved on since this case. The Nationality, Immigration and Asylum Act 2002 further restricted the provision of local authority social care services for adults, including under s. 17 Children Act 1989 and under s. 2 Local Government Act 2000, to unlawful immigrants. However, this restriction does not apply where provision of services is necessary to avoid a breach of ECHR or EU rights: s. 54 of and Sched. 3 to the 2002 Act. Furthermore, a subsequent Court of Appeal decision has made it clear that s. 17 Children Act 1989 can cover provision of accommodation or financial assistance towards accommodation: *R (W) v London Borough of Lambeth* **[2002]** (see Chapter 5). An amendment to the Children Act 1989 by the Adoption and Children Act 2002 has now put beyond doubt that s. 17 Children Act 1989 can be used to provide accommodation. In *R (W) v London Borough of Lambeth* the Court of Appeal also expressly approved the view expressed in the *Enfield* case about s. 2 Local Government Act 2000. The *Lambeth* case went to the House of Lords but there the issues were about the general nature of the s. 17 duty and about whether the local authority was entitled to offer accommodation for the child alone. See Chapter 5 for the arguments about that.

The idea behind the 1970's legislation was to outlaw discrimination – a concept embracing both direct discrimination (less favourable treatment) and indirect discrimination (creating unjustifiable disadvantage) – in the fields of employment, housing and the provision of facilities and services. Civil remedies were made available and in some circumstances criminal sanctions applied. This system of prohibitions and sanctions has remained intact whilst there has developed an increasing emphasis on proactive steps by public authorities to promote equal opportunity through strategies, policies and action. The Equality Act 2006 provides for the establishment of a single

Commission for Equality and Human Rights with responsibilities for promoting the broad notions of equality and diversity as well as for enforcement of the specific equality enactments (broadly, the enactments set out in Box 2.4). The Commission replaces the separate race, disability and equal opportunities commissions and has the additional role of promoting human rights awareness and compliance with s. 6 Human Rights Act 1998.

Box 2.4   UK ANTI-DISCRIMINATION LEGISLATION

Discrimination on grounds of	UK legislation
Race, colour, nationality, ethnic or national origin	Race Relations Act 1976, Race Relations (Amendment) Act 2000, Race Relations (Amendment) Regulations 2003
Sex and marital status	Sex Discrimination Act 1975, Equal Pay Act 1970
Disability	Disability Discrimination Act 1995, Special Educational Needs and Disability Act 2001, Disability Discrimination Act 2006
Religion and belief	Equality Act 2006
Sexual orientation	Equality Act 2006

None of the UK equality enactments addresses discrimination against children on the grounds that they are children. The Equality Act 2006 confers on the Commission for Equality and Human Rights a very broad remit to promote good relations between 'groups'. A 'group' may be defined by age, amongst other criteria, so that children could be a 'group' for this purpose. This provision falls short of a duty of non-discrimination or even a duty to promote equality of treatment but could conceivably be used to promote better access by children to facilities and services. It is early yet to determine what if anything this might add to the role and remit of the Children's Commissioners (see Chapter 3). The important point for present purposes is that the Commission for Equality and Human Rights represents a development from reactive measures (penalties and remedies for unlawful discrimination) to add requirements for proactive measures to be taken by public bodies generally by promoting equality and diversity in carrying out their functions. The same trend is reflected in the overarching requirement in s. 77 Government of Wales Act 2006 for the Welsh Assembly Government to ensure that all its functions are exercised with due regard to the principle of equality of opportunity for all people.

Social workers owe a professional duty of confidentiality to their clients. This duty is consistent with legal duties relating to the handling of personal and confidential information. The law is partly judge-made (for example, the common law duty of confidentiality and the rules of natural justice) and partly statutory (for example, the Freedom of Information Act 2000 and the Data Protection Act 1998). Like anti-discrimination law, it represents a combination of domestic legislation, human rights law and EU law.

In certain circumstances there is a legal duty not to disclose information without the consent of the person concerned. In limited circumstances there is a legal duty to disclose. In between there is a large area where disclosure is a matter of discretion which must be exercised in accordance with legal principles and professional ethics. This area of the law is explained further in Chapter 4 in relation to inter-disciplinary working.

International law: the development of children's rights

The history of children's rights in international law has already been touched upon in Chapter 1 in connection with the origins of the UNCRC. International recognition of children as a group deserving and requiring special provision and protection goes back to the League of Nations' 1924 Declaration of the Rights of the Child, which was later taken up and developed by the United Nations.

Children's rights and the United Nations

The foundation stone of modern human rights law is the United Nations' Universal Declaration of Human Rights 1948. It contained provisions of application to all persons, but also singled out motherhood and childhood as entitled to special care and assistance and all children, 'whether born in or out of wedlock', as entitled to enjoy the same social protection.

A UN Declaration on the Rights of the Child emerged in 1959. Unlike the 1924 Declaration, the 1959 Declaration adopted the language of rights in its content, not just in its title. This was a bold step, because the notion that children can be holders of rights at all has proved problematic. The difficulties are not just legal, but also philosophical or rooted in theories of child development or concern for the protection of children. However, a Declaration, unlike a Convention, has no binding effect – it is simply a statement of principle – so the promoters of the 1959 Declaration did not have to worry too much about the difficulties of enforcement.

The UNCRC 1989 constituted a sea change. First of all it was not merely declaratory; it has binding effect on the national governments that sign up to it. It established an enforcement mechanism in the form of a reporting and monitoring system whereby States Parties have to submit initial and periodic reports to the UN Committee on the Rights of the Child. Further, it went beyond the rights to protection and provision with which the 1924 and 1959 Declarations had been concerned and conferred also participative rights recognising the agency of children as citizens in the societies in which they live. In that, it reflects a very different view of children and of childhood compared to the earlier declarations.

Box 2.5 shows the content of the UNCRC and highlights the themes to which the UN Committee on the Rights of the Child has attached particular importance. Often the Convention rights are described in terms of 'protection, provision and participation' but in order to make connections with the law of England and Wales, they are here categorised in terms of the 'three principles' of best interests and development, support for family unity and the agency of the child. A further category, 'enforcement', notes UNCRC articles which provide for implementation by States Parties and the monitoring system under the UN Committee on the Rights of the Child.

Box 2.5   THE UNCRC

Best interests and development	General right to protection: children's best interests to be a 'primary consideration' in all governmental action concerning them (Art. 3)* Protection from discrimination (Art. 2)* Right to life, survival and development (Art. 6)* Protection from violence, injury or abuse, neglect or exploitation (Art. 19) Special protection for children deprived of family environment (Art. 20), regulation of adoption (Art. 21) and right to periodic review of treatment and care (Art. 25) Special protection for refugee children (Art. 22) Special care and facilities for disabled children (Art. 23) Right to health care services (Art. 24) Right to an adequate standard of living and to benefit from social security (Arts. 26 and 27) Right to and purpose of education (Arts. 28 and 29) Protection from economic exploitation and harmful employment (Art. 32) Protection from illicit drug use, trafficking, sexual and other forms of exploitation and from participation in armed conflict (Arts. 33 to 36, Art. 38) Protection from torture, cruel, inhuman or degrading

	punishment, protection of liberty and provision of rehabilitative care (Arts. 37 and 39) Special protection and treatment under penal law (Art. 40)
Support for family unity	Respect for rights and responsibilities of parents and families (Art. 5) Right to know and be cared for by parents (Art. 6) Coercive separation only by judicial order and only in the best interests of the child (Art. 9) Support for family reunification and suppression of illicit trafficking (Arts. 10 and 11, Art. 22) Support for parents to exercise primary responsibility for upbringing and development (Art. 18)
Agency of the child	Right to identity, name and nationality (Arts. 6 and 7) Right to express a view and have it taken into account, in particular in judicial and administrative proceedings (Art. 12)*
	Civil and political rights: freedom of expression, thought, conscience and religion, freedom of association and peaceful assembly, right to privacy and access to information (Arts. 13 to 17) Facilitation of participation by disabled children (Art. 23) Cultural and linguistic rights of indigenous and minority children (Art. 30) Right to participate in cultural life and the arts (Art. 31)
Enforcement	State Parties to undertake 'all appropriate legislative, administrative and other measures' to implement rights, 'to the maximum extent of their available resources' (Art. 4) State Parties must promote awareness of the Convention amongst adults and children (Art. 42) Submission of initial and periodic reports on implementation to the UN Committee on the Rights of the Child (Arts.43 and 44) Co-operation between UN agencies on implementation (Art. 45)

*The UN Committee has adopted these four provisions as key themes which must be applied by States across the board in implementing the Convention.

The way in which the UNCRC was developed, over a period of 10 years, by consensus building involving not only governments but non-governmental organisations as well, gave it a particular strength and credibility which no doubt contributed to its becoming the most widely ratified human rights treaty ever. It represents a global acceptance that:

* children have rights, including participation rights;
* national governments have obligations to ensure respect for those rights;
* the international community will police the performance of national governments in carrying out those obligations.

Other UN texts

While the UNCRC is the most important UN text on children's rights, others are also relevant and provide greater detail of children's rights in specific settings. These include the UN Standard Minimum Rules for the Administration of Juvenile Justice 1985 ('the Beijing Rules'), the UN Rules for the Protection of Juveniles Deprived of their Liberty 1990 and UN Guidelines for Action on Children in the Criminal Justice System 1997. Although these texts do not have the binding force of a treaty they have an indirect effect on implementation of the UNCRC since the UN Committee on the Rights of the Child has indicated that in monitoring the action taken by States Parties it will expect that the rules and guidelines contained in the texts are observed.

Children's rights and the Council of Europe

Within the Council of Europe, the most important source of international law conferring rights on children remains the ECHR. Unusually for an international agreement, the ECHR confers rights of individual action on individuals, enabling them to bring a complaint to the European Court of Human Rights (ECtHR) alleging that their Convention rights have been violated by a public authority in their country. The ECHR makes little specific reference to children, but certain of the Convention rights have a direct bearing on policy and practice with children and families. The case-law of the ECtHR and, since the Human Rights Act 1998, the UK courts, demonstrates that in applying the Convention to child care practice the principles of the best interests and development of the child and support for family unity are prominent. There is also a rather patchy but growing recognition of the need for respect for the agency of the child. Box 2.6 indicates the main points of impact on social work practice with children.

Some ECHR rights are absolute, that is to say there can be no justification for interference with them, and some are qualified. Interference with qualified rights may be justified where there is a legitimate aim and where in the individual case the interference is proportionate to achieving that aim. Article 8, for example, guarantees enjoyment of private and family life but this can be

Box 2.6   ECHR ARTICLES OF PARTICULAR RELEVANCE FOR SOCIAL WORK WITH CHILDREN

ECHR Article	Impact on social work with children
Art. 2: right to life Art. 3: right not to be subjected to torture or to inhuman or degrading treatment	Arts. 2 and 3 generate a positive obligation on the State to protect children from suffering injury or dying at the hands of others This means that the criminal law must prohibit injury and abuse and that in certain circumstances a failure by a local authority to remove children from an abusive environment may violate their rights. *Z v United Kingdom (2001)* (see Chapter 1, Box 1.6) established that possible legal liability for failure to remove children from an abusive home cannot be excluded. Equally, poor conditions for children in institutional settings may reach a sufficient threshold of severity to violate Art. 3. In *D G v Ireland* **[2002]** it was held that keeping a child in a penal institution and using reasonable restraint measures do not in themselves violate Art. 3, but in *Lukanov v Bulgaria* **[1995]** the ECtHR said that conditions detrimental to physical or mental health may do so. It should therefore be assumed that failure to take adequate steps to protect children from serious abuse in residential settings could violate Art. 3 In *A v United Kingdom* **[1998]** the defence of 'reasonable chastisement' did not provide adequate protection from ill-treatment amounting to a violation of Art. 3. Although the Children Act 2004 has restricted this defence to charges of common assault, there remains a difference in the protection provided by the criminal law to children and to adults
Art. 5: right to liberty and security	Restriction of liberty is permitted only for the purposes and under the conditions set out in Art. 5. Legislative provisions allowing for the restriction of children's liberty need to be interpreted compatibly, as in *Re K (Secure Accommodation: right to liberty)* **[2001]** (Chapter 1, Box 1.7). Judicial authority is necessary, but will not be adequate if the purposes do not fall within Art. 5: *Bouamar v Belgium* **[1989]**. Social workers and health professionals should beware of

(Continued)

45

relying solely on parental consent for 'voluntary' detention in an institution, at least where older children are concerned. This was sanctioned in **Nielsen v Denmark [1989]** for a 12-year-old boy but the decision has been much criticised

Art. 6: right to a fair hearing in the determination of any 'civil right or obligation' and guaranteed minimum rights in criminal cases	Difficulties arise over the ability of young defendants to participate effectively in criminal trials, especially in the Crown Court. See Chapter 8 for discussion of **V and T v United Kingdom [1999], S.C. v UK [2004]** and **R (S) v Waltham Forest Youth Court and Others [2004]** Art. 6 applies to some administrative as well as judicial processes, but for many social work decisions the procedural guarantees implied by Art. 8 are more significant. See Chapters 6, 7 and 8
Art. 8: right to respect for private and family life, home and correspondence	Interference is permitted where it is authorised by law for a legitimate aim and is proportionate to the end to be achieved. Child protection interventions normally satisfy this test, and the ECtHR accepts that in some cases the child's best interests must override the rights of parents. See further Chapter 6. The ECtHR case law emphasises: • the duty to work towards continued family contact and family reunification: **Johansen v Norway [1996], Olsson v Sweden [1988], Yousef v Netherlands [2003]**; • the need for procedural safeguards, especially proper representation of or participation by child and family: **McMichael v United Kingdom [1995], W v United Kingdom [1988]** 'Family life' often involves cohabitation but also extends to parents and children separated following divorce, separation or public care proceedings: **Hendriks v Netherlands [1983], W v United Kingdom [1988]**: the right then becomes a right to contact subject only to permitted interference. 'Private life' includes not only a person's personal, 'inner circle' but also the right to establish and develop relationships: **Niemitz v Germany [1992]**, a right to physical and psychological integrity

ECHR Article	Impact on social work with children
	and to develop one's personality: ***Botta v Italy* [1998]** (see Chapter 1, Box 1.8). The State has a positive obligation to protect and facilitate enjoyment of Art. 8 rights: this has a bearing on care planning and children's services provision generally
Art. 9: freedom of thought, conscience and religion	Case law has tended to focus on parents' rather than children's rights – e.g. in making health care or educational choices for their children. Greater emphasis on the agency of the child can be expected to generate more claims by children. See, for example, the case of the 13-year-old girl excluded from school for wearing the jilbab: ***R (Begum) v Headteacher and Governors of Denbigh High School* [2006]**
Art. 14: right not to be discriminated against in the enjoyment of Convention rights	This is of general relevance to all children: it prohibits discriminatory treatment for any reason, including age. It must however be linked to another ECHR article: it is not freestanding. For example, in ***Sutherland v United Kingdom* [1997]** it was linked to Art. 8 to establish that it was unlawful to discriminate between homosexual and heterosexual young people with regard to the age of consent
Art. 2, Protocol 1: right to education	This is not a right to be educated at any particular school but is a guarantee of fair and non-discriminatory access to the 'educational system' within a member State: ***Ali v Lord Grey School* [2006]**. The article highlights parental rights to ensure education and teaching in conformity with their own religious and philosophical convictions

interfered with where the law so allows in the interests of (amongst other things) the rights and freedoms of others. Since so much social work with children and families engages Article 8, there is a constant need to be aware of the requirement of proportionality. This will often involve a careful, measured balancing of different interests and making sure there is a clear record of the reasons for decisions. In the discussion of its application to individual case-work in Part Two of this book, Article 8 is presented as requiring constant attention to process, purpose and proportionality.

In addition to the ECHR, and taking account of the need for all Council of Europe members to implement their obligations under the UNCRC, the Council of Europe established the European Convention on the Exercise of Children's Rights 1996. This Convention is part of the Council of Europe's programme of harmonisation of laws (see below), in this instance seeking harmonisation of laws as to the way in which States implement Article 12.2 of the UNCRC. The Convention prescribes in some detail children's procedural rights in certain judicial proceedings. The UK has not as yet agreed to be bound by this Convention.

Children's rights and the European Union

The European Union has also taken a position on children's rights. Article 24 of the EU Charter of Fundamental Rights sets out, as a statement of rights, essentially the 'three principles' of the best interests and development of the child, support for family unity and the agency of the child. The article is worth quoting in full. Although as yet lacking formal legal status (see further below: *The authority of EU law*), it reflects a conceptual position underlying a nascent EU policy on children and families:

Article 24
The rights of the child

1. Children shall have the right to such protection and care as is necessary for their well-being. They may express their views freely. Such views shall be taken into consideration on matters which concern them in accordance with their age and maturity.
2. In all actions relating to children, whether taken by public authorities or private institutions, the child's best interests must be a primary consideration.
3. Every child shall have the right to maintain on a regular basis a personal relationship and direct contact with both his or her parents, unless that is contrary to his or her interests.

International law: mutual assistance

This strand of international law has a longer history than that of children's rights. As long ago as 1893, the Hague Conference on Private International Law was established with the aim of improving mutual co-operation in legal matters between countries around the world. Such co-operation includes recognition and enforcement of foreign judgments, agreement of rules as to applicable law, co-operation between judicial and administrative authorities in case preparation, provision and certification of documents, ensuring admissibility of evidence and so on. When children and their families move from one country to another, or more particularly when there is dispute as to whether and with whom children should live, such matters have obvious significance. The two Hague Conventions of most likely relevance to the practice of social work with children and families are:

- the Hague Convention on the Civil Aspects of International Child Abduction 1980, which seeks to give international protection to rights of custody; and

- the Hague Convention on Protection of Children and Co-operation in respect of Inter-country Adoption 1993, which is concerned with the prevention of the abduction, sale or traffic of children and the regularisation of inter-country adoption where this is in the best interests of the child.

European institutions have contributed further to the international law on mutual assistance in family matters. The Council of Europe's European Convention on the Recognition and Enforcement of Decisions Concerning the Custody of Children 1980 provides for mutual recognition and co-operation between State Parties in the enforcement of court decisions about custody of children. And the European Union (EU) has added to the collection, the most recent instrument being Council Regulation (EC) No. 2201/2003 ('Brussels II'). That the EU should concern itself with family law may seem surprising, since the EU is generally associated with economic and commercial matters, not with family and social policy. However, the free movement of persons has always been a core EU objective and since this generates (in the words of the Preamble to 'Brussels II') the need to create 'an area of freedom, security and justice', the EU promotes judicial co-operation across a wide range of matters which impact on people's life choices. This includes questions of movement, settlement and upbringing of children which fall to be decided by the courts in family proceedings. Significantly, Brussels II reflects the principle that the voice of the child must be heard by making this a pre-condition for enforcement of an order and by providing the child a further opportunity to be heard at the enforcement stage, unless it is inappropriate having regard to the child's age and understanding.

International law: harmonisation of laws

One of the aims of the Council of Europe is to promote harmonisation of the laws of member States. A number of its measures have been aimed at achieving similarity in the way in which national laws deal with children and families. Such measures form part of the context in which legislation for England and Wales is created. They include provisions aimed at protecting children in employment and the provision of social security and welfare in the European Social Charter 1961 (revised in 1996), the European Convention on the Adoption of Children 1967, the European Convention on the Legal Status of Children Born out of Wedlock 1975, the European Convention on the Exercise of Children's Rights 1996 (above) and the European Convention on Contact Concerning Children 2003.

Authority of the sources of law

Thus far, we have seen that the sources of laws impacting on social work with children are various and have developed in different contexts. We have also seen that the three principles of the best interests and development of the child, support for family unity and the agency of the child are pervasive in these sources, albeit not always formulated in the same way. While there is broad consistency on these principles, there is also scope for conflict as to specifics: the devil, it is often said, is in the detail. This raises the question: what is the relative authority of these sources of law: in the event of conflict, which one prevails?

Legislation

In the legal system of England and Wales, the general rule is that Acts of the UK Parliament carry the highest legal authority: a provision in an Act of Parliament cannot be declared unlawful by the courts even if it is in breach of a provision of international law binding on the UK. The exception to this rule relates to directly enforceable EU rights. It flows from s. 2 of the European Communities Act 1972, which requires courts in the UK to give effect to such rights. So far this exception has been of little practical relevance to social work with children and families, but this could change if EU social and family policy develops further. The ECHR has far greater and more obvious relevance, but ECHR rights cannot override a provision in an Act of Parliament. The impact of EU law and the ECHR on law made within the UK is explained further below (under *International law*) but first it is necessary to say a little more about UK legislation, in particular about the different 'layers' of legislation and about the territorial application of it, and also about the authority of case law decided in the courts.

Primary and subordinate legislation

Acts of Parliament may be referred to as 'primary legislation'. The Acts of Parliament with which we are concerned contain many provisions which have the effect of creating law without more ado. They also contain many provisions, known as 'enabling powers', which permit another authority, usually the Secretary of State, or Welsh Assembly Government, to create law. This law may be referred to as 'secondary legislation' or sometimes as 'delegated legislation'. It usually takes the form of regulations, rules or orders. The most relevant to child care social work are regulations which are commonly used to set standards for the delivery of statutory services and rules which govern the conduct of court proceedings.

Unlike a provision in an Act of Parliament, a provision in secondary legislation may be challenged in the courts and the courts may in certain circumstances hold it to be unlawful. Those circumstances include incompatibility with the ECHR, unless a provision in primary legislation prevents removal of the incompatibility.

Legislation may extend to the whole of the UK or only to one or more parts of it. The parts of the UK for this purpose are England, Wales, Scotland and Northern Ireland. Much of the primary legislation referred to in this book has a territorial extent limited to England and Wales. Scotland and Northern Ireland have separate legislation dealing with social work with children and families. Some legislation, including the Human Rights Act 1998, extends throughout the UK.

Devolution has made it much more important to be aware of the territorial application of legislation. Following the Government of Wales Act 1998, in 1999 all the Secretary of State's functions under the Children Act 1989 and many of the Secretary of State's functions under the Adoption Act 1976 were transferred to the Welsh Assembly. In post-devolution Acts impacting on social work with children and families, it is very common for separate and different provisions to be made for England and for Wales even though the Act as a whole 'extends' to both England and Wales. The Children Act 2004 is typical of this. It contains separate parts about the provision of children's services in England and the provision of children's services in Wales, a part setting up a Children's Commissioner for England (Wales already had one, established under the Care Standards Act 2000 and the Children's Commissioner for Wales Act 2001), a part dealing solely with the transfer of responsibility for the Child and Family Court Advisory and Support Service (CAFCASS) to the Welsh Assembly and lastly, separate provisions enabling the Secretary of State to regulate private fostering in England and enabling the Welsh Assembly to do so in Wales.

When it comes to secondary legislation, separate legislation for England and Wales is now the norm, with the Welsh Ministers making the secondary legislation for Wales and the Secretary of State making the secondary legislation for England.

Consequently, social workers carrying out child and family work in Wales and in England need to refer to different provisions in both primary and secondary legislation. The same applies to statutory guidance, informal guidance, directions, strategy documents and good practice guides. The differences are not just in form: there are important policy and institutional differences. These are likely to become more marked as the process of Welsh devolution continues under the Government of Wales Act 2006.

Guidance

Many documents are issued by the UK Government for England and the Welsh Assembly Government for Wales, directing the way in which statutory functions relating to children are to be carried out. Some of these are 'statutory guidance', meaning that they are issued under statutory authority. Examples are *Working Together to Safeguard Children* (DfES, 2006 / WAG, 2006) and the *Framework for the Assessment of Children in Need and their Families* (DoH, 2000; NAW, 2001), which are issued under s. 7 Local Authority Social Services Act 1970, and guidance about partnership working and children and young people's plans under ss. 17 and 26 Children Act 2004. Such statutory guidance carries considerable legal authority even though, as such guidance usually states, it is not 'law' and cannot undermine or override anything in legislation. Its legal authority comes from the fact that the courts will take it very seriously where any question arises as to the legality of action taken: in the absence of 'good reason, articulated in the course of some identifiable decision-making process', deviation from statutory guidance is likely to be regarded by the courts as a breach of the law (***R v Islington London Borough Council, ex parte Rixon* [1996]**).

Guidance not issued under statutory authority of this kind carries less legal authority but may still have a bearing on any determination of the legality of social work action. If such guidance, which might come in the form of circulars, practice guides or advice, were to be ignored, a decision to take a particular course of action might be held to be legally flawed if challenged by an application for judicial review (see Chapter 3).

Case-law

The legal framework for social work practice with children and families is essentially a statutory framework, but there are two important qualifications to this concerning the role of the courts.

First, only the courts have authority to interpret and declare the law. Any statutory provision means, ultimately, what a court decides it means. The words in the statute may therefore tell only part of the story. For example, the words 'likely to' suffer significant harm in s. 31 Children Act 1989 have been interpreted in a particular way (see Chapter 6).

Of course, the courts can only decide issues that are raised in cases brought before them. If an issue arises as to the meaning of a statutory provision and it has not been decided on by the courts, legal advice can be sought and different opinions may be offered but none can be regarded as authoritative. This can be a source of frustration when social workers naturally wish to know that a proposed course of action is legally sound and their legal advisers are unable authoritatively to assure them that it is: they can only give their best advice in the light of their professional knowledge about the way in which courts approach statutory interpretation.

Second, the courts play an important part in making law as well as in interpreting statutes. Many legal remedies were devised by the courts in England and Wales by means of the system of judicial precedent rather than by Act of Parliament. Such law is sometimes referred to as 'common law' (as opposed to statute law). For social work with children, probably the most important are the remedies for breach of the common law duty of care in negligence, breach of a statutory duty, breach of the common law duty of confidentiality and the remedies available on judicial review. These are explained in Chapter 3, as judicial mechanisms for accountability.

International law

The most important source of international law in relation to children is law contained in treaties, a term which covers written and binding legal agreements entered into by States, whether they are called a treaty or by some other name such as 'charter' or 'convention'. When the UK Government becomes a party to a treaty, the treaty's provisions become binding in international law but this does not make them directly enforceable in either the courts in England and Wales or the UK generally. For that to happen an Act of Parliament must be passed, and the Act may deal with the relative authority of international and national law. There is no set formula and a variety of approaches have been used.

The European Communities Act 1972, as amended by the European Communities (Amendment) Act 1993, requires the courts to give effect to directly enforceable EU rights and those rights may take precedence over any conflicting provision in national law, even if contained in an Act of the UK Parliament. The Human Rights Act 1998 adopts a different approach, imposing duties on the judiciary and on public bodies generally to act compatibly with the ECHR but maintaining the ultimate law-making supremacy of the UK Parliament. The Child Abduction and Custody Act 1985 adopts a different approach again, providing that the two Conventions to which it gives effect 'have the force of law' in the UK, but subject to the provisions in the Act which then sets out the processes to be followed in dealing with matters under the Convention in the UK.

The authority of EU law

The EU Treaties themselves confer certain rights and obligations. Others come in the form of EU secondary legislation, of which Regulations such as 'Brussels II' (see above, under *International law: mutual assistance*) are one variety. Treaty provisions and Council Regulations are directly applicable. Thus at the end of 'Brussels II' it is stated, 'This Regulation shall be binding in its entirety and directly applicable in the Member States ...' It is the combination of the binding nature of the Regulation with s. 2 of the European Communities Act 1972 which means that the Regulation will be given direct effect in the UK courts. It is directly imported into our law without the need for legislation by the UK Parliament or the Welsh Assembly. The EU Charter of Fundamental Rights does not as yet have this status: it has not yet become one of the Treaties to which s. 2 European Communities Act 1972 gives effect.

Nonetheless, EU law can provide a means of asserting a human rights claim before a national court, because fundamental rights, including those set out in the ECHR and any others resulting from the constitutional traditions common to the Member States are part of the 'general principles' of EU law. In the event that the subject matter of a dispute falls within the scope of EU law (as may be the case where a family's travel to or from or settlement in a EU Member State is involved) human rights under the ECHR are automatically relevant even without relying on the ECHR, and it could also be argued that notice must be taken of the extent to which respect for children's rights under the UNCRC has become established as a constitutional tradition common to Member States.

The authority of the law of the ECHR: the Human Rights Act 1998

The Human Rights Act 1998 does not give precedence to the ECHR over provisions in Acts of the UK Parliament. It gives further effect to the ECHR by creating three mechanisms: first, a strong interpretative obligation on the courts in the UK coupled with means of promoting compatible national legislation; second, a duty on public authorities to act compatibly; and third, the possibility of a claim in the UK courts arising out of a breach of that duty.

Interpretative obligation, declarations of incompatibility and remedial action: ss. 3, 4 and 10 Human Rights Act 1998

Section 3 provides that 'so far as it is possible to do so', primary legislation and subordinate legislation must be read and given effect in a way which is compatible with the Convention rights. Where it proves impossible to interpret primary legislation compatibly, the higher courts (High Court and above) may make a declaration of incompatibility under s. 4 of the Act. This signals to the government that change in the legislation is necessary in order to achieve compliance. It is up to the government then to decide what to do: s. 10 of the Act empowers but does not require the government to change the law by bringing forward secondary legislation. Under s. 19, new primary legislation has to be accompanied by a declaration of compatibility signed by the responsible Minister.

Duty of public authorities to act compatibly: s. 6

'Public authorities' include government departments, local authorities, organisations like CAFCASS, courts and tribunals. Accordingly, the Convention rights must be respected by these authorities and those working for them in everything they do. As the courts themselves are public authorities, they must act compatibly in making their decisions on all cases that come before them. This makes the Convention rights relevant in private family proceedings (not involving any other public authority) as well as public family proceedings (where the State, normally in the form of a local authority, is a party, as in care proceedings).

Enforcement by individual claim against a public authority: s. 7

The Act provides two methods of individual enforcement for a person who is a victim of an act which is unlawful by virtue of s. 6. Either a free-standing claim can be brought (s. 7(1)(a)) or the claim may be raised within existing proceedings (s. 7(1)(b)). Section 8 provides for remedies, which may include damages.

Authority of other international law

Where no Act of Parliament has been passed making the provisions of a treaty part of our law, the treaty's provisions may nonetheless be relevant in a number of ways:

- when interpreting statutes the courts apply a long-established rule that in case of ambiguity, they will follow an interpretation that is consistent with the international obligations of the UK;
- in developing the common law, the courts will seek to avoid conflict with the international obligations of the UK;
- incremental incorporation may occur, as appears to be happening with the UNCRC. This may take the form of adoption of the Convention as a set of overriding policy objectives (as has been done by the Welsh Assembly and by some local authorities) or of statutory references short of giving full legal effect to its provisions, as in the references to the UNCRC in the legislation governing the UK's four Children's Commissioners (see Chapter 3);
- indirect incorporation may occur, when a court determining an issue under the ECHR refers to another treaty such as the UNCRC for guidance as to how to interpret the ECHR: examples of this in cases relevant to social work with children include the *Howard League* case (Chapter 1) and *V and T v United Kingdom* (Chapter 8);
- the fact that the UK has accepted international obligations can act as a powerful force for change in domestic law and policy, especially when, as in the case of the UNCRC, the obligations include reporting and monitoring processes in which non-governmental organisations play a part;
- international law influences debate and thinking in professional, public and political spheres.

Box 2.7 lists the treaties that have been referred to in this chapter and indicates whether the UK is a party and, where applicable, the legislation giving effect to the treaty in the law of England and Wales.

Conclusion

This chapter has given an overview of the sources of law governing social work with children and families. Several themes emerge.

First, the relevant law in England and Wales takes account of international law so that in some areas such as human rights, discrimination law, the law on

Box 2.7   TREATY OBLIGATIONS RELATING TO CHILDREN

Treaty	UK a party	Legislation giving effect in the law of England and Wales
EU treaties and other directly applicable EU legislation ('Brussels II')	Yes	European Communities Act 1972 European Communities (Amendment) Act 1993
ECHR	Yes	Human Rights Act 1998
Hague Convention on the Civil Aspects of International Child Abduction 1980	Yes	Child Abduction and Custody Act 1985
European Convention on the Recognition and Enforcement of Decisions Concerning the Custody of Children 1980	Yes	Child Abduction and Custody Act 1985
UNCRC	Yes	Children's Commissioner for Wales Regulations 2001; Children Act 2004 (limited to the provisions describing the role of the children's commissioners)
Hague Convention on Protection of Children and Co-operation in Respect of Inter-country Adoption 1993	Yes	Adoption (Inter Country Aspects) Act 1999
European Convention on the Exercise of Children's Rights	No	
European Social Charter 1961	Yes	Various
European Convention on the Adoption of Children 1967	Yes	Adoption Act 1976, Adoption and Children Act 2002
European Convention on the Legal Status of Children Born out of Wedlock 1975	Yes	Family Law Reform Act 1987 removed most of the remaining legal disadvantages
European Convention on Contact Concerning Children 2003	No	

information and child abduction, national legislation represents a clear intention to give effect to international law as well as national and sub-national policy.

Second, this is not so clear in relation to the majority of legislation specifically about children in England and Wales: that is, the child welfare and child protection legislation based around the Children Act 1989. Here, there has been resistance to use of the language of rights. Consequently it falls to practitioners, guided by court judgments, to make the necessary connections between national and international law, in particular, between the powers and duties in England and Wales legislation and the requirements of the ECHR and UNCRC.

Third, both national and international laws have evolved in different contexts, in which different concepts – welfare, rights, protection and control – are dominant. This can create tension, but there are also principles which are evidenced in all the sources and which are wholly consonant with social work values for child care: promoting the best interests and development of the child, support for family unity and respect for the agency of the child.

Fourth, the different sources of law are inter-connected. It falls to the courts to interpret specific provisions compatibly or to give precedence to one source over another, following a quite complex set of legal rules.

Lastly, the requirements of human rights law including the ECHR and the UNCRC are not sufficiently known, understood and adhered to in social work practice with children and families. This situation is not helped by the fact that children's legislation for England and Wales eschews the language of rights and speaks instead of welfare, risk, protection and control. As will be seen in the next chapter, matters have not been improved by the changes introduced by the Children Act 2004. It is left to the child care social worker to become aware of the combined effect of national and international law and to interpret subject-specific powers and duties in a way which protects and promotes the rights and welfare of children.

Further Reading

A good general reference book is Andrew Bainham's *Children: The Modern Law*, 3rd edition. Jordan Publishing (2005).

On the impact of children's rights on the law in England and Wales, the best text is Jane Fortin's *Children's Rights and the Developing Law*, 2nd edition. LexisNexis Butterworths (2003).

The same author's article 'Accommodating children's rights in a post-Human Rights Act era', *Modern Law Review*, 69 (2006), pp. 299–326 provides an interesting critique of the absorption of rights-based thinking in judicial reasoning concerning children. She highlights the variation in this in different legal and/or policy contexts. This begs questions, including about the influence of the underlying child views and policy imperatives, touched upon in this chapter and in Chapter 1.

3

Accountability for Child Care Practice in England and Wales

- **Introduction**
- **Why devolution matters**
  A public law function
  Public bodies and private individuals
  Devolution
- **Organisational structures and policy development**
  Children's services within local authorities: the Children Act 2004
  Children and young people's plans
  Local authorities' wider and cognate functions
  Community strategies
  Joining up health and well-being: Wales
  Universal provision: education and training (England) and youth support services (Wales)
  Youth justice plans and community safety
  Drug Action Teams
  Central government policy on children and young people
  Social exclusion, poverty, 'outcomes' and rights
  Child protection
  Community safety and public order: the anti-social behaviour issue
  Domestic violence
- **Structures for accountability**
  Judicial remedies
  Actions in negligence
  Actions for breach of statutory duty
  Judicial review
  Human rights challenges
  Administrative machinery
  Inspection, review and audit of children's services
  Review and complaints in individual cases
  A 'children's champion'
  Children's Rights Director: England
- **The court system**
  Children Act 1989 proceedings
  Other civil proceedings
  Appeals
- **Conclusion**

This chapter considers accountability for child care social work practice in England and Wales. Child care social work is carried out within a layered and interconnected set of laws, policies and structures. Devolution under the Government of Wales Acts 1998 and 2006 brought the separation out of many of these for England and Wales. There is significant divergence between the Welsh and UK governments in policy on children and young people, still too frequently overlooked within a 'for Wales, see England' mentality. The immediate organisational context for statutory interventions remains the local authority. Most central government functions in relation to local authorities in Wales are now exercised by the Welsh Assembly Government rather than the Secretary of State, and, increasingly, separate laws are made for England and Wales in matters of public service delivery and social policy generally. Before surveying the post-devolution landscape in more detail, it is worth reminding ourselves why devolution of governmental functions matters in child care social work practice.

Why devolution matters

A public law function

As seen in Chapter 1, the definition of social work says that it 'intervenes at the points where people interact with their environments' (BASW, 2003). Put another way, social work operates at the intersection, or perhaps more accurately the overlap, between the private and public spheres of people's lives.

In a legal analysis, child care social work is a public law function. It is carried out on behalf of the State and represents the State accepting responsibility for supporting children in need and protecting them from harm. As such it fits within a scheme of checks and balances on the exercise of State power, characterised in a democratic constitution by the formal separation of 'legislative', 'judicial' and 'executive' functions. Local authority social work functions in relation to children are 'executive' functions of the State. The checks and balances on the exercise of these functions comprise:

- controls established by Parliament (the 'legislative function');
- administrative systems established by legislation (e.g. complaints procedures, inspection, audit and commissions); and
- control by the courts (the 'judicial' function).

Legislative controls include delineation of the circumstances in which it is lawful to take action and the creation of administrative frameworks for inspection and review. Judicial controls enable disputes about the lawfulness of action to be adjudicated upon.

Public bodies and private individuals

Social work, whether with children or any other group, can only happen either with the voluntary engagement of the client or, failing that, with clear statutory authority for the intervention. In either case, any social worker employed by a public body (like a local authority) can do, ultimately, only what the law authorises. This is because the law distinguishes between the powers of private individuals and public bodies. In a case that had nothing to do with social work with children, a senior judge put it like this:

To the famous question asked by the owner of the vineyard ('Is it not lawful for me to do what I will with mine own?' St Matthew Chapter 20, verse 15) the modern answer would be clear: 'Yes, subject to such regulatory and other constraints as the law imposes'. But if the same question were posed by a local authority the answer would be different. It would be: 'No, it is not lawful for you to do anything save what the law expressly or impliedly authorises. You enjoy no unfettered discretions. There are legal limits to every power you have.' (Sir Thomas Bingham, MR, in *R v Somerset County Council, ex parte Fewings* [1995])

Applying this principle to social work with children, a social worker working privately can do with her expertise, professional training and judgement whatever she wishes, subject to such constraints as the law imposes. A social worker working within a local authority social services department can do with her expertise, professional training and judgement only that which the law 'expressly or impliedly authorises'. Put another way,

The social work 'job' within a local authority is not to be a good social worker – it is to apply good social work and managerial skills to the task of carrying out statutory functions. (Spicer, 2006: 196)

Authorisation is to be found principally in statutory sources. For some purposes the statute alone is enough: support for children in need and their families, for example, is authorised by s. 17 Children Act 1989 without the need for any further authorisation. For other purposes judicial authority is required, typically where the intervention sought will interfere with private family rights. Any intervention must also be carried out in a lawful manner. This involves exercising discretion in a way that is fair, takes into account all that should be taken into account and is not influenced by extraneous considerations, prejudice or bias.

The structures and systems dealt with in this chapter can be seen as mechanisms for policing the intersection, or overlap, between the public and private spheres of people's lives, these points where 'people interact with their environments'. Their function is to direct or guide the way in which social workers carry out statutory functions in relation to children and families and to ensure accountability for any action taken.

Devolution has resulted in the separation out, for England and Wales, of the majority of legislative and administrative controls relating to social work. In other words, post-devolution statutory provisions are mainly generated and/or made for Wales by the Welsh Assembly and administrative controls are mainly exercised by separate institutions for England and Wales. Judicial controls are relatively untouched by devolution: there remains a single courts system for England and Wales although there is some administrative separation and an important difference in the right to use the Welsh language in court proceedings in Wales (s. 22 Welsh Language Act 1993).

The separate law for Wales and England is not always very obvious. A single primary legislative source (for example an Act of the UK Parliament such as the Children Act 2004 or the Learning and Skills Act 2000) often masks a different set of provisions for Wales and England. Parts or sections of an Act may provide for separate Welsh and English structures and beneath that, separate subordinate legislation and guidance is issued by the Welsh Assembly Government or the relevant UK government department – usually the Department of Health or the Department for Children, Schools and Families.

Box 3.1 illustrates the organisational structures and policy responsibility for England and Wales. Box 3.2 shows the separate structures for accountability.

Organisational structures and policy development

In **Box 3.1** it can be seen that the occupational standards for child care social work are the same for England and Wales, although they are issued separately by the English and Welsh bodies responsible for registration of social workers: the General Social Care Council and the Care Council for Wales respectively. The standards set out the broad areas of work undertaken by child care social workers in which they are expected to be able to demonstrate professional competence. These are shown in Box 3.3.

Children's services within local authorities: the Children Act 2004

The immediate statutory context for social work with children is to be found in the Children Act 2004, which builds on a structure dating back to the Local Authority Social Services Act 1970. The Children Act 2004 is quite prescriptive about the way in which children's services are to be organised and directed at the local level. It was part of the UK Government's response, set out in the Green Paper *Every Child Matters* (HM Treasury, 2003), to the report of the inquiry into the death of Victoria Climbié (Laming, 2003). It aimed to improve co-operation between local authorities and their 'relevant partners' as defined by the Act (that is, other agencies which have functions in relation to safeguarding children or promoting their welfare).

Box 3.1 POLICIES AND ORGANISATIONAL STRUCTURES FOR CHILD CARE SOCIAL WORK

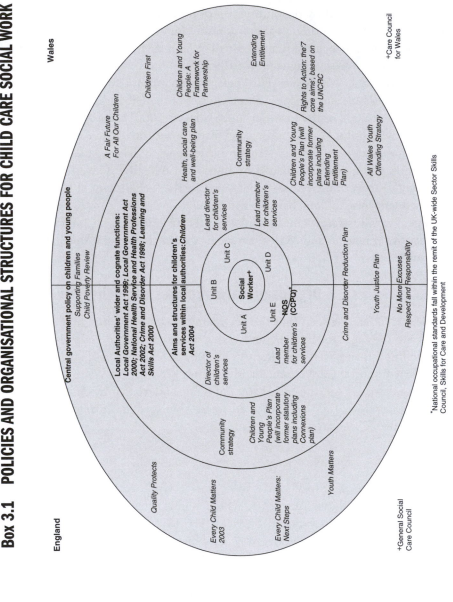

England

Wales

Central government policy on children and young people
Supporting Families
Child Poverty Review

A Fair Future For All Our Children

Children First

Local Authorities' wider and cognate functions:
Local Government Act 1999; Local Government Act 2000; National Health Service and Health Professions Act 2002; Crime and Disorder Act 1998; Learning and Skills Act 2000

Children and Young People: A Framework for Partnership

Aims and structures for children's services within local authorities: *Children Act 2004*

Health, social care and well-being plan

Extending Entitlement

Community strategy

Community strategy

Lead director for children's services

Children and Young People's Plan (will incorporate former plans including Extending Entitlement Plan)

Rights to Action: the 7 core aims', based on the UNCRC

Director of children's services

Unit C

Lead member for children's services

Unit B

Social Worker⁺

Unit D

Unit A

Unit E

NOS
(CCPq)⁺

Lead member for children's services

Children and Young People's Plan (will incorporate former statutory plans including Connexions plan)

Crime and Disorder Reduction Plan

Youth Justice Plan

All Wales Youth Offending Strategy

Quality Protects

No More Excuses
Respect and Responsibility

Every Child Matters 2003

⁺Care Council for Wales

Every Child Matters: Next Steps

Youth Matters

⁺General Social Care Council

*National occupational standards fall within the remit of the UK-wide Sector Skills Council, Skills for Care and Development

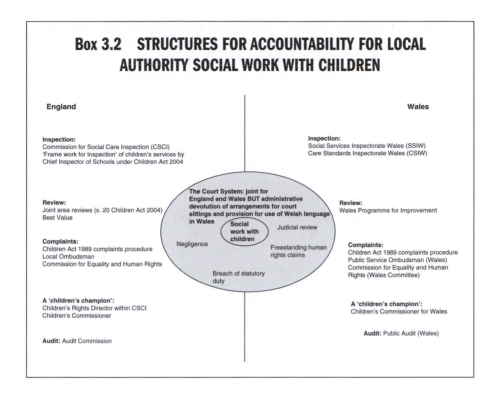

Box 3.2   STRUCTURES FOR ACCOUNTABILITY FOR LOCAL AUTHORITY SOCIAL WORK WITH CHILDREN

England

Inspection:
Commission for Social Care Inspection (CSCI)
'Frame work for Inspection' of children's services by Chief Inspector of Schools under Children Act 2004

Review:
Joint area reviews (s. 20 Children Act 2004)
Best Value

Complaints:
Children Act 1989 complaints procedure
Local Ombudsman
Commission for Equality and Human Rights

A 'children's champion':
Children's Rights Director within CSCI
Children's Commissioner

Audit: Audit Commission

Wales

Inspection:
Social Services Inspectorate Wales (SSIW)
Care Standards Inspectorate Wales (CSIW)

Review:
Wales Programme for Improvement

Complaints:
Children Act 1989 complaints procedure
Public Service Ombudsman (Wales)
Commission for Equality and Human Rights (Wales Committee)

A 'children's champion':
Children's Commissioner for Wales

Audit: Public Audit (Wales)

The Court System: joint for England and Wales BUT administrative devolution of arrangements for court sittings and provision for use of Welsh language in Wales

Social work with children

Judicial review

Negligence

Freestanding human rights claims

Breach of statutory duty

The Act makes provisions aimed at improving processes for collecting, sharing and using information effectively. In some respects it merely puts on a statutory footing pre-existing arrangements: for example under s.13 (for England) and s. 31 (for Wales), Area Child Protection Committees are given a formal status and role as Local Safeguarding Children Boards.

Box 3.3   NATIONAL OCCUPATIONAL STANDARDS FOR CHILD CARE SOCIAL WORK

Unit A: working directly with children and young people

Unit B: working with parents, families, carers and significant others to achieve optimal outcomes for children and young people

Unit C: undertaking and/or co-ordinating work with networks, communities and agencies to achieve optimal outcomes for children and young people in need

Unit D: contributing to the development of services, policies and practices which optimise life chances for all children and young people

Unit E: taking responsibility for the continuing professional development of self and others

The Act uses the term 'children's services' to refer to local authorities' educational, health and social services functions so far as they relate to children, coupled with the arrangements made by local authorities in partnership with other bodies to improve the well-being of children, safeguard them and promote their welfare. The term 'children's services authority' refers to a local authority carrying out these functions: the precise definition in s. 65 of the Act differs for England and Wales because of differences in types of local authorities in the two countries. The intention is to join up the organisation and direction of targeted (welfare) and universal (education and health) children's services.

In England, children's services authorities are required by the Act to appoint a director of children's services to take responsibility for these functions (the specific functions are listed in s. 18(2)). In many English authorities this entailed the merger of parts of former education and social services departments, bringing them under the responsibility of the director of children's services. In Wales, the Act imposes no such requirement, but local authorities must appoint a lead director to oversee arrangements for co-operation with other agencies and the development of the children and young people's plans as required by the Act (s. 27(1)). In both England and Wales a lead member (elected councillor) must be identified.

Children and young people's plans

The children and young people's plans drawn up under s. 17 (for England) and s. 26 (for Wales) Children Act 2004 provide the immediate, local policy context for social work with children. Guidance and regulations about the local partnerships and plans are issued for Wales by the Welsh Assembly and for England by the Secretary of State (DfES, 2005/WAG, 2006). In this implementing role, the Secretary of State has pursued strategies for England flowing from the Green Paper *Every Child Matters*, and the Welsh Assembly Government has pursued its own strategies for Wales flowing from its *Rights to Action* policy (WAG, 2004a). While the two strategies have much in common, there are also important differences, notably in the approach to absorption of rights-based policy and practice based on the UNCRC. This is discussed further later in this chapter.

Local authorities' wider and cognate functions

Beyond their responsibilities for 'children's services' under the Children Act 2004, local authorities have a range of wider and cognate statutory functions which have an important bearing on social work with children. Local authorities are required by law to produce plans and strategies in relation to these functions and these, in addition to the children and young people's plan, need to be taken into account as they too frame the exercise of child care social work functions. Box 3.4 shows those of most direct relevance to child care social work, but it is not exhaustive. A brief explanation of each follows.

Box 3.4   LOCAL PLANS AND STRATEGIES

Plan/Strategy	Statutory/ Policy base	Lead authority	Partners
Community Strategy	Local Government Act 2000	Local authority	Statutory and non-statutory agencies, voluntary organisations, community groups, etc., in 'local strategic partnerships'
Health, Social Care and Well-Being Strategy (Wales only)	National Health Service Reform and Health Care Professions Act 2002 / NHS (Wales) Act 2006	Local authority, together with Local Health Boards	Health bodies, voluntary organisations, the Welsh Assembly, private health and well-being services providers
Children and Young People's Plan	Children Act 2004	Local authority	Statutory partners include police, probation, youth offending teams, health and education bodies
Youth Justice Plan	Crime and Disorder Act 1998	Local authority	Police, probation, social services, youth services
Crime and Disorder Reduction Strategy (England) Community Safety Strategy (Wales)	Crime and Disorder Act 1998	Local authority together with chief officer of police	Police and probation, services must co-operate in the formulation of the strategy
Drug Action Team Plan	10-year national strategy *Tackling Drugs to Build a Better Britain* (TSO, 1998a)	Local authority	Range of statutory and non-statutory stakeholders

If the array of plans and strategies appears daunting, some comfort may be derived from the fact that the Local Government Act 2000, while itself imposing a new requirement for local authorities to prepare a community strategy, also introduced a system of review and plan rationalisation which may have the effect of reducing the burden on local authorities to some extent. The aspiration is for all the plans and strategies to complement and speak to each other within an overall set of priorities set by the local authority's community strategy.

Community strategies

Community strategies are produced under guidance issued separately for England and Wales under s. 4 Local Government Act 2000 for Wales and England (NAW, 2001; Defra, 2000). The community strategy is intended to reflect a vision for development of an area, shared by the community as a whole. Most strategies identify a number of themes or strategic aims, amongst which some form of commitment about children and young people is, unsurprisingly, ubiquitous. Perhaps the most significant thing about the requirement to produce a community strategy is the way in which they are required to be developed and implemented: there is great emphasis on the widest possible participation of statutory and non-statutory agencies, voluntary organisations, community groups and individuals, especially those most hard to reach by reason of social exclusion.

Joining up health and well-being: Wales

The National Health Service and Health Professions Act 2002 was one of a series of enactments reflecting a divergence in health policy that developed remarkably quickly after devolution. The 2002 Act provided for the establishment of primary care trusts as key commissioning bodies for health services in England, whereas for Wales the Act empowered the Welsh Assembly to establish Local Health Boards. The areas of the Local Health Boards so established are coterminous with local authority areas and the Boards have a remit to work jointly with local authorities to produce health and well-being strategies. Regulations made by the Welsh Assembly direct how these strategies are to be drawn up and what they are to contain (Health, Social Care and Well-being Strategies (Wales) Regulations 2003). Under these Regulations, Local Health Boards are required to integrate the health and well-being strategies with local plans for children's services. The first health, social care and well-being strategies drawn up pursuant to these requirements run from April 2005 for a period of three years and subsequent strategies run for five-year periods. These strategies do not exist in England. The Welsh provisions have now been consolidated within the NHS (Wales) Act 2006.

The Learning and Skills Act 2000 provides a framework for the provision:

- in England, of services to 'encourage, enable or assist' effective participation of 13- to 19-year-olds in education and training (s. 114); and
- in Wales, of 'youth support services' for 11- to 25-year-olds (s. 123).

Within this framework sit the Connexions service for England and the *Extending Entitlement* strategy for Wales.

Connexions is a network of 47 partnerships comprising local authorities, voluntary and statutory youth services, employment and training services, schools and colleges, health and youth justice services. They are promoted and directed by central government and supported by funding provided through local authorities and provide, somewhat uncomfortably (for example, Wylie, 2004), both universal services (principally the careers advisory service) and services targeted at socially excluded groups. Connexions personal advisers may offer a valuable resource for some children who come into contact with local authority social services, especially older children and those to whom duties are owed under the Children (Leaving Care) Act 2000 (see Chapter 8).

Extending Entitlement operates somewhat differently. It is the name given to the Welsh Assembly's direction and guidance to local authorities under s. 123 of the Learning and Skills Act 2000. It sets out a 'universal entitlement' for 11- to 25-year-olds in Wales and requires local authorities in Wales to develop strategies to deliver the entitlement. Consistent with the Assembly's commitment to the UNCRC (discussed below), the Entitlement ranges widely across provision, protection and participation issues and emphasises a positive approach to children's agency and achievement. There is no separate organisation responsible for delivery of the Entitlement: the main tools were initially young people's partnerships and plans established by local authorities, now subsumed in the arrangements for children and young people's plans under the Children Act 2004.

Youth justice plans and community safety

The Crime and Disorder Act 1998 requires local authorities to produce an annual plan setting out how youth justice services in its area are provided and funded and the functions, composition and funding of youth offending teams. The content of these plans is prescribed by the Youth Justice Board for England and Wales and the plans have to be submitted annually to the Board. The 1998 Act also requires local authorities together with the relevant chief officer of police to draw up a strategy setting out objectives and performance targets aimed at reducing crime and disorder. In England these are known as crime and disorder partnerships and in Wales, as community safety partnerships.

These plans and strategies are an important part of the context for social work with children at risk of offending and a number of other commonly encountered issues such as domestic violence.

Although criminal justice functions are not devolved to the Welsh Assembly, the separate framework for cognate services including social services, health, housing and education, means that there is scope for differences in implementation. To reflect these differences, and to establish a shared foundation for youth services providers in Wales, the Welsh Assembly Government and the Youth Justice Board issued an All Wales Youth Offending Strategy (WAG/YJB 2004). The Welsh Strategy makes explicit links with the UNCRC and prioritises children's welfare needs: young offenders are 'children first, offenders second'. The Strategy promotes the idea of universal entitlement set out in *Extending Entitlement* as the basis for preventative work at various levels of potential or actual involvement in the youth justice system. There is no equivalent document in respect of England, nor is there in any other Youth Justice Board publication such an overt association between youth justice policy and children's rights. Within the Youth Justice Board there is a consultative committee for Wales, chaired by a Board member, with responsibility for overseeing the delivery of the Welsh Strategy. The extent to which the Strategy can make an impact on practice in youth offending teams and associated agencies in Wales, whilst the institutional structure of the youth justice system remains a joint England and Wales one, has yet to be seen.

Drug Action Teams

Drug Action Teams were established in each local authority area in the late 1990s pursuant to a UK-wide government strategy, within which responsibility for implementation in Wales is substantially devolved to the Welsh Assembly Government (Home Office, 2002: 66, and see NAW, 2000). The primary functions of local strategies are prevention (aimed primarily at young people), reducing supply, reducing the impact of drug abuse on communities and promotion of treatment and support. Typically, local Drug Action Teams will involve a wide range of stakeholders and a number of groups: a steering group, commissioning group and various working groups.

Central government policy on children and young people

So far, we have seen that local authority social work with children is situated in a statutory construct of 'children's services' within local authorities and that this is linked to other statutory roles and responsibilities of local authorities. Direction and often a high degree of prescription come from central government, that is to say (mainly) the Welsh Assembly Government for Wales and (mainly) the Department for Children, Schools and Families. In turn, this is driven by the wider policy agendas of the two governments. It is worth noting certain features of this wider environment. Most remain common to England and Wales but there are some significant differences in emphasis, and in important respects there is an international dimension.

Social exclusion, poverty, 'outcomes' and rights

The social exclusion agenda focuses on the groups from which most child and family social workers' clients come. As Henricson and Bainham remarked, 'Combating social inequality is a core governmental function undertaken both for humanitarian reasons and to preserve the social fabric and cohesion of the State' (2005: 36). There is a human rights perspective, illustrated by the interpretation of Article 8 ECHR as creating a positive obligation to promote social rights (see Chapter 1) and by the UNCRC, especially Article 27 which requires State Parties to recognise the right of every child to a standard of living adequate for the child's physical, mental, spiritual, moral and social development. Article 4 UNCRC requires that States undertake measures 'to the maximum extent of their available resources' to implement children's economic, social and cultural rights.

There is an EU dimension too, since social cohesion is considered necessary for economic growth, and reduction in social exclusion is necessary for social cohesion. EU leaders, meeting at the European Council of Lisbon in 2000, produced an agreement requiring member States to produce, implement and monitor National Action Plans on Social Exclusion. The UK's National Action Plan is submitted by the Department for Work and Pensions. In line with objectives set by the EU, the UK's plan includes as key objectives the elimination of child poverty and improving access to quality services including health and social care (DWP, 2006). Thus, the measurement and reduction of children's social exclusion is integrated into EU economic and social policy, and the Lisbon agreement has stimulated development of more sophisticated, multi-dimensional indicators of social exclusion, taking into account such matters as access to education, housing, health and technological resources as well as relative income poverty (for example, Levitas et al., 2007).

The UK Government made a commitment to eradicate child poverty by 2020 and set targets for reduction of numbers of children living in relative low-income households and numbers of children suffering a combination of material deprivation and relative low income (HM Treasury, 2004). The Welsh Assembly Government has published its own strategy on child poverty (WAG, 2004b). Both the HM Treasury and the Welsh Assembly documents specifically acknowledge the UNCRC obligations and the Assembly's strategy makes explicit links with the Assembly's seven core aims (see 'Rights to Action', above) which are themselves based on the UNCRC.

The Children Act 2004, formulated roughly contemporaneously with these policy developments, makes no such explicit link with this international agenda. The Act's five 'aspects of well-being' include social and economic well-being but, as already noted in Chapter 2, the UK Government deliberately avoided adopting the UNCRC or the language of children's rights as explicit references for the direction of children's services. To some extent this is ameliorated in Wales by the Welsh Assembly's adoption of the UNCRC as an overarching policy framework within which children's services are delivered. This seems more coherent than the English position, since the international context is relevant to both the employment/fiscal aspects for which the Department for Work and Pensions and HM Treasury have the main responsibility and the children's services aspects which fall mainly to the Department for Children, Schools and Families and the Welsh Assembly. The Childcare Act 2006 represents something of a fusion of these different areas of responsibility.

Presented as a measure to help meet the government's commitments on child poverty, it built on the Treasury-driven Sure Start and Children's Centres initiatives. For England, but not Wales, the 2006 Act replicates the five 'aspects of well-being', together with a duty to reduce inequalities, in setting out local authorities' general functions in relation to young children. New duties to provide support, advice and assistance to parents in procuring child care services are placed on local authorities in both Wales and England.

Child protection

The protection of children from abuse is an obligation under Article 18 UNCRC and is an aspect of the positive duty of the State under Articles 2, 3 and 8 ECHR. It is a longstanding objective of children's legislation for England and Wales, dating back to the late nineteenth century. Legal protection takes the form of criminal offences and the protective powers and duties of local authorities under the Children Act 1989.

Public inquiries and serious case reviews have repeatedly identified failures of local authorities and other agencies to protect children who come to their attention. There are some consistent themes:

- inadequate collaboration between agencies;
- inadequate systems for recording and using information within agencies, or failures in using the systems that exist;
- lack of sufficient experienced front-line staff, and lack of supervision of less experienced staff;
- insufficient attention to support for children and families in need, as opposed to 'child protection';
- failure to focus on the child rather than the adults in the family;
- failure to strike an appropriate balance between respect for cultural difference and standards of child care and protection that should be universal;
- failure to protect looked after children from abuse within the care system, especially in institutional settings;
- lack of sufficient resources, especially for support of children and families in need.

The Laming Report found that the legislative framework for protecting children, based on the powers and duties in the Children Act 1989, was not the problem. The gap was not caused by a deficiency in the law but in its implementation, and this was a matter of both structures and skills (Laming, 2003: para 1.30). The Children Act 2004 introduced measures attempting to address some of these problems. Its focus was on improving processes within and between agencies, formalising inter-agency collaboration and seeking to tighten up on handling and use of information. However, neither the 2004 Act nor the Children Act 1989 directly addresses the problems of staffing levels, professional competence and resources, nor the factors which contribute to failures in practice to put the child's needs at the centre of an investigation or assessment. A clearer presentation of a basic level of support and protection as a matter of right, in accordance with the UNCRC, would have gone further towards achieving this. The mismatch between the Children Act 2004's 'aspects of well-being' and the rights of the child under the UNCRC is not just a matter of language.

Community safety and public order: the anti-social behaviour issue

The Labour government which came to power in 1997 had adopted the slogan 'tough on crime, tough on the causes of crime'. The Home Office White Paper *No More Excuses* (Home Office, 1997) set out plans for whole-sale reform of the youth justice system, creating new national and local structures and a range of new powers and orders that the courts can make. The Crime and Disorder Act 1998 provided for the setting up of the new structures and introduced anti-social behaviour orders (ASBOs) and associated requirements for the development of local strategies to improve community safety. The White Paper *Respect and Responsibility* (Home Office, 2003) developed further the government's agenda on anti-social behaviour. By the end of 2005, these policies had generated 6,500 ASBOs and 13,000 acceptable behaviour contracts in England and Wales (Home Office, 2006). Over half of all ASBOs are made against children. There are serious concerns, discussed further in Chapter 9, about their compatibility with children's welfare and rights. This is reflected in a wide academic literature, has featured in a number of legal challenges (including an unsuccessful attempt by the Northern Ireland Commissioner for Children and Young People to prevent the introduction of similar measures in Northern Ireland) and has attracted adverse commentary from the UN Committee on the Rights of the Child (UN, 2002a).

The UK Government insists that its anti-social behaviour measures must be seen in the context of other measures aimed at reducing disadvantage, such as Sure Start, child tax credits and the development of youth support services and sports facilities. It is striking that little attempt is made to situate the community safety policies within a rights-based framework. The Government explains that its 'Respect' agenda is based on 'shared commitment to a common set of values' which include 'respect for others, their property and privacy ... a recognition that everyone has responsibilities as well as rights' (Home Office, 2006a: 5). These values and legal measures designed to protect individuals and communities from the effects of anti-social behaviour can readily be expressed in terms of a balancing of rights: ECHR case-law has recognised that some form of protection by the State may be required by Article 8 (see further Chapter 9), and there is nothing in the UNCRC to suggest that children's rights include being allowed to behave anti-socially. There are perhaps two related reasons for eschewing a rights-based framework in this arena. The first is the problem of public perception of the problem of youth offending, which is thought to feature high in voters' priorities. The second is that on the children's rights side of the equation, there ought to be greater allowance for children's immaturity and developmental needs than can be accommodated within the 'robust response' demanded by the Respect agenda (Home Office, 2006: 7). Whatever the reasons for it, this suppression of rights and child welfare considerations in approaches to youth justice creates yet more complexities in the organisational and policy environment for child care social work.

Domestic violence

There has long been official awareness of domestic violence as an issue requiring particular legal and policy responses. In 2004, a UK Government-commissioned report documented the economic and social cost of domestic violence (WEU, 2004). This report galvanised governmental activity and a seeming tidal wave of activity followed across agencies, including changes in legislation and the adoption of policies and training initiatives by the police, probation and prosecution services, statutory and voluntary support agencies and non-governmental organisations. The UK Government's *Safety and Justice* strategy (TSO, 2003) included changes, effected by the Domestic Violence and Victims of Crime Act 2004, to tighten legal protection in the form of court orders and enforcement measures, building on the system contained in the Family Law Act 1996. In Wales, the Welsh Assembly Government produced the *All Wales Domestic Violence Strategy* (WAG, 2005b). These strategies promote a pro-active, inter-agency approach to identification and prosecution of domestic violence, support for victims and rehabilitation of offenders. They endorse a wide notion of domestic violence covering a range of abusive behaviour which occurs in the context of personal relationships. Whilst the focus is mainly on relationships between adults, an important feature of these recent developments is the recognition that when a child witnesses or lives with domestic violence, it is a child protection issue. This is reflected in an amendment to the statutory definition of 'harm', which can trigger compulsory measures under the Children Act 1989, to embrace harm caused by witnessing violence to another. This is discussed further in Chapter 6.

Box 3.2 above showed the main structures for accountability for social work decisions. They are judicial (actions brought before the courts seeking redress for wrongful or sub-standard action) and administrative (mechanisms for inspection, review, complaints and audit). Judicial remedies remain common to England and Wales. The administrative mechanisms are separate.

Judicial remedies

The judicial checks and balances on the exercise of child care social work functions can conveniently be dealt with under four headings: actions for damages for negligence, actions for damages for breach of statutory duty, applications for judicial review and human rights claims. These are the legal claims most likely to be made where things go wrong – where it is alleged that a social worker has exceeded or misinterpreted his authority to act or acted in a less than professionally competent way.

Actions in negligence

When it is reasonably foreseeable that a person (C) will suffer harm if another person (D) acts or fails to act, and there is a relationship of sufficient proximity between C and D for it to be fair, just and reasonable to impose a duty on D for the benefit of C, the law imposes such a duty. It is often referred to as the 'common law duty of care'. C will have a claim for compensation if D breaches the duty by failing to act to a reasonable standard of care and, as a result, C suffers harm. This is known as an action in negligence.

Social workers working with children may develop a relationship which puts them in the position of 'D' with their child client in the position of 'C'. Box 3.5 illustrates this with a fictitious example. Here, David owed a duty to Carl and breached the duty by failing to record and communicate information in a manner consistent with a reasonable professional standard of care: he should have sought expert medical assessment of the allergy issue.

This form of liability is relatively new in social work. The courts used to reject the idea of a social workers' liability in negligence for two reasons. Firstly, the duties owed by a social worker were owed to the public generally, not to the individual client. Secondly, it would be contrary to the public interest to place the burden of risk of litigation on professionals carrying out very difficult and sensitive work in child protection. This approach has not survived the influence of the ECHR and Human Rights Act 1998. A line of cases starting with *X (Minors) v Bedfordshire* [1995], which went to the ECtHR as *Z v United Kingdom* [2001], has effectively removed any public interest immunity from legal action previously enjoyed by child care social workers.

Box 3.5   AN ACTION IN NEGLIGENCE

Carl, aged 5, was referred to Blankshire Social Services because of concerns that he might be suffering neglect at home. David, a social worker in Blankshire's child and family team, was assigned to the case. Following investigation and assessment an interim care order was applied for and obtained and Carl was placed in short-term foster care. David omitted to record information given to him by Carl's parents that suggested he might have a food allergy. This information was not in Carl's medical records and David took the view that Carl's parents were being untruthful in an effort to cover up their own shortcomings. Consequently, the information was not communicated to the foster carers. Carl became acutely ill after eating a peanut butter sandwich in the foster home.

Nevertheless, in practice, it will still be an exceptional case that meets all the criteria for a claim in negligence. Even if all the requirements for a duty of care are made out, cases may founder on issues of whether the duty was in fact breached (i.e. whether the conduct of the social worker fell below a reasonable professional standard) and whether the damage was caused by the breach or was too remote from it. As yet, the courts have not been prepared to countenance an extension of any possible duty of care to include parents (as opposed to the child) in a child protection investigation. The development of this area of the law, and its non-application to parents, was considered in the House of Lords decision in *JD (FC) v East Berkshire Community Health Trust and others* [2005] (Box 3. 6).

Actions for breach of statutory duty

A claim for damages for breach of statutory duty may be made alongside a claim in negligence or independently. To establish the claim it must be shown that a person (D) was under a duty imposed by statute and that the statute should be so interpreted as to confer a right of individual action on a person (C) who was intended to benefit. Then, if it can be shown that D breached the statutory duty (which may be a matter of showing a want of reasonable care or may be a matter of strict liability) and if C can show that s/he suffered damage as a result, C may be entitled to compensation.

On the whole, the duties imposed on local authorities in relation to social work with children do not give rise to actions of this kind: this aspect of the decision in *X (Minors) v Bedfordshire* remains good law notwithstanding the subsequent developments in relation to the common law duty of care. This is either because duties are general duties (like s. 17 Children Act 1989 – to provide services to children in need generally, not to provide a specific service to a specific child) or because the courts take the view that in passing the legislation

Parliament did not intend to confer an individual right of action. An important qualification to this arises where it can be shown that a person's ECHR rights are engaged, and in this respect the law is also, to borrow Lord Bingham's phrase in the *JD* case at Box 3.6, 'on the move': see further, the discussion of *R (G) v Barnet London Borough Council and others [2003]* and *R (J) v Enfield London Borough Council [2002]* in Chapter 5.

Box 3.6   DUTIES TO CHILDREN AND PARENTS IN CHILD ABUSE INVESTIGATIONS

In *JD (FC) v East Berkshire Community Health Trust and others* [2005], three separate cases were considered by the House of Lords. In each case, a child was suspected to have suffered abuse at home but it subsequently turned out that this was not so. In fact, the children's symptoms were attributable to wholly innocent medical causes (which were, respectively, a generalised allergic condition, Schamberg's disease and brittle bone disease). The misdiagnosis had led to separation of the children from their parents and the question arose whether the parents, as well as the children, could claim damages for negligence against the authorities concerned. Four of the five law lords in the case held that they could not: the fifth, Lord Bingham, noted that the law in this area was 'on the move' under the influence of the ECHR and felt it ought to be allowed to develop incrementally. He was not prepared to say that a duty could never be owed to parents in such cases.

Judicial review

Judicial review is a key constitutional mechanism whereby administrative decisions or executive action can be challenged and scrutinised by the courts. It is a form of judicial control of the executive function of the State and is available in relation to a wide range of decisions made pursuant to statutory powers. An application may be brought with the leave of the court by a person having a sufficient interest in the decision. It is not an appeal or review of the substance of the decision. Rather, its role is to ensure that decisions are made lawfully, that is to say that they are within the proper scope of the powers conferred on the decision-maker, are reached rationally and that a fair process is followed. The grounds for judicial review were famously summarised by Lord Diplock, in a case not concerned with social work, as 'illegality, irrationality and procedural impropriety' (*Council for the Civil Service Unions v Minister for the Civil Service* [1985]). To this list must be added the further ground of proportionality, imported from ECHR case-law. As noted in Chapter 2,

75

proportionality is relevant whenever the court has to consider whether interference with a qualified Convention right (like Article 8) is justified.

Generally, judicial review is not appropriate where there are other means by which a court can determine whether a particular social work decision is legally sound. Thus, the question whether a care order should be made is one which falls to the court and it is in that context that the content of a care plan may fall to be considered. In care proceedings the court is concerned with the substantive question whether the proposed plan is in accordance with the child's welfare, but the court can also deal with issues about the legality and rationality of the plan and the fairness of the process which led to it. Judicial review is therefore inappropriate as a means of challenging a care plan drawn up for the purposes of care proceedings. It may be appropriate in relation to a range of decisions which could not otherwise be scrutinised by a court, for example:

- a decision to place a child's name, and information about a suspected abuser, on the child protection register (now, the Integrated Children's System: see Chapter 6): **R v Norfolk County Council ex parte M [1989]**, although usually there should first be recourse to the complaints procedure under s. 26 Children Act 1989: **R v Hampshire CC ex parte H [1999]**;
- a decision relating to a care plan drawn up outside care proceedings, where services are being provided on a voluntary basis under s. 17 and/or s. 20 Children Act 1989 and an application for a care order is not warranted: **CD v Isle of Anglesey [2004]**: see further Chapter 5;
- a decision not to provide services or to provide services which are alleged to be inadequate to meet a child's needs: see further the cases about needs assessment and support under s. 17 Children Act 1989 in Chapter 5;
- a decision to separate a mother and baby where the mother is serving a term of imprisonment (the decision would be for the prison service rather than social services but local authority social workers would invariably be involved): e.g. **CF v Secretary of State for the Home Department [2004]** (Chapter 2).

Human rights challenges

Under the Human Rights Act 1998, an issue about a person's Convention rights can, if relevant, be raised in any legal proceedings in the UK. This is because

- the courts, as public authorities under s. 6 of the Act, must act compatibly with the Convention rights;
- s. 3 requires the courts to interpret legislation in a way which gives effect to Convention rights;
- s. 7 entitles a person who claims to be a victim of a breach of s. 6 to rely on Convention rights in any legal proceedings; and
- as an alternative, s. 7 entitles a person claiming to be a victim of a breach of s. 6 to bring proceedings against the public authority concerned.

Usually the courts will prefer the Convention points to be raised in the course of any existing legal proceedings rather than starting separate proceedings. Thus a claim may be made in the course of family proceedings, a claim for negligence or breach of statutory duty or a judicial review application.

So far as care proceedings are concerned, the High Court has held that human rights issues arising while proceedings are still ongoing should be dealt with in those proceedings rather than by starting a separate claim (*Re L (Care Proceedings: Human Rights Claims)* [2003]). Where the care proceedings have finished, it may be appropriate to issue a free-standing claim but equally the claim could be made within another application, such as an application to discharge a care order or an application for contact.

Administrative machinery

Administrative machinery for accountability in child care social work comprises processes for inspection, review, audit and complaints. This machinery is neither legislative nor judicial and is, in terms of the traditional separation of powers referred to at the beginning of this chapter, part of the executive function of the State. It represents one executive agency supervising another, each pursuant to a statutory remit and therefore subject ultimately to the supervision of the courts by way of judicial review. It performs an important function in ensuring that services are carried out lawfully and effectively. Since devolution there has been an incremental but quite rapid separation out of this administrative machinery for Wales and England.

Inspection, review and audit of children's services

For England, the Commission for Social Care Inspection (CSCI) has a remit covering social care services generally, in adult and children's services and in the public, private and voluntary sectors. It was set up under Health and Social Care (Community Health and Standards) Act 2003 and is the lead inspectorate of social care for England. Under s. 76 of the 2003 Act, the CSCI is required, in exercising its functions, to be concerned in particular with:

(a) the availability of, and access to, the services;
(b) the quality and effectiveness of the services;
(c) the management of the services;
(d) the economy and efficiency of their provision and their value for money;
(e) the availability and quality of information provided to the public about the services;
(f) the need to safeguard and promote the rights and welfare of children; and
(g) the effectiveness of measures taken by local authorities for the purpose specified in paragraph (f).

Under the Children Act 2004, the CSCI is required to work in an integrated way with the inspectorates covering the prisons, health care, probation,

ACCOUNTABILITY FOR PRACTICE

education, police, prosecution and courts services. Annual performance assessments for children's services are carried out jointly by CSCI and Ofsted (Office for Standards in Education), and these assessments make judgements about local authorities' achievements against the five 'aspects of well-being' and their capacity to improve services. In addition, a more wide-ranging appraisal of the well-being of children is required, with each children's services authority area undergoing a periodic joint area review involving some or all of the nine inspectorates listed in s. 20 of the 2004 Act.

All of these inspectorates, including CSCI, are expected to use a framework for assessment of children's services issued under s. 21 Children Act 2004 (Ofsted, 2005a) in addition to the specialist frameworks already used by the individual inspectorates. The scope of the assessment framework under the 2004 Act is very wide, covering statutory, voluntary and private providers of services to 0- to 19-year-olds and those receiving services as care leavers. The purpose is to ensure that the inspections evaluate services against the five 'aspects of well-being', from which the assessment framework derives eight principles for inspection. Consistent with the 2004 Act itself, the Framework makes no explicit reference to the rights of service users, although one of the eight principles requires inspectors to 'take account of the views of children and young people and seek to involve them in inspections in other ways' (Ofsted, 2005a: 5).

The Children Act 2004 requires that in addition to the annual performance assessments there must be joint area reviews for each children's services authority area in England. Again, the focus is on measuring achievement against the five 'aspects of well-being' and 'key judgements' are specified in relation to each of them (Ofsted, 2005b). These are at a fairly high level of generality. For example, Box 3.7 shows the key judgements for 'protection from harm and neglect' (one of the five 'aspects of well-being'), translated by Ofsted as 'staying safe'.

Joint area reviews (JARs) will normally be arranged to coincide with periodic assessment by the Audit Commission of local authorities' corporate performance (Ofsted, 2005b). An Audit Commission inspector will be a member of the 'JAR' team as well as carrying out the corporate performance assessment. The Audit Commission's role is to report on the economy, efficiency, effectiveness and performance of local government. The aims of holding the reviews together are to reduce the burden of inspection, to avoid duplication in evidence-gathering where possible and to enable relevant links to be made between organisation and delivery of children's services and the overall performance of local government in an area.

For Wales, there are two inspectorates which carry out, broadly, the inspection and review functions carried out for England by CSCI. They are the Social Services Inspectorate for Wales (SSIW) and the Care Standards Inspectorate for Wales (CSIW). Both are operationally independent branches of the Welsh Assembly Government, to which they also provide advice.

A third inspectorate, covering health care, is similarly situated. Under the Public Audit (Wales) Act 2004, a Wales Audit Office was established to carry out for Wales broadly the same functions as the Audit Commission continues to carry out for England.

The Children Act 2004 provisions about annual performance assessment and joint area reviews do not apply to Wales. Instead, under s. 30 of the 2004 Act, inspection and review of children's services is brought within the previously existing responsibilities of the Welsh Assembly under the Health and Social Care (Community Health and Standards) Act 2003. Under s. 93 of the 2003 Act, SSIW carries out a cycle of reviews of adult services, children's services and joint reviews with the Wales Audit Office. In carrying out these functions, SSIW is required under s. 97 of the 2003 Act to be concerned in particular with the same matters as set out for CSCI in s. 76 (quoted above).

The additional layer of inspection and review requirements linked to the five 'aspects of well-being' under the Children Act 2004 has not been applied to Wales. SSIW and the Wales Audit Office have devised their own matrix for measurement of performance in joint reviews, based on just two questions: first, how good are the services? and second, how well placed is the authority to sustain and improve performance (SSIW, WAO, 2005)? Seven 'domains' are used to make judgements on these questions and in these domains there are resonances with some of the matters with which SSIW is required to be particularly concerned under s. 97 of the 2003 Act. Thus, in measuring how good the services are, the domains are access to services, assessment, care management and review, range of services provided, quality of services provided, arrangements to protect vulnerable people and success in promoting independence and social inclusion. Given the Assembly's declared commitment to the UNCRC as an overarching set of principles, it is disappointing to note that there is no clear reflection in this list of a 'particular concern' to safeguard and promote the rights and welfare of children. For the time being, therefore, the framework for inspection and review of children's services in Wales as well as England tends to suppress consideration of UNCRC compliance as a measure of success.

Review and complaints in individual cases

Complaints procedures and advocacy services are services the local authority must provide under Pt. III Children Act 1989 (as amended by the Adoption and Children Act 2002: see Chapter 5). Section 26 Children Act 1989 requires each local authority to have a complaints procedure to deal with complaints about any aspect of the broad range of local authority functions under the 1989 Act. The courts have made it plain that they will normally expect this procedure to be used before any application for judicial review is made: *R v Royal Borough of Kingston upon Thames ex p. T* [1994]. Judicial review is possible either of the panel's decision or of a local authority's decision not to implement the complaints panel's recommendation. The latter situation was the subject of *Re T (Accommodation by Local Authority)* [1995] where it was held that the local authority could not, however, be compelled to follow a panel recommendation that a looked after child should reside with particular foster carers: judicial review would be limited to the legality of the decision in question rather than its merits.

For children looked after by a local authority there is also a system of regular review of implementation of the individual care plan, regardless of whether any complaint has been made. This procedure was introduced by the Adoption and Children Act 2002 as a response to judicial recognition, in *Re S, Re W* [2002], that the lack of regular review may lead to breaches of Article 8 ECHR. Concerns for the position of looked after children had also been raised by the Utting Report, *People Like Us* (TSO, 1997) and the Waterhouse Report, *Lost in Care* (TSO, 2000). The most important changes in the system are the requirement for the appointment of an independent reviewing officer in respect of every looked after child and for the provision of advocacy services for children who wish to make representations.

Regulations made under ss. 26 and 26A prescribe the procedure, the qualifications and role of the independent reviewing officer and the arrangements for provision and monitoring of advocacy services. These are dealt with in Chapter 8. On the face of it, the system provides protection for children in care and supports their participation in decisions made about them by the local authority as corporate parent. There are links between the system for review of individual cases and the general inspection and review processes, in the form of performance indicators for such things as the percentage of children directly communicating their views to a statutory review. It remains to be seen what difference this will make in terms of securing respect for children's substantive rights – to survival and development, educational opportunity and to support in overcoming physical, social and economic disadvantage. Important as it is, participation should not be regarded as an end in itself.

A 'children's champion'

The role of a children's commissioner has been described as that of a 'children's champion' – an advocate for children's rights and interests. Wales and England have separate children's commissioners with different statutory remits. There are also children's commissioners for Scotland and Northern Ireland.

An independent 'children's champion' at national level, either in the form of a children's commissioner, ombudsperson or as part of a national human rights institution, is regarded by the United Nations Committee on the Rights of the Child as central to implementation of the UNCRC (UN, 2002b; UN, 2003a). The Council of Europe supports this approach (Council of Europe, 1998). A children's commissioner's functions may include review of services and dealing with complaints but the idea is more broadly based than either or even both of these. The UN Committee's reasons for supporting the establishment of children's commissioners include those in favour of the establishment of national human rights institutions generally: that is, to promote changes in policy and practice and to support individual complaints in order to ensure effective respect for human rights. In respect of children, the UN Committee cites additional factors: their vulnerability, their lack of voice in society, their exclusion from the political process and the particular problems they encounter in accessing and using the judicial and administrative remedies that are formally available to them. In its concluding observations on the UK's initial report, the UN Committee recommended the establishment of a children's commissioner (UN, 1995a). This lent weight to lobbying from a variety of voluntary and statutory bodies. For Wales, the establishment of a children's commissioner was the first recommendation of the Waterhouse Report into child abuse in health and social care settings in North Wales (TSO, 2000).

The Children's Commissioner for Wales was established in two stages, under Pt. V Care Standards Act 2000 and under the Children's Commissioner for Wales Act 2001. The Commissioner's functions include reviewing and monitoring the arrangements made by care providers for complaints, whistle-blowing, advocacy, advice and support, providing advice, information and assistance to children, examining individual cases and making reports. The Commissioner's 'principal aim' is 'to safeguard and promote the rights and welfare of children' (s. 72A of the 2000 Act) and, under Reg. 22 of the Children's Commissioner for Wales Regulations 2001, the Commissioner must 'have regard to' the UNCRC in exercising all his or her functions.

Of the four children's commissioners within the UK, the Children's Commissioner for Wales (CCfW) has the most extensive powers to provide advice and assistance and to deal with complaints and investigations in individual cases. In 2005–6 the Commissioner's advice and support service dealt with cases involving 566 children and young people (CCfW, 2006: 13). Education, especially special educational needs, and social services are the most frequent subjects of these cases (CCfW, 2006: 16). Often the role of the Commissioner's office is limited to liaising with other statutory bodies, advocating for concerns raised by or on behalf of the child, or simply referring on as appropriate.

The Welsh Commissioner has powers of independent investigation and review. An early example was the Clwych Examination into allegation of child sexual abuse in schools (CCfW, 2004). The inquiry made numerous findings of fact and recommendations for changes in process and practice to which the Welsh Assembly Government responded, undertaking to take forward some of the recommendations in the process of its implementation of the Children Act 2004 in Wales. The Commissioner has made clear that in the event of the government's response to such recommendations being less than satisfactory, he would be ready to use his powers to investigate the government's own decision-making processes (CCfW, 2006: 42).

The English Commissioner (technically, the Commissioner established under the Children Act 2004 for non-devolved matters throughout the UK but otherwise, for children in England) has a remit closely tied to the *Every Child Matters* agenda. This is considerably narrower than envisaged in the Laming report's recommendations on national structures. Laming had recommended that a Ministerial Children and Families Board should be established, to which a new National Agency for Children and Families should report. This proposed Agency would have a chief executive whose role would incorporate the responsibilities of a children's commissioner. The Agency's functions would have included advising on implementation of the UNCRC, child impact assessments, scrutiny of proposed legislation, conduct or oversight of serious case reviews and an annual report to Parliament on the quality of services to children and families.

Every Child Matters did propose that a children's commissioner be established by statute, but without many of the functions specified by Laming. In particular, the advisory role on UNCRC implementation and the serious case review functions were omitted. Instead, the commissioner's function would be to collect and represent the views of children, and to represent the 'interests' of children, in government policy processes directed at the five 'aspects of well-being'. This is the formulation enacted in Pt. I of the 2004 Act.

The English Commissioner has the general function of 'promoting awareness of the *views and interests* of children in England' (s. 2(1) Children Act 2004, emphasis added). In particular, the Commissioner may:

(a) encourage persons exercising functions or engaged in activities affecting children to take account of their views and interests;
(b) advise the Secretary of State on the views and interests of children;
(c) consider or research the operation of complaints procedures so far as relating to children;
(d) consider or research any other matter relating to the interests of children;
(e) publish a report on any matter considered or researched by him.

The Commissioner is 'in particular' to be concerned with the views and interests of children so far as relating to the five 'aspects of their well-being' set out in s. 2(3) of the 2004 Act. There is a reference to the UNCRC in the 2004 Act but only as an aid to interpretation as to what the 'interests' of children might be: in considering this, the Commissioner 'must have regard to' the Convention.

The English Commissioner has powers of investigation in individual cases, but only where the case raises some issue of public policy of relevance to other children, where the Commissioner is satisfied that the inquiry would not duplicate work that is the function of some other person and after consultation with the Secretary of State. This means that the consequence of a referral to the Children's Commissioner for Wales could be quite different from the consequences of a referral to the English Children's Commissioner, as shown in Box 3.8.

Children's Rights Director: England

The CSCI includes a Children's Rights Director whose role is to secure that in carrying out its functions the CSCI safeguards and protects the rights and welfare of children and young persons who are receivers of social care services and gives proper consideration to their views and the views of their parents. The Children's Rights Director is required to monitor, and report to the CSCI on, the effectiveness of measures taken by local authorities for the purposes of safeguarding the rights and welfare of children and young persons and the effectiveness of service providers' complaints and whistle-blowing arrangements. The office is also intended to provide a conduit for the views of service users to be made known to the CSCI and to alert CSCI to improvements that may need to be made in national standards. The office does not investigate individual cases but has a statutory duty to report to the police or relevant local authority any case where there is reasonable cause to suspect that a child who is a service user is suffering, or is likely to suffer, significant harm.

Box 3.8   COMPLAINTS TO THE CHILDREN'S COMMISSIONERS: WALES AND ENGLAND

Referral	Children's Commissioner for Wales	English Children's Commissioner
Leah, a disabled child, is awaiting provision of home support services before being able to be discharged from hospital and resume schooling. There have been repeated delays	Could provide advice, contact relevant agencies and make representations on Leah's behalf	No power to provide advice or assistance
Leah's case suggests a systemic problem in the provision of home support services	Could conduct an examination if satisfied the case raises a question of principle of more general application or relevance to the rights or welfare of relevant children. Report would be published and sent to Leah, the Welsh Assembly and the UK Parliament	Could hold an inquiry if satisfied that the case raises issues of public policy of relevance to other children, and that the inquiry would not duplicate the work of others. Must first consult the Secretary of State. Report would be published and sent to the Secretary of State

The office is not replicated for Wales because the functions are carried out independently by the Children's Commissioner for Wales.

Obvious questions arise about overlap between roles of the Children's Rights Director and the English Children's Commissioner under the Children Act 2004. In a statement issued jointly in 2005, they dealt with this question by explaining the Commissioner's role as a 'generalist' one, linked to the UNCRC, and the Director's role as a 'specialist' one, focusing on vulnerable groups and linked to the CSCI's inspection role, but that they work together on issues of application to all children.

Box 3.9 shows the court system so far as relevant to those social work interventions requiring judicial authority and the judicial machinery for review described in this chapter. It includes the courts in which applications are made for orders under the Children Act 1989 and those in which civil actions for negligence or breach of statutory duty and applications for judicial review may be brought. It does not include the criminal courts.

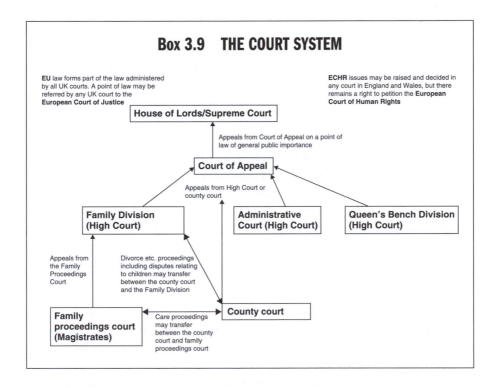

Box 3.9   THE COURT SYSTEM

EU law forms part of the law administered by all UK courts. A point of law may be referred by any UK court to the **European Court of Justice**

ECHR issues may be raised and decided in any court in England and Wales, but there remains a right to petition the **European Court of Human Rights**

House of Lords/Supreme Court

Appeals from Court of Appeal on a point of law of general public importance

Court of Appeal

Appeals from High Court or county court

Family Division (High Court)

Administrative Court (High Court)

Queen's Bench Division (High Court)

Appeals from the Family Proceedings Court

Divorce etc. proceedings including disputes relating to children may transfer between the county court and the Family Division

County court

Family proceedings court (Magistrates)

Care proceedings may transfer between the county court and family proceedings court

Children Act 1989 proceedings

The Courts Act 2003 introduced structural changes in the court system of England and Wales. The most important change so far as children's proceedings are concerned is the creation of 'local justice areas' served by county courts and magistrates courts administered by a unified courts administration service. This should mean improvements in the efficiency of allocation of children's cases and transfers of cases between the courts. Almost all public law children's cases under the Children Act 1989 begin in the family proceedings courts. Whether and at what point they are transferred from the magistrates court to the county court (in practice, this means one of the 53 county courts in England and Wales which are designated as 'care centres') or from the county court to the Family Division of the High Court depends on a range of issues including the complexity of the legal and evidential issues involved and any connection with other proceedings (e.g. divorce) that may be pending in the other court. In deciding whether and when to transfer, the courts are always required to consider what would be in the interests of the child concerned. Allocation and transfers of cases are governed by subordinate legislation made under s. 92 Children Act 1989: the Children (Allocation of Proceedings) Order 1991.

Other civil proceedings

Applications for judicial review are always made to the Administrative Court, a division of the High Court. Claims for damages for negligence or breach of statutory duty may be commenced either in the county court or the High Court.

Appeals

The diagram indicates the courts to which appeals lie from the decisions of the lower courts. Under the Constitutional Reform Act 2005, the role of the Appellate Committee of the House of Lords as the highest UK appeal court is transferred to a new Supreme Court for the UK, thereby ending a constitutional anachronism in which both legislative and judicial functions were vested in the House of Lords.

Conclusion

This chapter has sought to situate the practice of child care social work in a structural context which is established and regulated by law. It has shown how different areas of public policy have contributed to create the current systems of control and accountability for social work action.

The immediate organisational context for child care social work may seem dominated by a culture of managerialism: target-driven, outcome-oriented and subject to continuous review. This is indeed the thrust of much of the changes introduced by the Children Act 2004. There are dangers with this approach. Emphasis on process and quantitative measures may mask failures to deliver services consistent with principles of good social work practice which are also *legal* principles – promoting the best interests and development of the child, support for family unity and respect for the agency of the child. Measurements counting things like the percentage of review meetings held within specified time periods or the percentage of children registered as at risk for more than a specified period do nothing to indicate quality of service in an individual case nor whether the rights of service users are being protected and promoted. The meeting attended by the 'woefully unprepared' social worker in *CF v Secretary of State for the Home Department* [2004] (see Chapter 2) may have been timely and attended by the right people, without managing at all to protect the right of the baby to proper representation of her interests in a crucial decision about whether she could continue to be with her mother.

These dangers are exacerbated by the omission of references to human rights requirements, including the UNCRC, in much of the legislation and guidance which sets out the aims of children's services and the arrangements for their inspection and review. It leads to a situation where, at the point at which services are delivered, there is only a partial presentation of the legal framework governing those services. Social workers have to look beyond office requirements for returns of figures and forms, and constantly remind themselves of the totality of legal and professional requirements governing their interaction with clients, colleagues and other agencies.

On the other hand, recent legislative measures also include provisions designed to secure better protection for some aspects of children's rights. The changes introduced by the Adoption and Children Act 2002 to the system of reviews of looked after children and the requirements for the provision of advocacy services and reviews were a welcome and necessary step towards ensuring that children do not disappear from view once in care and that they are helped to participate in decisions affecting their care. The challenge must be to ensure that this process, as indeed all the prescribed processes, serves the substantive purpose of safeguarding and protecting the rights and welfare of children. This requires experience and knowledge of the law, the legal principles of decision-making, human rights and the legal framework of child welfare. The success of the system depends very much on the degree to which the independent reviewing officers and the social work case managers acquire this experience and knowledge. Equally important in terms of securing the best possible package of support for children's rights and welfare is effective inter-agency working, in which the players fully understand their own and others' roles and, critically, how they can interact towards the common purpose. This is the subject of the next chapter.

Further Reading

A critical and thought-provoking analysis of the strands of policy contributing to the *Every Child Matters* agenda is J. Williams, 'What matters is who works: why every child matters to New Labour', *Critical Social Policy* (2004), 406.

John Murphy's article 'Children in need: the limits of local authority accountability', *Legal Studies* 23 (2004), pp. 103–134, critically examines the effectiveness of various mechanisms for accountability for decisions under Pt. III Children Act 1989. Part III of the 1989 Act is dealt with in this book mainly in Chapter 5, but Murphy's argument, that a lack of effective accountability may seriously undermine the purpose of the Act, might usefully be considered here as well as in conjunction with Chapter 5. It is referred to again in the End Note in this book.

It may be useful to refer also to government guidance on complaints: for Wales, *Listening and Learning: A Guide to Handling Complaints and Representations in Local Authority Social Services in Wales* (Welsh Assembly Government, 2006), and for England, *Getting the Best from Complaints: Social Care Complaints for Children, Young People and Others* (Department for Education and Skills, 2006), available on-line on the Welsh Assembly Government and *Every Child Matters* websites respectively.

4

Inter-agency Working and Information Sharing

Introduction

Inter-agency working, with which this chapter is concerned, is:

- a rule of professional good practice: this is laid down in the NOSCCPQ (Sector Skills Council, 2005: 17; 22) and has been a constant theme in messages from research and reports of inquiries where things have gone wrong;
- required by law: there are specific requirements in legislation and statutory guidance for consultation, disclosure, exchange of information and provision of support for social work with children and families;
- further bolstered by legal requirements to consult and co-operate at strategic level: for example through the children's trusts and Local Safeguarding Children Boards established under the Children Act 2004;
- characterised by legal and practice issues about control and use of information, the discrete yet supposedly complementary functions of the various agencies involved and the difficulties in achieving commonality of purpose and approach.

Why inter-disciplinary working matters

The first and most obvious point is that the quality of decision-making and the quality of any service provided to children and their families is likely to be better if the knowledge and resources of all the relevant statutory and voluntary agencies can be harnessed effectively. Any practitioner will know of cases in which, if some piece of information had been known, a different and better decision could have been made or a different and better service could have been provided, and where the information in question was in the possession of another person or agency but not brought to bear at the critical time. Likewise any practitioner will know of cases where delays caused by communication, structural or administrative issues have resulted in detriment to a child.

Delay and system abuse

The impact of delay is recognised in s. 1(2) Children Act 1989 which states that in determining a question about the upbringing of the child the court must have regard to 'the general principle that any delay in determining the question is likely to prejudice the welfare of the child'. Delay in dealing with care proceedings has been a persistent source of concern and has been the subject of a number of official reports and responses, discussed further in Chapter 6. In such reports it has repeatedly been found that lack of effective inter-agency communication and co-operation is an important factor contributing to delay within the court system. Delay also contributes towards increased cost both for the family and for the system as a whole, and is linked to poorer outcomes for the family, particularly in terms of the potential for maintaining positive family relationships.

Without effective inter-agency working, the quality of decision-making and service provision may be not only less good than it might be, but also positively harmful, to a child. This was identified by the National Commission of Inquiry into the Prevention of Child Abuse and Neglect as a variety of system abuse which occurs when the operation of law, procedures or practices within systems or institutions is avoidably damaging to children and their families (TSO, 1996). Furthermore, there are good professional and legal reasons for striving to ensure that inter-agency collaboration is effective.

Professional standards

The NOSCCPQ require social workers to 'liaise and work with other professionals, departments and agencies to achieve optimal outcomes' for children and young people in need (Sector Skills Council, 2005: Unit B). The associated performance criteria include knowledge and understanding of different professional and agency roles, responsibilities and perspectives, developing strategies for collaborative working and contributing to effective inter-agency working to provide an integrated service and range of resources. Child care plans are highlighted as a means of optimising the delivery of multi-agency services, both for individual children and their families and in the context of planning, managing and reviewing services. In other words, at the same time as the social worker must strive to promote the best multi-agency 'package' for the individual child, she should also identify any gaps in provision and pursue these within her own organisation and through inter-agency protocols and joint systems for planning and review. Awareness of the policy and operational environment discussed in Chapter 3 is thus essential.

Legal risks

If we apply a more legalistic lens, it can be seen that a failure to ensure that all the available information and expertise is harnessed effectively may undermine the lawfulness of any action taken. This could be because the action is seen to be irrational (in the sense used in judicial review: see Chapter 3) or not proportionate (in the sense used in ECHR case-law: see Chapter 2) to the aim to be served. Equally a failure to take appropriate action could, in an extreme case, expose a local authority to potential legal liability in negligence or for breach of its duty to act compatibly with the ECHR (see Chapter 3).

Risks to children

In the end of course, the most important reason for getting inter-agency collaboration right is the need to safeguard and protect the rights and welfare of children and to reduce risk, whether the risk is from neglect, impaired development or deliberate harm. A graphic and powerful reminder of the possible consequences of failure to do this was provided by the inquiry into the circumstances surrounding the death of Victoria Climbié. The introduction to the Laming Report recorded the harrowing findings that:

during the days and months following her initial contact with Ealing Housing Department's Homeless Persons' Unit, Victoria was known to no less than two further housing authorities, four social services departments, two child protection teams of the Metropolitan Police Service (MPS), a specialist centre managed by the NSPCC, and she was admitted to two different hospitals because of suspected deliberate harm. The dreadful reality was that these services knew little or nothing more about Victoria at the end of the process than they did when she was first referred to Ealing Social Services by the Homeless Persons' Unit in April 1999. The final irony was that Haringey Social Services formally closed Victoria's case on the very day she died. The extent of the failure to protect Victoria was lamentable. Tragically, it required nothing more than basic good practice being put into operation. This never happened. (Laming, 2003: para 1.16)

Inter-agency collaboration

Both *Working Together to Safeguard Children* (DfES, 2006/WAG, 2006) (*'Working Together'*) and the *Framework for the Assessment of Children in Need and their Families* (DoH, 2000 / NAW, 2001) ('the *Framework'*) identify many statutory and voluntary agencies, professionals and others who may need to be involved in a case concerning the protection or welfare of children. *Working Together* contains a long but no doubt not exhaustive list, including local authorities as a whole as well as in their social services functions, state and private schools and education services, youth services, cultural and leisure services, all medical, psychiatric and community health services, Drug Action Teams, the police and accident emergency services, probation, prison and youth justice services, voluntary and private sector services carrying out a range of child and family oriented work, housing authorities, court services including children's guardians and child and family reporters working for CAFCASS and the armed forces. The general point is that if any one of the agencies fails to play its part, the result could be delay and detriment to the child concerned and to other family members. Two examples will help to illustrate this.

Box 4.1 indicates the agencies that may be involved in a typical child protection case under the Children Act 1989. It builds on an example used in the UK Government consultation paper (LCD, 2002a), which led to the establishment of the Family Justice Council (the role of which is explained later in this chapter).

In this case there is a clear focus on preparation for court, but the need for inter-agency working is not confined to cases where court proceedings are contemplated. It is a pervasive theme throughout social work generally and in social work with children in particular. Assessments under s. 17 Children

Box 4.1 JAKE: A CHILD AT RISK OF IMMEDIATE HARM

Police respond to an emergency call made by the neighbour of 9-year-old *Jake's* family. The neighbour reports a domestic fight and hearing Jake crying. The police refer the family to *social services*, who apply for an emergency protection order. In the application social services are represented by the *local authority legal department*. A child protection conference is held: *social services* and other agencies – *police, health visitor, child advocacy service and/or solicitors for child and parents, education services*, etc.

The application is heard by *justices' clerk/magistrates* at the local family proceedings court. A *children's guardian* is appointed to represent Jake's interests. The guardian appoints a specialist *solicitor* and instructs that solicitor.

Magistrates make an interim care order and the case is transferred to the county court where proceedings are already pending concerning **Ben**, Jake's 4-year-old brother. *Court staff* at the family proceedings court and at the county court liaise over the listing of the case at the county court and the transfer of files. The *judge* at the county court gives further directions to the *solicitors* for each party to the proceedings as to the filing of reports including an expert report from a *paediatrician*.

The final hearing takes place before a *circuit judge*, with presentation of the case by the *local authority legal department* and *counsel* for the family. Jake and Ben are made the subject of a care order, but the plan is to work with the family towards rehabilitation: *specialist counselling and therapeutic services* will work with *social services* to that end.

Act 1989, for example, are not directed towards court proceedings (although matters may be discovered in the course of a s. 17 assessment indicating that a court order should be sought because of risk of significant harm to a child), but these assessments can only be carried out effectively with good inter-agency co-operation. Box 4.2 indicates the agencies that may be involved in a core assessment carried out in accordance with the *Framework*.

The legal framework for inter-agency collaboration

Requirements to assist in specific interventions

Partnership working, which includes both partnership between professionals and families and also partnership between professionals, was a central theme of the policy underlying the Children Act 1989. Section 27 of the Act provides that local authorities carrying out functions under Pt. III (support for children and families) can call for help from other local authorities, education,

Box 4.2   EMMA: A YOUNG CARER

Emma, aged 14, is referred, with her consent, to **social services** by a **children's drop-in centre** run by a national children's **voluntary organisation** because she is suffering a variety of stresses due to an increasing need to support her mother **Jane** in caring for Emma's 6-year-old disabled brother **Iwan**.

Apart from the obvious need for **social services** to work with the whole family in this situation, agencies that are likely to be able to contribute to the assessment include Emma's **school**, **GP**, **education welfare services** and the **drop-in centre**. Full investigation of Emma's needs in the context of her family will also involve obtaining information from **health bodies** and other **social services** staff about Iwan.

housing and health authorities. Such an authority receiving a request for help is obliged to comply unless to do so would be incompatible with their own functions. Under s. 47(9), similar requests for help can be made in relation to a child protection investigation under Pt. IV, and the requested agency must respond positively unless it would be unreasonable to do so.

Legislative provisions also recognise the need for specific instances where collaboration between agencies and professions is likely to be required. Thus s. 48 Children Act 1989 empowers a constable to request to be accompanied by a doctor, nurse or health visitor when exercising a warrant to recover a child pursuant to an emergency protection order, and s. 213A Housing Act 1996 (added by the Homelessness Act 2002) allows a local authority dealing with a child in need under s.17 Children Act 1989 to request help from a housing authority even though the family is ineligible for housing assistance (this situation has been the subject of a number of legal cases and is considered in Chapter 5).

Structural and organisational requirements

As well as providing for specific instances of assistance, the law imposes requirements as to structure and organisation of services, intended to promote multi-disciplinary working or inter-agency collaboration. Multi-disciplinary working is different from inter-agency or inter-disciplinary working. Multi-disciplinary working occurs where members of a number of disciplines are involved in a team effort to provide a particular service or produce a particular outcome. Thus a multi-disciplinary package for a particular child may involve a team comprising a social worker, educational welfare officer and occupational therapist. Inter-agency or inter-disciplinary working occurs where various agencies or members of different disciplines exchange information or provide other forms of support for one another even though they are not engaged on a joint project or activity. An example would be the provision of information by a school or police force for the purposes of a needs assessment or child protection investigation.

YOTs: a statutory multi-disciplinary team

Youth offending teams, or YOTs, are perhaps the best example of a statutory multi-disciplinary team carrying out front-line responsibilities. YOTs were a central plank of the youth justice reforms introduced by the Crime and Disorder Act 1998. They have responsibility for assessment of, and provision of programmes and support for, young offenders and those deemed to be at risk of offending. Members include police and probation officers, social workers and officers from health, education, substance abuse teams and housing. The YOT manager is responsible for co-ordinating the work of the youth justice services in accordance with strategies agreed by a local management board. The idea is that because the YOT includes members from a wide range of services, it can respond to the needs of young offenders in a comprehensive way. The YOT uses 'ASSET', a centrally prescribed assessment tool, to identify the needs of each young offender, to assess the risk the young person poses to others and to help identify suitable responses.

Accompanying these front-line teams is a system of joint inspection, an important mechanism for promoting centrally set priorities. YOT inspections are carried out by a multi-disciplinary team reflecting the composition of the YOTs themselves: the inspection teams include representatives of the Audit Commission, the Commission for Health Improvement, Estyn (HM Inspectorate for Education and Training in Wales), HM Inspectorate of Constabulary, Ofsted (Office for Standards in Education), HM Inspectorate of Prisons, HM Inspectorate of Probation, the Social Services Inspectorate and the Social Services Inspectorate for Wales.

The child protection model: Local Safeguarding Children Boards

Some respondents to consultation in the course of the Laming Inquiry saw the YOTs as the model that ought to be adopted for protecting children and promoting their welfare (Laming, 2003: 17.53). In the event the Children Act 2004, which formed part of the government's response to the Laming Report, did not follow this suggestion, but did institutionalise a multi-disciplinary approach at strategic (as opposed to front-line) level. Section 13 (for England) and s. 31 (for Wales) of the 2004 Act provide for the establishment of Local Safeguarding Children Boards (LSCBs). The LSCBs comprise representatives of each children's services authority (as defined in s. 65) and their 'Board partners', who are the police, probation, health and prison services and the YOT. The Act imposes a duty of co-operation on each of these bodies in the setting up of LSCBs, and empowers the Secretary of State, for England, and the Welsh Assembly, for Wales, to make detailed provision about the LSCBs' functions and procedures and to issue guidance (ss.16 and 34). The LSCBs have the task of promoting more effective inter-agency and inter-disciplinary working for the purposes of safeguarding and promoting the welfare of children in their area. They absorb the functions of their non-statutory predecessors, the Area Child Protection Committees, which operated under an earlier version of *Working Together*, but also have a wider role, linked to other provisions of the Children Act 2004 about children's services. This represents a clear attempt, consistent with Laming's approach, to 'join up' child protection with support for children and families in need, at least at a strategic level.

Children's services, children's trusts and mutual co-operation under the Children Act 2004

In addition to providing for LSCBs, the Children Act 2004 makes other structural provision intended to enhance inter-agency working and to ensure a clearer focus by a wide range of bodies on safeguarding children and promoting their welfare. The list of bodies includes children's services authorities themselves, health bodies, the police, probation and prison services, YOTs and Connexions (England). The Act places a duty of co-operation on these bodies (s. 10 for England and s. 25 for Wales) and also requires them to make arrangements to ensure that their functions are discharged having regard to the need to safeguard children and promote their welfare (s.11 for England and s. 28 for Wales). This latter duty extends not only to what these authorities do themselves but also to the arrangements they make for any of their functions to be serviced by others such as private and voluntary sector bodies carrying out work under contract.

For England, statutory guidance on inter-agency co-operation pursuant to s. 10 requires the establishment of 'children's trusts' (DfES, 2005). For Wales, this additional layer does not exist and the equivalent guidance deals with the setting up and maintaining of arrangements between the key persons and bodies themselves (WAG, 2005a).

The Children Act 2004 promotes a multi-disciplinary approach within local authorities by formalising the notion of 'children's services' as embracing health, education and social services and providing for lead managerial and political responsibility. There is provision for inspection to be on a multi-disciplinary basis, with joint review and inspection of children's services for England and inspection by the Welsh Assembly in Wales.

The Children Act 2004 thus represents an attempt to achieve more effective inter-agency co-operation through structural reform, including multi-agency working at strategic level by administrative bodies with local authorities in the lead, co-ordinating role as children's services authorities.

Meanwhile, developments in the family justice system have also been focused on achieving better inter-agency collaboration.

Inter-agency collaboration and the family court system

When the Children Act 1989 was enacted, the government recognised that implementation of the Act required an inter-disciplinary effort. To that end the Children Act Advisory Committee (CAAC) was set up, comprising representatives of the legal, social services, health and academic disciplines. The CAAC reported annually to the relevant UK government ministers and to the President of the Family Division on issues arising from cases brought under the 1989 Act. In 1997 the CAAC published a practitioner's Handbook of Best Practice in Children Act Cases. After the CAAC was disbanded, similar work was carried out by the Children Act Sub-Committee of the Lord Chancellor's Family Law Advisory Board. This work was mainly focused on the implications of domestic violence for contact with children and the implementation of the Family Law Act 1996 (that Act would have introduced radical changes in the law on divorce, had it been fully implemented). When the Family Law Advisory Board was in turn disbanded, the lacuna in high-level inter-disciplinary structure was filled to some extent by an Interdisciplinary Forum promoted by the President of the Family Division and the work of a non-governmental organisation, the National Council for Family Proceedings. These groups facilitated conferences and papers that influenced government thinking and promoted changes in the law on matters such as care planning and judicial overview of treatment of children in care.

The Family Justice Council

From the late 1990s, reform and restructuring of the court system in England and Wales provided an opportunity to create a more solid and wide-ranging structure for this kind of high-level, policy-oriented activity. The Family Justice Council ('the Council') was established in 2004 by the Department for Constitutional Affairs (DCA). The Council's membership includes representatives of the family judiciary, the magistrates' courts, local authority children's services, the legal professions, mediation services, academics and child health specialists. *Ex officio* members include the Children's Commissioner for Wales, government officials from the DCA, the Department of Health, Home Office, Foreign and Commonwealth Office, the Department for Children, Schools and Families, Her Majesty's Courts Service and representatives of CAFCASS, the Legal Services Commission and the Association of Chief Police Officers. The Council's terms of reference are 'to facilitate the delivery of better and quicker outcomes for families and children who use the family justice system' and it aims to fulfil this remit by promoting consistency and best practice, disseminating information, providing advice and guidance, encouraging relevant research and making recommendations to Government (FJC, 2006).

At local level, a number of local family court business committees had already established an inter-disciplinary forum to facilitate training and exchange of information amongst professionals, including social workers whose work involved cases under the Children Act 1989. The Council declared that an early and urgent priority was to formalise links with these local groups and to promote their establishment in areas where they did not yet exist. Such a forum may provide a useful means by which social workers can engage regularly with local practitioners from all the different disciplines involved in court cases, many of whom will also have a role in delivery of wider children's services. Box 4.3 gives an example of the activities of one such forum, and demonstrates how this kind of local activity can serve to stimulate improvements in local service, research and evaluation as well as providing regular training and dissemination of relevant research.

Box 4.3   THE SWANSEA FAMILY COURT INTER-DISCIPLINARY FORUM

The Forum was established in 2001, meeting twice yearly, with around 100 to 150 delegates drawn from local family judges, magistrates, solicitors and barristers, social workers, CAFCASS guardians and reporters, court service managers, health professionals, voluntary organisations, adoption and fostering agencies, the police and academics. Topics included the impact of the Human Rights Act 1998 on family court cases, the introduction of CAFCASS, domestic violence, case preparation and delay, the Adoption and Children Act 2002 and the use of experts. Issues identified at the Forum led to changes in local practice: for example, a protocol for more effective co-ordinated support for children and families in cases of suspected sexual abuse. The Forum disseminates research from across England and Wales and identifies further research needs: examples of projects stimulated by the Forum are an investigation of the effectiveness of supervised and conditional contact orders and an inquiry into assessment and placement of children for adoption by same sex couples.

Conclusions on the frameworks for inter-agency collaboration

Recent years have seen intensified efforts to improve inter-disciplinary and multi-disciplinary working in children's cases through changes in the law governing the structure and organisation of key services and the imposition of legal duties of mutual co-operation and support. Many of the changes represent a formalisation in law of practices already in existence and the subject of earlier non-statutory guidance. It is to be hoped that this process will help to resolve some of the difficult legal and practical issues involved in achieving effective 'joined-up' working and thereby help to achieve Lord Laming's aspiration of reducing the likelihood of a repetition of the multiple failings exposed by the Victoria Climbié Inquiry. However, as with any major structural change, an initial concentration on organisational issues means that it must be some time before the impact of the changes can be measured. It should be remembered that another common finding in child death inquiries and serious case reviews is that restructuring of services can itself place additional strain on case handling teams, support staff and managers and that this forms part of a context in which errors occur (see, for example, the North East Lincolnshire Serious Case Review following the conviction of Ian Huntley for the murders of Jessica Chapman and Holly Wells (NE Lincs, 2004)). Structural reorganisation will not, of itself, improve the intelligent, analytical skills of social workers. Changes in systems for information-sharing and expansion of information collected about children will not, of themselves, produce more effective interventions without the application of those skills. It is a practical reality that reorganisation can place strain on consistency in responsibility for both paper and electronic records and generally places strain on staff. Of course, none of this is an argument against necessary reorganisation, it is merely to sound a cautionary note about the practical implications of transitions to new systems.

Legal and practice issues in inter-disciplinary and inter-agency working

This section explores those issues in inter-agency collaboration where the legal framework might be expected to have most impact: these are the use and disclosure of confidential information, the allocation of roles and responsibilities and the quest for a 'common purpose'.

Confidentiality and disclosure of information

The Laming Report was far from alone in noting that uncertainty over the legality of sharing information was a contributory factor in failures adequately to protect children at risk of significant harm. There are two dangers, pulling in opposite directions: the danger of not passing on crucial information that could lead to action to prevent a child suffering significant harm and the danger of passing on unvalidated information which may give a misleading picture equally to the detriment of the child and family concerned. This was clear from the comments of many of those responding to the Laming Inquiry's consultation, who agreed there was confusion as to when professionals are allowed to share information with each other without the consent of the child or carers (Laming, 2003: 17). Laming recommended that the government should issue guidance on the Data Protection Act 1998, the Human Rights Act 1998

99

INTER-AGENCY WORKING

and common law rules on confidentiality. A similar recommendation was made by Sir Michael Bichard in his report arising from the murders of Holly Wells and Jessica Chapman. He found that misunderstandings about the impact of data protection legislation in particular were common amongst the police and said that 'better guidance is needed on the collection, retention, use and sharing of information so that police officers, social workers and other professionals can feel more confident about using information properly' (Bichard, 2004: Introduction and Summary, para. 23).

New government guidance has indeed been issued (for example DfES, 2006a) and may well help to improve understanding and consistency in practice, but the fact remains that the question whether and to whom to pass on personal information in an individual case is often far from easy and requires the exercise of professional judgement. The proper balance has to be struck between all the different rights and interests concerned. Before exploring how this is to be done in practice, we first need a brief outline of the law.

Legal protection from disclosure of confidential or personal information

There are four main legal inhibitors to the sharing of personal information between agencies. These are:

- the common law duty of confidentiality;
- the right to protection for private and family life in Article 8 ECHR;
- data protection (Data Protection Act 1998, derived largely from EU law (EU, 1995));
- the possibility of judicial review if a decision to disclose goes beyond the powers of the agency, is irrational or unfair.

A brief explanation of each of these is given below.

The common law duty of confidentiality arises when a person discloses information to another (e.g. a service user or carer to a social worker, or a patient to a clinician) in circumstances where it is reasonable to expect that the information will be held in confidence. This legal obligation is the result of case-law decided by the courts over many years. It is also a rule reflected in the Code of Practice for Social Workers (Care Council for Wales, 2002; General Social Care Council, 2002) and is a standard term of employment for local authority and NHS employees, linked to disciplinary procedures. Breach of the common law duty may give rise to an action for damages, and other remedies such as an injunction to restrain publication may be sought from the court.

Article 8 ECHR is engaged when disclosure constitutes an interference with the right to respect for private and family life. It is well established that confidential information is protected by Article 8. Because s. 6 Human Rights Act 1998 prohibits a public authority from acting incompatibly with Convention rights, social workers have no power to make disclosures which breach this right and a legal claim may be made under s. 7 of the 1998 Act if they do. Furthermore, professional standards require social workers to respect and protect the human rights of service users. Disclosure which is compatible with the common law duty of confidentiality and with data protection legislation should normally satisfy the requirements of Article 8, but it must also be considered whether in the individual case the disclosure can be justified as necessary to serve a legitimate aim (such as the protection of the rights or interests of a vulnerable child, the child's health, etc.) and whether the action taken is proportionate to the need.

Data protection applies when 'personal data' is 'processed' within the meaning of the Data Protection Act 1998. 'Processing' includes holding, obtaining, recording, using and disclosing information held electronically or on paper, including images. 'Personal data' includes all confidential service-user information but also goes much wider and includes any information from which a living individual can be identified. The Act imposes constraints on 'data controllers' (which term will invariably cover social workers dealing with information about children and families) and sets out eight data protection principles for information handling. The data protection principles most likely to impact on social work with children and families are:

- the first principle, which requires processing to be fair and lawful and to comply with one or more of a list of reasons why the processing is necessary;
- the second principle, which requires processing to be for one or more specified and lawful purposes;
- the seventh principle, which requires that personal data be protected against unauthorised or unlawful processing and against accidental loss, destruction or damage.

Judicial review may be available to a person aggrieved by a social work decision to use information, if the decision is legally flawed. The courts have stated that judicial review should not be much used in relation to child protection, as other avenues of complaint are likely to be more appropriate, but it is nonetheless potentially available in a case where disclosure clearly exceeded the powers of the discloser, was unfair or irrational.

The 'broader societal interest' principle

The detail of each of these legal topics is, undoubtedly, complex (with the prize for complexity going to the data protection legislation). However, the most important thing for practitioners to remember is that all of these inhibitors on disclosure are subject to the principle that disclosure may be made where there are circumstances that justify overruling the right of an individual to confidentiality in order to serve a broader societal interest. This principle is put in a more or less elaborate way in all the relevant statute and case-law. It will invariably cover disclosure which is necessary for the purposes of child protection (i.e. where a child is perceived to be at risk of significant harm) and disclosure for the purpose of preventing or reporting a criminal offence. Of course, the decision to disclose still needs to be made rationally and lawfully. This means seeking validation of information where possible and paying careful attention to the extent to which disclosure is required and how it can be contained (i.e. to whom should the information be given and what limitations, if any, should be placed on its use).

The 'broader societal interest' principle will not necessarily cover disclosures for the purposes of assessment where the child is not perceived to be at risk of significant harm and no criminal conduct is suspected: in that case, normally, the consent of the person concerned or someone able to consent on behalf of that person should be sought. Where the person concerned is a child, a judgement about the competence of the child to consent needs to be made. In this regard, it may be useful to note that the Data Protection Registrar's own guidance suggests that consideration needs to be given to obtaining the consent of a child from the age of 12.

Box 4.4 suggests how confidentiality and disclosure issues may apply in the cases of Jake and Emma (Boxes 4.1 and 4.2 above).

Statutory authority to disclose for certain purposes

Legislation clarifies the power to disclose information in certain circumstances. Some provisions are quite broad, such as s. 115 Crime and Disorder Act 1998 which empowers any person to disclose information to a local authority, the police, health or probation authorities where it is 'necessary or expedient' for the purposes of the Act, or s. 54 Domestic Violence and Victims of Crime Act 2004 which empowers a person to disclose information to a relevant authority for the purpose of fulfilling its functions under the Act. Others are directed at specific circumstances, such as the Health and Social Care Act 2001 which enables patient information to be used without consent to the extent that it is needed for the purposes of clinical audit, record validation, research or public health, or the Health and Social Care (Community Health and Standards) Act 2003 which enables health and social care inspectorates to access personal information for the purposes of carrying out their inspection functions or dealing with complaints.

Legal requirements to disclose

Unlike some jurisdictions, in England and Wales there is no mandatory reporting duty where professionals suspect child abuse. However, there are certain

Box 4.4   CONFIDENTIALITY AND DISCLOSURE

Disclosure of information between agencies is relatively unproblematic in **Jake**'s case, since the purpose of disclosure is a child protection investigation. In **Emma**'s case, disclosure is not necessarily justified under the 'broader societal interest' principle and Emma's consent needs to be sought for disclosure of information from her school record or from her GP. **Jane**'s consent would need to be sought for disclosure of information about her own condition and that of **Iwan**. However, it should be borne in mind that the Laming Report recommended that 'in cases that fall short of an immediately identifiable section 47* label ... the seeking or refusal of parental permission must not restrict the initial information gathering and sharing. This should, if necessary, include talking to the child'. In Emma's case, since she is 14 and has already taken the step of seeking help from a drop-in centre, this may be straightforward. If the referral had been about Iwan, it may well have been more difficult.

Even in a child protection case like **Jake**'s, the situation becomes more complex once care proceedings are under way, because Rule 4.23 of the Family Proceedings Rules 1991 prevents disclosure of documents held by the court relating to the proceedings, except with the leave of the court. Particular issues arise if criminal proceedings are contemplated as well as care proceedings, especially with regard to admissions made to a social worker or children's guardian. These are discussed further in Chapter 6.

---

*Section 47 Children Act 1989: duty to carry out child protection investigation.

requirements for inter-agency disclosure or notification once a case is being dealt with. Examples are para. 2.14 of the National Minimum Standards for Youth Justice (see Chapter 9) which requires the police to inform a YOT within one working day whenever a young person under 18 has been charged with an offence or given a reprimand or bailed for a final warning, and ss. 85 and 86 Children Act 1989 which require health authorities, local education authorities and care homes to notify the relevant local authority where they are providing accommodation for a child. Statutory guidance makes clear that certain disclosures are to be expected as routine: *Working Together*, for example, states that social services should always inform the police of any suspected criminal offence against a child.

As already noted (Chapter 2, and further discussed in Chapters 5, 6 and 7), the procedural fairness requirements read by the courts into Article 8 ECHR mean relevant information must be disclosed to the children and parents concerned. Case-law provides useful and quite detailed guidance as to the way in which social services records should be kept and disclosed to parents and children as well as other agencies involved. Take, for example, a social services meeting at which decisions are taken about a child being looked after: numerous documents, including correspondence, agendas and minutes, will be generated. In *Re G (Care: Challenge to Local Authority's Decision)* **[2003]**, the court considered the practical effect of Article 8 ECHR on the use and disclosure of such documents:

(a) the local authority is under a duty to make full and frank disclosure to those whose Article 8 rights are engaged of all key documents in its possession or available to it, including in particular attendance notes of meetings and conversations and minutes of case conferences, core group meetings and similar meetings;

(b) social workers should at all times keep clear, accurate, full and balanced notes of all relevant conversations and meetings between themselves and/or with parents, other family members and others involved with the family;

(c) where important meetings are held there should be a written agenda circulated in advance to all concerned;

(d) clear, accurate, full and balanced minutes of the meeting (identifying in particular what information has been given to the meeting and by whom) should be taken by someone nominated for that task before the meeting begins;

(e) as soon as possible after the meeting, the minutes should be agreed by those present as being an accurate record of the meeting and then be immediately disclosed to all parties.

Guidance on protection and use of confidential information

Following the Laming Report's recommendation, Codes of Practice have been issued on confidentiality. There are separate Codes for England and Wales. The Welsh Code covers health and social care and for England there are separate Codes for health and for social care (DoH, 2003; WAG, 2005c). These have the status of non-statutory guidance.

The Codes adopt a 'confidentiality model' comprising the four requirements to 'protect, inform, provide choice and improve' and emphasising the need to ensure that service users are aware of their rights and know what choices they can make about how their personal information is used. To assist with decision-making in individual cases, the Codes of Practice contain 'disclosure models' charting the considerations which apply where disclosure is sought for different purposes: these provide a useful checklist for practitioners and should be referred to routinely.

To supplement this guidance, the government expects that protocols and practices will be developed locally. In Wales, a detailed scheme called the 'WASPI' (Wales Accord on Sharing Personal Information) has been developed (WAG, 2006a). The WASPI is applicable to all public sector organisations, voluntary sector organisations and private organisations contracted to deliver relevant public services. It does not have the force of law but is offered as a package that can be adopted and applied at different levels within the services and organisations. It contains four tiers aimed respectively at strategic organisational level, at operational management level, at individual operational level and at service user level. If implemented as intended by the organisations concerned, the WASPI should support greater understanding and consistency about the use and disclosure of information.

Conclusions on the law relating to confidentiality and use of information

Law imposes constraints on use of confidential information but also requirements to disclose. For social workers working with children and families, the starting point, both as a matter of law and as a matter of professional ethics, is that service users are entitled to respect for their private life, which includes protection of confidential information about them. However, it is plain that a social worker's legal and professional responsibilities cannot be carried out effectively without access to and exchange of information with other agencies. Consequently such access or exchange of information should be regarded as a normal, integral part of the job. The law should not be regarded as an impediment to this but rather as a set of rules governing how it is to be done. The legal rules cover the way in which information is recorded and retained, the considerations as to when, how and to whom it should be communicated and certain express limitations or permissions which are required along the way. Recent government guidance is aimed at enhancing professionals' understanding of what these legal rules require them to do in practice, and at achieving greater consistency and transparency, without changing the rules themselves.

Different roles and responsibilities

The Laming Report emphasised the need for professionals to deepen their knowledge about other disciplines and to enhance their skills in working across professional boundaries. The different professions involved in working with vulnerable children and their families have, by definition, discrete areas of knowledge and experience and they develop a particular way of interrogating, thinking about and discussing issues. Most of them also work within a discrete legal and professional framework which gives them a focus on particular people as patients, clients, suspects or service users in the context of a particular set of statutory responsibilities. Even within services, the Laming Inquiry found variation in approach, for example as to the identification and assessment of need, and considerable variation as to the interpretation of guidance. Laming concluded that it was necessary to develop a 'common language' that could be used by those working with children and families, which would inform common referral practices, assessment and training (Laming, 2003: 18, Recommendation 13).

The structural changes made by the Children Act 2004 are to some extent a response to this. As already noted, the Act formalises multi-disciplinary activity at the strategic level of the LSCBs, brings together children's services within local authorities under common professional and political leadership and prescribes a set of desired outcomes for children towards which planning and delivery of children's services must be directed.

These changes may help to create an environment in which it is easier for members of the different disciplines to achieve mutual understanding of one another's roles and responsibilities, but no one would argue that structural change alone is enough. Take, for example, **Emma**'s case (above). An appropriate response to her needs might well involve support from educational welfare, home-help services and her GP, co-ordinated by a social work case-handler. Each would need to know what the other was doing and alert the case-handler to any problems that arise. The case-handler would need to know what action to take. The structural changes in the Children Act 2004 may have the effect of bringing the social worker physically and organisationally closer to the educational welfare officer, but probably not any closer to the home-help services or the primary care unit in which the GP works. Effective liaison between the professionals and others involved still depends on their own individual understanding of the case as a whole and their own role in it, together with a culture of mutual respect where there is shared confidence that each is working towards the same defined goals and will deal with information received in a lawful and professional manner.

It is perfectly possible for there to be good inter-agency relationships, with individuals working well together and exchanging information, yet still failing to work *effectively* because of a lack of role clarity or consistency in handling referrals. Examples of this can be seen in some of the cases examined in the North East Lincolnshire Serious Case Review mentioned earlier in this chapter. After his conviction, it became publicly known that Ian Huntley had come to the attention of police and social services on some 11 occasions between 1995 and 2002, most of which involved allegations or suspicions of sexual exploitation of teenage girls. In several cases it was clear that if these allegations or suspicions were well founded, Huntley had committed a criminal offence. The Serious Case Review examined the cases and found unexplained inconsistency in the way decisions were made as to whether the police, social services or the two agencies jointly should conduct an investigation. There was also inconsistency in the allocation of cases within the social services department and in decisions about referral of possible criminal offences to the police. There was a lack of clarity about roles and responsibilities. The Bichard Report commented that a good indication that something was wrong was that it was not clear what particular meetings and exchanges were for, both at the time of the meeting and in associated records:

we were struck by the looseness of terminology used in the case notes to describe the nature of particular meetings ... it is much more than a question of semantics. Lack of clarity about the status of meetings can often mean the absence of rigour in determining who should be there, whether it is simply for information or decisions are required, who is responsible for chairing and summing up, who is going to be responsible for taking any follow up action and so on. (Bichard, 2004: para 154)

If, as seems to be the case, government guidance is not enough, mutual understanding of roles and responsibilities is perhaps best promoted by joint training. A blueprint for training of 'family justice professionals' has been developed by the President of the Family Division's Interdisciplinary Family Law Committee and is being promoted by the Family Justice Council (FJC, 2005). It is aimed at members of all the professions that have a role in child protection and contains modules dealing with child and adolescent development, children, family and human rights legislation, legal and administrative processes and support and therapy for vulnerable children, their parents and carers. To be effective, such a programme would need to be taken up by the respective professional bodies as part of initial and continuous professional training. This development has yet to emerge.

A common language and a common purpose

The promotion of a common language and common purpose which can be shared by all the different disciplines involved in protecting children and promoting their welfare is a laudatory aim, but not easy to realise. On one understanding, it is actually impossible because the different disciplines each develop a specialist language through which they work so that full understanding would only be achieved by a person who became competent in all of the disciplines: law, medicine, social work, policing, education, etc. Furthermore, as King and Piper (1995) have argued with particular reference to law and the legal system, the tendency of different disciplines to develop their own styles, constructions and systems of communication is an insular tendency, pulling against effective inter-disciplinary working. The challenge is to work within each of the disciplines, and at an inter-disciplinary level, to reduce this insularity, without losing the essential specialist knowledge and skills.

All those involved may at least be able to agree that they share an interest in achieving solutions that serve the best interests of the child, so this looks like at least a base line for a 'common purpose'. The priority attached to the child's best interests would vary – for some it would be the paramount consideration as a matter of law, for others simply one of a number of interests to which they must have regard, but all would agree that it was of great importance. However, the best interests principle is limited by the fact that it is, despite its apparent universality, notoriously variable according to whose particular lens is being applied to it in an individual case (for example, Mnookin, 1975 and Eekalaar, 2002).

The Children Act 2004 does not derogate from the best interests formula, nor does it attempt to gloss it by changing the way in which it is interpreted by the courts making decisions under the Children Act 1989. But the 2004 Act does prescribe a common purpose towards which the efforts of statutory agencies involved in delivering children's services and safeguarding and promoting children's welfare are to be directed. It does this by requiring that arrangements made between children's services authorities and their partners (health, police, probation, youth justice and youth services) must be directed towards improving the well-being of children, in particular so far as relating to:

(a) physical and mental health and emotional well-being;
(b) protection from harm and neglect;
(c) education, training and recreation;
(d) the contribution made by them to society;
(e) social and economic well-being.

This prescription therefore forms part of the 'common purpose' to which the various agencies' efforts are directed. Thus far, then, this 'common purpose' can be seen to comprise a 'best interests' concept enshrined in the Children Act 1989 and interpreted primarily by the courts, and a concept of 'well-being' defined and interpreted largely through government guidance pursuant to the Children Act 2004. Yet this cannot be the end of the story: neither the Children Act 1989 nor the Children Act 2004 make express reference to the rights of children and families, but as shown in Chapter 2, rights as understood under the ECHR and UNCRC also form a part of the legal framework and anyone carrying out public functions must ensure that they act in accordance with these rights as required by law. The opportunity to make this explicit in the Children Act 2004 was side-stepped. The result is that the law is, to put it mildly, less coherent than it might be in defining the 'common purpose' of inter-disciplinary working for and with children.

Assessment

One area where the need for a common purpose and a common language can be best demonstrated is assessment. The Laming Inquiry found that the national assessment framework that had been designed for use by all relevant disciplines, in practice tended to be seen, wrongly, as exclusively or predominantly for social services. In response to this, and in the context of implementation of the Children Act 2004, the Common Assessment Framework (CAF) has been developed and is being promoted by DfES for England and the Welsh Assembly Government for Wales for use as an initial assessment and referral tool by all relevant agencies. The CAF is intended to promote the use of a common language across agencies, to lead to better sharing of information and earlier identification of problems and appropriate referrals. The system is considered further in Chapter 5: at the time of writing it is early yet to seek to assess how successful it may be in helping to promote a common language and purpose.

Another problem noted by Laming was the effect of limited resources and targeting on assessment:

> There appeared to be a widely held view that in practice, social work tends to be service-led rather than needs-led. The majority of service users tend to receive services that are available, not necessarily the services they require. This is the result of limited resources, administrative convenience, and the failure to recognise the need for individual assessment to determine the service to be provided. (Laming, 2003: para 17. 62)

Article 4 UNCRC requires States Parties to undertake measures to implement the economic, social and cultural rights of children 'to the maximum extent of their available resources'. This is the only legal requirement directed at the general issue of allocation of funds to provide adequate levels of support for children in need. It is not directly enforceable in law, although non-governmental organisations can use the reporting and monitoring process under the UNCRC to identify areas that appear to be under-funded and to urge allocation of more resources. The limited extent to which lack of provision may generate an individual legal claim is discussed in Chapter 5. For present purposes, the point is that lack of resources will undermine effective inter-disciplinary collaboration in various ways, creating competition for resources between services that ought to be operating collaboratively, contributing to failures in continuity and communication and reducing opportunities for essential training – and that all of these can properly be seen as UNCRC implementation issues.

Culture

In seminars conducted during the course of the Laming Inquiry, it was noted that 'For some, the problem lay in society's attitude to children. Children were not sufficiently valued and some level of violence towards them was tolerated. The solution would be nationally agreed outcomes for children, which everyone involved could work to' (Laming, 2003: para. 17.48). The expression by the Children Act 2004 of the five 'aspects of well-being' to which all children's services must be directed was no doubt an attempt to supply this solution. However, it was done in the context of deliberate suppression of the language of children's rights: the 2004 Act does not even use the 'rights and welfare' formula employed in earlier Acts such as the Care Standards Act 2000 and the Health and Social Care (Community Health and Standards) Act 2003 but repeatedly uses the formula of safeguarding and promoting welfare. The 2004 Act was also the context for a heated debate about, and ultimately the retention (albeit in a more limited form) of, the defence of reasonable chastisement for assaults committed against children by their parents. The result is that Parliament has succeeded in setting out nationally agreed outcomes in the context of an Act which undervalues children by failing to acknowledge their internationally recognised entitlements and which perpetuates this particular manifestation of tolerance of a level of violence against children. This seems less than an adequate response to the issue of culture raised in the Laming Inquiry.

Conclusion

In practice, inter-organisational relationships only work through human relationships. Hudson et al. (1999) identified reciprocity, choice, consensus, purpose and trust as essential elements of collaborative working. Neither law nor administrative systems can supply these qualities but they can provide conceptual and organisational frameworks designed to nurture them or, at the very least, not to inhibit them. In this chapter it has been seen that the law provides:

- an organisational framework in which the 'stakeholders' are identified;
- a set of specific requirements and permissions intended to facilitate collaborative working; and
- certain expressions of purpose towards which the efforts of the stakeholders must be directed, formulated in terms of welfare, well-being and rights.

The law is clearer in the way it supplies the first two than the third of these prerequisites, although clarity is not always the same as simplicity. That there is something of a fudge in relation to the third, expressions of purpose, reflects pervasive contemporary themes in our legal and administrative culture. These themes are firstly an uneven adjustment to the absorption of human rights and secondly, ambivalent about the place of children's rights in a system designed to meet paternalistic concerns about welfare and control. The professional requirements for child care social work are, by comparison, clear: practice should reflect the values that are drawn from human rights obligations and the UNCRC. In seeking to operationalise these values in a multidisciplinary, inter-agency context, social workers will derive support from acquiring knowledge of the case-law decided by the courts rather than relying solely on the plethora of official guidance. Ultimately, it falls to the courts to interpret the law compatibly with human rights obligations, whether or not those obligations appear explicitly on the face of the subject-specific legislation and guidance.

Further Reading

Social work students and practitioners should become thoroughly familiar with the relevant government guidance on confidentiality and information-sharing: *Information Sharing: A Practitioner's Guide* (Department for Education and Skills, 2006: available on the *Every Child Matters* website) and *Confidentiality: Code of Practice for Health and Social Care in Wales* (Welsh Assembly Government, 2005).

Salutary reading on inter-agency working is to be found in almost any child death inquiry or serious case review: reference has been made here to the Laming Inquiry, Bichard Inquiry and North East Lincolnshire Serious Case Reviews. A useful summary of findings from a number of such reviews is *Learning from Past Experience – a Review of Serious Case Reviews* (Department of Health, 2002).

Part Two
Social Work Practice with Children

INTRODUCTION: Key Concepts in Case-work Interventions

Part Two of this book is concerned with the application of the law, policies and systems discussed in Part One to individual case-work with children and families. This Introduction explains the key legal concept of parental responsibility and the terms 'voluntary engagement' and 'compulsory measures', used in this Part to distinguish social work involvement which depends on the consent of the child and/or persons with parental responsibility from that which does not. The Introduction concludes by suggesting a general, rights-based approach to case-work and the social work role.

Chapters 5, 6 and 7 consider four instalments of a typical case where a referral is made to social services by a health professional. As the case unfolds, the social worker to whom it is allocated must apply core areas of knowledge, underpinned by legal and professional values, as shown in **Box In.1**

The social worker will need to work collaboratively – with the children, parents, other professionals and agencies. As explained in Chapter 3, a legal basis is necessary for any social work action carried out on behalf of a local authority. It is convenient to divide consideration of the legal basis by looking separately at what are here called 'voluntary engagement' and 'compulsory measures', not least because the latter generally require the authority of the court whereas the former do not. A key difference is that compulsory measures generally impact on the exercise of parental responsibility whereas voluntary engagement does not. This calls for some further explanation.

Voluntary engagement and compulsory measures

Voluntary engagement with children and families is usually based on powers and duties set out in Pt. III Children Act 1989, although other statutory powers and duties may be relevant, notably in the case of disabled children and their families, under the Chronically Sick and Disabled Persons Act 1970, Carers and Disabled Children Act 2000 or Education Act 1996. These powers and duties confer lawful authority on the local authority to offer a range of specific services, from advice and counselling to practical assistance in the home or provision of equipment and facilities. In some cases cash payments may be made or accommodation offered.

Box In.1

Core areas of knowledge	Legal and professional values
The rights of the children and other persons involved	Human rights and social justice
The powers and duties of local authorities and the court orders that can be applied for and made	Lawful authority
Legal considerations in the exercise of statutory discretion, including the impact of cognate statutory schemes	Principles and standards bearing on lawful authority in the individual case
The social work process: Assess → Plan → Implement and Sustain → Review and Record, together with legal processes and timescales and proper preparation and presentation of evidence	Professional competence, partnership working
Relevant administrative and judicial processes for supervision and complaints	Accountability

Compulsory measures are actions taken, mainly under judicial authority, which have the effect of changing the legal position as to exercise of parental responsibility. The legal concept of 'parental responsibility' was introduced by the Children Act 1989, marking a deliberate departure from the previous language of 'parental rights'. However, parental responsibility remains linked to the bundle of rights and duties previously recognised by the courts as attaching to the relationship of parent and child. Section 3(1) Children Act 1989 defines parental responsibility as 'all the rights, duties, powers, responsibilities and authority which by law a parent of a child has in relation to the child and his property'. This 'bundle' includes determining the child's religious and educational upbringing, having physical possession of the child and administering discipline, naming the child, maintaining the child and ensuring s/he receives an education, authority to give various consents such as consent to medical treatment, to the taking of blood for testing, to the child's marriage or adoption and to the temporary removal of the child from the jurisdiction. It includes the right to represent the child in legal proceedings, appoint a guardian, to administer the child's property, to allow the child to be interviewed and to allow confidential information relating to the child to be published.

The Children Act 1989 also provides for the acquisition of parental responsibility. In the absence of compulsory measures, the position is that the child's mother always has parental responsibility and the father has it if either married to the child's mother, registered on the birth certificate, or if he has a parental responsibility agreement with the mother, a court order conferring parental responsibility or a residence order (ss. 2 and 4 Children Act 1989 as amended by s. 111 Adoption and Children Act 2002). Other persons may acquire parental responsibility by appointment or by court order in private law family proceedings: for example, a testamentary guardian or any person in whose favour a residence order under s. 8 Children Act 1989 is made.

Voluntary engagement has no legal effect on parental responsibility but is generally aimed at supporting parents in their exercise of it. Compulsory measures have the effect that either:

(a) a person not previously having parental responsibility is given lawful authority to exercise certain aspects of it (if necessary without the consent of any other person having parental responsibility); or

(b) some restriction is imposed on the way in which a person having parental responsibility exercises it; or

(c) both (a) and (b).

The change may be very limited, for example simply empowering a police officer to do what is reasonable to secure the immediate safety of a child (s. 46 Children Act 1989). It may be extensive, yet still not extinguish the parental responsibility of the parent(s), as where a care order (s. 31 Children Act 1989) or placement order (s. 21 Adoption and Children Act 2002) is made. Only an adoption order has the effect of wholly extinguishing parental responsibility: the adopted child is treated in law as if born as the child of the adoptive parent or parents (s. 67 Adoption and Children Act 2002). The table in Box In.2 shows the effect on parental responsibility of the various measures available to local authorities (or in some cases the police) in England and Wales.

'Child protection', 'child and family support' and resource issues

Another way of distinguishing between social work action taken on the basis of voluntary engagement and that which is based on compulsory measures is to speak in terms of 'child and family support' and 'child protection'. This distinction is out of step with current thinking. In a broad sense, all social work interventions with children and their families are concerned with child protection. Provision of support and services on the basis of voluntary engagement can be seen as protective in that it seeks to avoid or counteract disadvantage of one kind or another, thereby reducing the risk of poor outcomes for the child. Just as supportive work ought to reduce the need for

Box In.2 EFFECT OF COMPULSORY MEASURES OF PARENTAL RESPONSIBILITY ('PR')

Order/Power	Parental responsibility (PR)	Legislation
Removal and accommodation of children by police in cases of emergency	No change, but the designated officer 'shall do what is reasonable in all the circumstances for the purpose of safeguarding or promoting the child's welfare', bearing in mind the short duration of the power	s. 46(9) Children Act 1989
Emergency Protection Order	Limited PR conferred on applicant (local authority or NSPCC): exercisable only 'as far as is reasonably required to safeguard or promote the welfare of the child', bearing in mind the short duration of the order	s. 44(4)(c), s. 44(5)(b) Children Act 1989
Child Recovery Order	No change: the order is supportive of the offence of child abduction in s. 49 Children Act 1989	s. 50(3) Children Act 1989 sets out the effect of the order: it operates as a direction and authority for the recovery of the child and confers on a constable a power to enter and search premises
Child Assessment Order	No change but the order can authorise keeping the child away from home for specified periods for the purpose of assessment	s. 43(9) Children Act 1989
Care Order	Local authority gets PR without parents losing it but local authority can exercise certain aspects, e.g. deciding with whom a child should live, to the	s. 31(3) Children Act 1989

Order/Power	Parental responsibility (PR)	Legislation
	exclusion of any others with PR	
Placement Order	Adoption agency gets PR without parents losing it	s. 25 Adoption and Children Act 2002
Adoption Order	Child treated in law as if born to the adoptive parent(s), so adoptive parents get exclusive PR	s. 67 Adoption and Children Act 2002
Supervision Order	No change but the supervisor may require the child to live at a specified place, attend specified places, submit to medical/psychiatric examination and participate in specified activities	s. 35 Children Act 1989 Pts I and II Sched. 3 Children Act 1989
Educational supervision order	No change but child and parents required to comply with court and supervisor's directions. Parent's failure to comply may be a criminal offence	s. 36 Children Act 1989 Pt. III of Sched. 3 Children Act 1989
Interim Care/ Supervision Order	Local authority gets PR without parents losing it: court may give specific directions to support assessment for purpose of final hearing	s. 38 Children Act 1989

compulsory measures, equally an investigation directed towards the possible use of compulsory measures may reveal unmet needs that should be addressed by using child and family support and services. As stated in the key government guidance, *Working Together:*

> Effective measures to safeguard children are those which also promote their welfare. They should not be seen in isolation from the wider range of support and services already provided and available to meet the needs of children and families. (DfES, 2006 / WAG, 2006: para 1.13; para 7.32)

119

However, the phrase 'child protection' has often been used in a narrower sense, referring to the use of compulsory measures. There is a *gravitas* about compulsory measures which tends to render 'child protection' in this sense somehow in a different category from 'child and family support'. Perhaps this has contributed to a position identified in research wherein too much emphasis is placed on child protection at the expense of child and family support (DoH, 1995). In the context of limited resources within local authorities, addressing this problem has not proved easy and the Report of the Laming Inquiry, summarising messages from practitioners' discussions, showed that distortions persist (Laming, 2003: para. 17.36–38).

The Children Act 2004 represents an attempt to correct these distortions, promoting a more preventive, holistic approach within the concept of 'safeguarding children and promoting their welfare'. It remains questionable whether the desired improvements can be achieved within available resources. There is an international dimension to this because Article 4 UNCRC requires States Parties to implement the Convention 'to the maximum extent of available resources'. In its Concluding Observations on the UK's second periodic State Party report under the Convention (UN, 2002a), the UN Committee recommended that the UK undertake an analysis of all total and sectoral budgets to show the proportion spent on children, identify priorities and allocate resources in accordance with the Article 4 requirement. In particular, the UK needed to take all necessary measures to accelerate the elimination of the 'high proportion' of child poverty. Through the UNCRC reporting process, Article 4 may gain greater prominence as part of the wider picture in which children's services budgets and resource allocation decisions are negotiated. Service managers who use Article 4 as a source of external validation for arguments for more resources will make an important contribution to any such development.

The social work role and the social work process

In relation to both voluntary engagement and compulsory measures, the social work role is essentially one of assessment followed, where relevant, by one or more of the following:

(a) facilitation, or direct provision, of support or assistance;
(b) preparation of evidence to secure judicial authority for compulsory measures;
(c) co-ordination of services;
(d) review, evaluation and further assessment.

Carrying out the role requires application of the 'social work process', encapsulated in the NOSCCPQ as:

Assess → Plan → Implement and Sustain → Review and Record

Action taken in the course of this process is framed and constrained by:

(a) the duty under s. 6 Human Rights Act 1998 to act compatibly with ECHR rights;
(b) the professional duty to promote children's rights as set out in the UNCRC;
(c) the structures and objectives prescribed by the Children Act 2004;

as well as the terms of the specific power (under the Children Act 1989, etc.) being used.

Accordingly, it is suggested that the right approach to decision-making in individual cases is to consider, first, the rights of the child and other persons involved, second, the Children Act 2004 objectives and associated guidance and, third, the specific powers and duties that may be available for use in the particular case. In this way, it should be easier to ensure that the exercise of statutory discretion is properly informed by the relevant legal and professional values – and is less vulnerable to challenge. This is the approach adopted in dealing with legal and practice issues in Part Two of this book.

5

Engaging with Children and Their Families to Safeguard Children and Promote Their Welfare

Introduction

This Chapter is concerned with the social work process following a referral indicating that a child or children may be in need of support or services. To illustrate the process, we consider three instalments of a fictitious case study, starting with a reference from a non-social work professional. The referral suggests that there may be a need for the provision of support or assistance in order to secure the well-being of the children within their home. As we follow the story of Anne and Martin through this chapter and in its fourth instalment in Chapter 6, the two critical referrals both come from health professionals – in the first instance from a health visitor and in the second from a consultant paediatrician in an accident and emergency unit. A study in 2003–4 of 100 English local authorities indicated that health services were the most frequent, or amongst the most frequent, source of referral followed by police, schools and other educational services, then by relatives, acquaintances and the general public (Statham et al., 2004).

CASE STUDY (1)

Two siblings, Anne (3) and Martin (18 months) are referred to Blankshire Local Authority by their health visitor. Both children are asthmatic and the health visitor is concerned that their asthma has worsened since they moved with their parents, Elin and James, to their current accommodation three months ago. Also, Martin has not gained weight during that period. The health visitor reports that the flat is damp and inadequately heated and furnished. The children's mother, Elin, has just been diagnosed as suffering from depression and her GP has prescribed drugs for her. The health visitor has recently taken over the file and notes that there were no significant concerns in the past, that although Elin and James are not married, James is registered as the children's father (the health visitor has not met him and understands that he works away from home frequently) and that Elin's former accommodation was rented from the Council in her sole name. The health visitor suspects that the children's health is being affected by a combination of their living conditions and a recent deterioration in parental care.

These circumstances, coupled with the local authority's statutory duties, trigger a requirement for Blankshire to carry out an assessment. At this stage, the case presents as one where help may be needed in the form of provision of support and services rather than more drastic intervention. It is therefore necessary to consider the legal framework for assessing need and offering help on the basis of voluntary engagement with the children and family. Taking the approach suggested in the Introduction to Part Two, the starting point is consideration of the rights of the children concerned. The local authority social worker, operating within structures and systems generated by the Local Authority Social Services Act 1970, the Children Act 2004 and cognate statutory provisions (Chapter 3), mindful of the need to co-ordinate services towards achievement of the 2004 Act's five 'aspects of well-being' (Chapter 4), must then utilise specific statutory powers and duties in a way which ensures the children's entitlement whilst also respecting the rights of others involved.

Rights, powers and duties

Box 5.1 identifies the relevant UNCRC and ECHR provisions and lists the domestic provisions which might be argued to be consistent with the State's positive obligations under both Conventions to provide support for children and their families. There is not a direct correlation between the international and the domestic provisions. There is a fundamental conceptual difference between asserting a right to provision (UNCRC, and to a limited extent also ECHR) and conferring a power to provide services (domestic legislation). The difference between a right (UNCRC/ECHR) and a duty (domestic legislation) may be less significant, depending on to whom the duty is owed and how it can be enforced. There is no wholly satisfactory practical resolution to these conceptual differences. The social worker must strive to apply the domestic provisions in a way which is as consistent as possible with the UNCRC and with Convention rights under the ECHR, taking the UNCRC in particular as the 'value base' for actions and decisions.

Box 5.1   CONVENTION RIGHTS AND DOMESTIC LAW

UNCRC: rights and obligations	ECHR: rights and obligations	Law in England and Wales
The 'four pervasive themes':		
1. Protection from discrimination (Art. 2)	Non-discrimination in enjoyment of Convention rights (Art. 14)	Equality Act 2006 and anti-discrimination statutes (see Chapter 2, Box 2.4)
2. Best interests of the child a primary consideration in all actions concerning children (Art. 3)	The 'best interests' notion has been developed by the ECtHR in resolving conflicts between children's rights and the rights of others e.g. parents	The interests of the individual child are not paramount. Statutory provisions such as those in Pt. III Children Act 1989 authorise provision of support and services, but (with limited exceptions) do not require it in any individual case. Under the Children Act 2004 services must be directed in particular at five 'aspects of well-being'

UNCRC: rights and obligations	ECHR: rights and obligations	Law in England and Wales
3. Right to survival and development (Art. 6)	Art. 8 imposes positive obligations which may in practice imply provision of support in certain circumstances: ***Botta v Italy* [1998]** (Chapter 1)	The definition of 'need' in s. 17(10), (11) Children Act 1989 is based on the child's health and development compared to 'a similar child'
4. Right to have views taken into account (Art. 12)	Art. 6 applies only where there is a 'determination of a civil right or obligation' but fair process is required in relation to any action impinging on enjoyment of Art. 8 rights	s. 17(4A) Children Act 1989 requires the child's wishes and feelings to be given due consideration; s. 26 provides for complaints procedure
Special care and facilities for disabled children (Art. 23)	ECHR not designed to confer social and economic rights, but State support may be necessary to ensure respect for certain rights, e.g. Art. 8, Art. 3	Specialised assessment provision under Chronically Sick and Disabled Persons Act 1970, Carers and Disabled Children Act 2000 and Education Act 1996. A disabled child is a child 'in need' under s. 17(10) and (11) Children Act 1989
Right to health care services, an adequate standard of living and to benefit from social security (Arts. 24, 26 and 27). Right to education, rest, leisure and play (Arts. 28, 29 and 31)		Statutory bodies have duties to provide service and facilities, under, e.g. National Health Service Act 1977 and NHS (Wales) Act 2006; Education Act 1996; Learning and Skills Act 2000

(Continued)

UNCRC: rights and obligations	ECHR: rights and obligations	Law in England and Wales
Support for parents to exercise primary responsibility for upbringing and development (Art. 18)		Under s.17(1) Children Act 1989 powers must be exercised in such a way as to promote the upbringing of children in need by their families

The UNCRC

Most of the articles set out in the first column of Box 5.1 are essentially 'provision' requirements. (As explained in Chapter 2 the UNCRC is sometimes characterised as containing rights to provision, protection and participation.) In effect, the UNCRC asserts that children have a right to nurture. It requires the State to support parents as primary carers and, where parents will not or cannot fulfil this role, to ensure that substitute care is provided. Applying this analysis to **Case Study (1)**, Anne and Martin's development appears to be threatened either by the lack of an adequate standard of living or by want of parental care, or both, and the State is obliged to provide support and services to ensure that the children receive the nurture to which they are entitled.

The kind of support envisaged is indicated in the UN Committee's General Comments on implementing rights in early childhood (UN, 2006) and on adolescent health and development (UN, 2003b). These texts emphasise that approaches must be rights-based, non-discriminatory and multi-sectoral. They must also recognise the active agency of the child as well as the role of the family and must reflect the indivisibility of the rights set out in the Convention:

The Committee reminds States parties (and others concerned) that the right to survival and development can only be implemented in a holistic manner, through the enforcement of all the other provisions of the Convention, including rights to health, adequate nutrition, social security, an adequate standard of living, a healthy and safe environment, education and play (Arts. 24, 27, 28, 29 and 31), as well as through respect for the responsibilities of parents and the provision of assistance and quality services (Arts. 5 and 18). From an early age, children should themselves be included in activities promoting good nutrition and a healthy and disease-preventing lifestyle. (UN, 2006a: para.10)

As discussed below (under *Domestic provisions*), the social worker dealing with the referral of Anne and Martin has a tool-kit comprising powers, duties, assessment techniques, guidance and working practices. It may be possible to use these tools effectively to promote the children's rights as contemplated by the UN Committee in the above extract. Certainly, the social worker will strive to negotiate the best possible package of support. Yet two problems are likely to remain: first, the realities of limited resources, difficult allocation decisions and division of responsibilities across different agencies, and second, the legal position that under the relevant domestic provisions the individual child normally has no entitlement to provision of support and services. These two problems are properly to be seen as UNCRC compliance issues which are ultimately the responsibility of the UK under international law.

The ECHR

The ECHR does not expressly include economic and social rights (with the exception of the right of access to education and protection of property). However, as Palmer (2003) has shown, through its case-law the ECtHR has begun to recognise the scope for development of certain of the Convention rights in a way which embraces economic and social rights. In ***Botta v Italy* [1998]**, the ECtHR said that the right to respect for private life under Article 8 includes a right to 'personal development', including the enjoyment of relationships with other people, and that the State's duty was not only to protect people from interference with this right by others but could also embrace the provision of measures which will directly affect an individual's personal development. This did not amount to an automatic right to provision in accordance with individual need: the Court acknowledged that the State had to balance the general interest and the interests of the individual, and that it was legitimate to take resources into account. The importance of the case is that it establishes the principle that decisions about provision of support and services may be scrutinised by reference to Article 8 rights.

Botta was not a case about provision of support for children, but the reasoning can be applied as follows:

- a child has a right under Article 8 ECHR to personal development, including enjoyment of relationships with family and friends;
- the State must protect the child from interference with this right by others: examples might include intervening where a child is being prevented from attending school or is repeatedly kept away from hospital appointments;
- where there is a direct link between the provision of support or facilities and the child's personal development, the State may be required to provide the relevant support or facilities (for example by providing transport or other facilities to enable a disabled child to attend school, or by providing material support to enable a child to continue to live at home whilst also securing the child's health);

- the State has discretion as to how to allocate resources to these ends and how to balance the needs of the individual child against the general public interest, BUT it must be able to justify its decisions, showing that it has paid proper regard to the rights and interests of the persons involved.

In England and Wales, some judges have adopted this approach when dealing with disputes arising under Pt. III Children Act 1989, and it is a useful starting point when assessing need and service provision. Thus, a social worker carrying out an assessment of Anne and Martin's needs as described in Case Study (1) should consider the extent to which the children's personal development will be adversely affected if a particular service is not given. If the service is not available, the local authority should be able to give an explanation why this is so, demonstrating that an appropriate balance has been struck between the individual's needs and other demands.

Domestic provisions

Having identified the rights engaged in this situation, the social worker dealing with Anne and Martin's referral in Case Study (1) must turn to the specific powers and duties governing provision of support for children in need and their families and strive to apply these in a manner compatible with those rights. The domestic provisions are contained mainly in the Children Act 1989, Children Act 2004 and associated regulations and guidance.

Part III Children Act 1989

Part III Children Act 1989 sets out local authorities' powers and duties to provide facilities and services to children in need in their area. The idea is that there should be collaborative working between parents, social workers and other agencies in the provision of welfare services for children. Section 17 places a general duty on local authorities to provide services to children in need in their area (Box 5.2) and gives a definition of 'need' for this purpose (Box 5.3). Under Sched. 2 to the Act, certain services must be provided, others may be

---

Box 5.2   SECTION 17(1) CHILDREN ACT 1989: THE GENERAL DUTY TO 'CHILDREN IN NEED'

It shall be the duty of every local authority ... (a) to safeguard and promote the welfare of children within their area who are in need; and (b) so far as is consistent with that duty, to promote the upbringing of such children by their families, by providing a range of services appropriate to those children's needs.

CHILD LAW FOR SOCIAL WORK

Box 5.3 SECTION 17(10) AND (11) CHILDREN ACT 1989: THE DEFINITION OF 'CHILD IN NEED'

a child shall be taken to be in need if (a) he is unlikely to achieve or maintain, or to have the opportunity of achieving or maintaining, a reasonable standard of health or development without the provision for him of services by a local authority ... (b) his health or development is likely to be significantly impaired, or further impaired, without the provision for him of such services; or (c) he is disabled.

For this purpose, 'family' includes any person who has parental responsibility for the child and any other person with whom he has been living; 'disabled' means 'blind, deaf or dumb or suffers from mental disorder of any kind or is substantially and permanently handicapped by illness, injury or congenital deformity or such other disability as may be prescribed'; 'development' means physical, intellectual, emotional, social or behavioural development; and 'health' means physical or mental health.

provided (Box 5.4 and Box 5.5). Other provisions in Pt. III of the Act confer further powers and duties (Box 5.6). The Children Act 2004 superimposes overall aims towards which local strategies are to be directed, and structures within which the strategies are to be devised and services delivered.

Despite the prescription of specific services in Pt. III Children Act 1989, and despite the centrally set overall objectives added by the Children Act 2004, substantial local discretion remains both in individual case-work and in deciding what services to provide. In Sched. 2 Children Act 1989, even the 'must do' list (Box 5.4) is peppered with words such as 'reasonably practicable' or 'if the local authority considers that', which qualify the apparently mandatory nature of the duty. Likewise, the definition of 'need' in s. 17(10) and (11) Children Act 1989 (Box 5.3) is deliberately wide. It was intended to reinforce the emphasis on preventive support and service to families (DoH, 1991: para.2.4), but provided a local authority ensures that all the categories of need (that is, lack of a reasonable standard of health or development, significant impairment of health or development and disablement) are covered, it retains local discretion as to priorities and criteria.

Guidance

The exercise of discretion is of course always tempered by the legal duty to act rationally, fairly and compatibly with ECHR rights (See Chapter 3: Structures for accountability: *Judicial remedies*). Further, a local authority carrying out social services functions is under a duty to act in accordance with guidance issued by the Secretary of State or the Welsh Assembly Government

---

Box 5.4 SCHEDULE 2 CHILDREN ACT 1989: THINGS THE LOCAL AUTHORITY *MUST* DO FOR THE PURPOSES OF S. 17:

- take reasonable steps to identify the extent to which there are children in need in their area;
- publish information about their services and take reasonable steps to ensure that those who might benefit from services receive information relevant to them;
- open and maintain a register of disabled children within their area and provide services designed to minimise the effect on them of their disabilities;
- take reasonable steps, through the provision of services, to prevent children suffering ill-treatment or neglect;
- take reasonable steps to reduce the need to bring care or supervision proceedings (under Pt. IV of the Act) or criminal proceedings, against children, to reduce the need to place children in secure accommodation, and to encourage children not to commit criminal offences;
- make such provision as the authority considers appropriate for children living at home, e.g. advice, counselling, occupational and recreational activities, home help and other assistance;
- where appropriate, provide family centres, providing a range of services to children and families;
- take such steps as are reasonably practicable to enable children separated from their family to live with them, or to promote contact – if the authority considers this necessary to safeguard or promote the child's welfare;
- have regard to different racial groups when providing foster care or day care.

---

under s. 7(1) Local Authority Social Services Act 1970. For the purposes of dealing with Anne and Martin's referral in Case Study (1), the key statutory guidance is:

- the *Framework for the Assessment of Children in Need and Their Families ('the Framework')* (DoH, 2000 / NAW, 2001), from which the
- *Common Assessment Framework* ('CAF') (DfES, 2006b; WAG, 2007) has been developed, and
- *Working Together to Safeguard Children ('Working Together')* (DfES, 2006 / WAG, 2006).

Box 5.5   SCHEDULE 2 CHILDREN ACT 1989: THINGS THE LOCAL AUTHORITY *MAY* DO FOR THE PURPOSES OF S. 17:

- provide assistance to a person to obtain alternative accommodation where the local authority considers this may help protect a child (because the child is at risk of ill treatment at the hands of that person).

Box 5.6   OTHER POWERS AND DUTIES UNDER PT. III CHILDREN ACT 1989

Section 18: day care for pre-school and other children. A local authority *must* provide 'such care as is appropriate' for children under 5 who are in need and not yet attending school, and for children in need who are attending school, outside school hours or during school holidays. A local authority *may* provide such care for children not in need.

Section 20: provision of accommodation for some 'children in need'. A local authority *must* provide accommodation where a child in need within the area appears to require it as a result of: there being no person who has parental responsibility for him; his being lost or having been abandoned; or the person who has been caring for him being prevented (whether or not permanently, and for whatever reason) from providing him with suitable accommodation or care.

Under **s. 20**, a local authority *may* provide accommodation even though a person with parental responsibility is able to provide accommodation, if the authority considers this would safeguard or promote the child's welfare and provided (in the case of children under 16) the person with parental responsibility does not object. For those over 16, a local authority *must* provide accommodation if the authority consider the child's welfare to be 'likely to be seriously prejudiced' if accommodation is not provided.

Sections 22, 23 and 25: powers and duties in respect of children looked after by the local authority (see **Chapter 8**).

Sections 23A–D; 24A–C: duties to some people who have been in care (see **Chapter 8**).

Duty to carry out assessment

Case-law has established that a local authority is under a duty to carry out an assessment where it appears that an individual child may be 'in need': *R (AB and SB) v Nottingham City Council* [2001]; *R (S) v London Borough of Wandsworth, London Borough of Hammersmith and Fulham, London Borough of Lambeth* [2002]. Accordingly, in Case Study (1), it would not be lawful for Blankshire to refuse to assess Anne and Martin's needs, given what they have been told by the health visitor and applying the statutory definition of 'need'.

Process and Assessment

Chapter 5 (England) and Ch. 8 (Wales) of *Working Together*, read in conjunction with the *Framework*, prescribe a process which Blankshire must follow on receipt of the health visitor's referral in Case Study (1). This is shown in Box 5.7.

Box 5.7   PROCESS ON REFERRAL

1. Open a file (unless a file already exists). Record the name, address and age of each child.
2. Record details of the referral. Where the referral is from another professional, that professional is required to confirm it in writing within 48 hours, showing the nature of the concerns, how and why they have arisen, what appear to be the needs of the child and family, whether there are concerns about maltreatment and, if so, what is their foundation and whether urgent action is required to ensure the child's safety.
3. Within 1 working day of the referral, decide on next steps and, unless no action is to be taken, allocate the case to a lead worker.
4. Communicate the decision to the referrer (if a professional: if the referrer is not a professional, confidentiality considerations will restrict what information may be disclosed).
5. If it is decided that the child's needs should be assessed, carry out an initial assessment within 7 days of the referral.
6. Decide whether a core assessment is to be carried out: if so, complete it within a further 35 days (making 42 days in total from the date of the referral).
7. Identify whether and, if so, where intervention will be required to secure the well-being of the child.
8. Agree a realistic plan of action (including services to be provided) with a timetable, allocation of responsibility and review process.

The purpose of and statutory basis for assessment

The initial assessment is directed at ascertaining:

(a) whether the child concerned is in need;
(b) whether there is reasonable cause to suspect that this child is suffering, or is likely to suffer, significant harm.

These questions are based on the statutory criteria triggering different powers and duties under the Children Act 1989. If it is a 'need' case, the local authority response falls within Pt. III of the 1989 Act. If it is also a 'significant harm' case, the local authority also has to consider taking compulsory measures under Pt. IV or Pt. V. It is essential to be clear about the legislative basis for the assessment. It may be clear from the facts reported on referral that the child is at risk of significant harm, and immediate compulsory measures may be appropriate. In that case, the initial assessment will coincide with the preparation of the evidence required to obtain the court's authority, but should still also focus on assessment of need, since this will be relevant whether or not the compulsory measures are authorised.

In Case Study (1), there are probably insufficient grounds to suspect that Anne and Martin are at risk of 'significant harm'. The case should accordingly be allocated to a suitably qualified social worker to conduct an initial assessment before any further action is taken.

Requirements as to involving people and collecting information

The initial assessment should include collecting information from a range of sources – persons and organisations involved in providing support or services, the child and family members. Section 17(4A) Children Act 1989 (inserted by s. 53 Children Act 2004) emphasises the need to respect the agency of the child by requiring local authorities to ascertain the child's wishes and feelings about the provision of services and to give them due consideration before determining what, if any, services to provide. In Case Study (1), Anne and Martin are very young, but this does not mean that no effort need be made to ascertain their wishes and feelings. Age is relevant as to how, not whether, the children's own messages should be sought out. As the UN Committee has noted, research and theory confirm that 'young children are best understood as social actors whose survival, well-being and development are dependent on and built around close relationships' (UN, 2006: para 8). The requirement in the *Framework* for assessment always to be 'child centred' should be read in that light.

Inter-agency working

In order to support inter-agency working, s. 27 Children Act 1989 permits a local authority carrying out functions under Pt. III of the Act to request help from any other local authority, local education authority, local housing authority or health body. The requested authority must comply with the request 'if it is compatible with their own statutory or other duties'. Section 47(9), (10) and (11) makes similar provision for a s. 47 assessment (directed at the 'significant harm' criterion), but in that case it can only be refused if compliance 'would be unreasonable in all the circumstances of the case'.

It will no doubt help the social worker to whom Anne and Martin's referral is allocated if information can be obtained from Anne and Martin's GP, any health clinic or children's centre they have attended, any registered childminder or day-care provider and the housing authority. There should be local protocols dealing with inter-agency requests, pursuant to the arrangements explained in Chapter 4. However, there may be reluctance to disclose information without parental consent, and the overriding public interest condition would not normally apply unless there was at least a reasonable suspicion of risk of significant harm (see discussion of confidentiality in Chapter 4). The social worker will wish to see Elin as soon as possible in any event, and should seek Elin's consent to the disclosure of information from these other agencies.

Concurrent assessment

There is no indication in Case Study (1) of any other assessment being carried out. This may not always be so. Paragraph 3, Sched. 2 Children Act 1989 makes it clear that different types of assessments may be carried out at the same time and the *Framework* says that assessment should be carried out in parallel with other action and providing services. For example, it may be appropriate for an assessment of special educational need to be carried out under Pt. IV Education Act 1996, or an assessment for the purposes of provision of services under the Chronically Sick and Disabled Persons Act 1970. Often the purposes of such assessments are entirely complementary. Where they are not, care must be taken to avoid a conflict of interest. This may arise when considerations of welfare are the trigger for an assessment (as under s. 17 Children Act 1989) whilst at the same time community safety considerations have triggered another process within the same authority (such as collation of evidence to apply for an ASBO). Detailed guidance on how to ensure that neither process is delayed whilst conflict of interest is avoided in this situation was given in *R (M (A Child)) v Sheffield Magistrates Court* [2004] (see further Chapter 9).

Carrying out the assessment

The Laming Report stated that 'the basic aim of any assessment of a child should be to understand the child in his or her social situation' (Laming, 2003: para 17.33). Since 2000, assessment has been required to follow the 'three dimensional' approach set out in the *Framework*. On its face, this satisfies Lord Laming's description, since it examines the child's development, parenting capacity within the family home and the impact of the environment. The basic 'triangle' set out in Appendix A to the *Framework* is now very familiar (See Figure).

The Common Assessment Framework (CAF) builds on this approach, providing a preparatory checklist and an eight-stage procedure for gathering and analysing information, with associated forms. However, whereas the *Framework* is clearly directed at the exercise of social services functions, the CAF appears to be aimed at a much wider target, embracing the provision of any children's services and available for use by any practitioner (not just a social worker) who has concerns that a particular child may fail to achieve the five 'aspects of

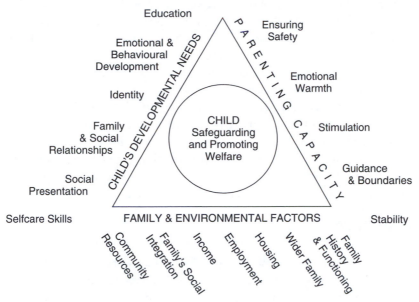

Health   Basic Care

Education

Emotional &
Behavioural
Development

Ensuring
Safety

Emotional
Warmth

Identity

Family
& Social
Relationships

CHILD
Safeguarding
and Promoting
Welfare

Stimulation

Social
Presentation

Guidance
& Boundaries

Selfcare Skills   FAMILY & ENVIRONMENTAL FACTORS   Stability

Community Resources   Family's Social Integration   Income   Employment   Housing   Wider Family   Family History & Functioning

Reproduced under the terms of the Click-Use Licence

well-being' prescribed by the Children Act 2004 (see Chapter 3). Accordingly, the CAF could in principle have been completed by the health visitor in Case Study (1) prior to making the referral to Blankshire. This would have to be done on a purely voluntary basis, with Elin's consent. Once the referral had been made, the fact that a CAF form had been completed by the health visitor would not in any way discharge the local authority's duty under s. 17 Children Act 1989, but the information so gathered might help focus the s. 17 enquiries. The CAF Practice Guidance (DfES, 2006b) does not address in any detail the application of the CAF to the disparate statutory functions of professionals dealing with children, rather optimistically leaving its application within the different statutory systems to be worked out through local inter-agency collaboration.

In addition to the *Framework* and the CAF, appended to both the English and Welsh *Working Together* is a collection of questionnaires and scales that can be used to support assessment and decision-making. The *Framework* contains guidance about assessment-planning and information-gathering and refers to numerous research studies and models indicating best practice. In all of this documentation there is an emphasis on identifying how families themselves may need to change, and on explaining to them what may happen if they don't, as well as on identifying facilities and services that may help them better to safeguard and promote the welfare of the child. The CAF Practice

Guidance (DfES, 2006b) discusses the 'continuum' of needs and services: in the nature of things, there will be change one way or the other. Paragraph 1.57 of the *Framework* envisages assessment as an active component of change, stating that 'the process of assessment should be therapeutic in itself'. There is, however, an implicit tension between scrutiny and therapy, and there is debate as to whether the increasing bureaucratisation of the process does anything to ameliorate this, or indeed makes it worse. (For example, see the discussion in Millar and Corby, 2006.) The unfolding story of Anne and Martin in the second instalment in Case Study (2) illustrates the potential for 'therapeutic assessment'. The initial assessment suggests the need for a core assessment to be carried out, but in the meantime a process that could bring about change may well have already started, since Elin has identified at least part of the problem and appears ready to discuss her options with the lead worker.

CASE STUDY (2)

In the course of the initial assessment, Elin tells the lead worker, Adi, that she would like to leave James because he has been threatening her. Elin says this is the reason for the depression for which she is now receiving medication. However, the flat they are living in is rented by James from a friend of his, and Elin has nowhere else to go. She has not applied to the local authority for housing as she left the council flat which she had occupied as sole tenant, leaving unpaid arrears of rent. The arrears accumulated, she says, because James had withheld money from her. She knows the children's health as well as her own is being affected but increasingly feels powerless to improve the situation. The housing department confirms the situation with regard to the rent arrears. On this information, and having discussed the case at some length with the health visitor, Adi forms the view that further assessment is required with a view to identifying services that might be provided under s. 17 Children Act 1989. Adi has not yet been able to contact James, who is working away during the period of the initial assessment.

Initial assessment, core assessment and a plan for the child

Following the initial assessment, under the *Working Together* process (Box 5.7), a decision to undertake a core assessment is one which must be made by the social care team (England) or social services (Wales), rather than the lead worker alone. Likewise, the question whether any core assessment should remain focused on the provision of services under Pt. III Children Act 1989 or on possible compulsory measures under Pts. IV or V (or a combination of both). At the end of the process set out in Box 5.7, the plan may accordingly be a children in need plan or a child protection plan or some other plan, depending on the circumstances and the results of the assessment. In the third instalment of the story of Anne and Martin, in Case Study (3), the plan is a children in need plan.

CASE STUDY (3)

A core assessment is carried out. It identifies both children as children in need. In Anne's case it concludes that a part time day nursery place would be beneficial to improve her social and language development. Martin is in need of better nutrition. Both children need to be living in more suitable accommodation. The consensus is that Elin is capable of providing the parenting both children need but requires continued counselling support in relation to the probable termination of her relationship with James and, urgently, practical support to obtain acceptable accommodation for herself and the children.

Provision of services

In Case Study (3), provision of a day nursery place for Anne, advice and perhaps provision of cash payments to assist with the nutrition issues for Martin, and counselling for Elin, are services falling within the ambit of Pt. III and Sched. 2 Children Act 1989 and ought to be readily implemented as part of the 'children in need' plan. The question of accommodation is more difficult. This is an example of a 'need' to which the Children Act 1989 does not provide a complete response, and where other statutory systems and policies, which do not necessarily put children centre-stage, have to be considered. The other statutory scheme in Case Study (3) is publicly-funded housing; in other circumstances it might be immigration or asylum, as illustrated in the case of *R (G) v Barnet London Borough Council* (one of the cases discussed below under *The problem of accommodation*). The particular problem of accommodation provides a good illustration of the way human rights law interacts with domestic powers and duties. First, it is necessary to examine the nature of the local authority's duty under s. 17 Children Act 1989.

The nature of the duty under s. 17 Children Act 1989

The first point is that an assessment under s. 17 Children Act 1989 identifying a child as a child in need of particular services does not normally create a legal duty on the local authority to provide those services. Section 17 has been described as imposing a 'target duty', not capable of generating liability to individuals (Latham J, in *R v Bexley London Borough Council ex parte B (Care Hours Provision)* [2000]). The welfare of an individual child in need is not the paramount consideration – the target of the provision in s. 17 is the welfare of all children in need in the local authority's area. This is the general principle, but there are some qualifications:

(i) *Disability:* Section 17A Children Act 1989, and associated Regulations (the Community Care, Services for Carers and Children's Services (the Direct Payments) (England) Regulations 2003 and the Community Care, Services for Carers and Children's Services (Direct Payments) (Wales) Regulations 2004) have the effect that where services have been assessed as necessary to meet the needs of a disabled child, a duty to provide direct payments may arise. The power to make direct payments might, for example, enable financial support to be given for the employment of a carer for a disabled child rather than the provision of a local authority carer. The Regulations impose a duty to provide payments but only where the local authority is satisfied of two things:

(a) that the person's needs for the relevant service can be met by securing the provision of it by means of a direct payment, and

(b) that the child's welfare will be safeguarded or promoted by securing the provision of the service by means of the payment.

Thus, in Case Study (3), even if Anne or Martin were assessed as falling within the definition of a 'disabled child', a duty to make direct payments would not arise unless Blankshire were so satisfied.

(ii) *ECHR/Human Rights Act arguments*

The argument here is that the positive obligation of the State (normally under Article 8 but other Articles may be relevant, e.g. Articles 2 and 3 in cases of severe deprivation), combined with the domestic power to provide services, can generate a duty to provide a particular service to a particular person. The reasoning in **Botta v Italy** has already been discussed. In **R (J) v Enfield London Borough Council and Secretary of State for Health [2002]**, Elias J held that the positive obligation under Article 8, read together with a local authority's power to promote well-being under s. 2 Local Government Act 2000, could generate such a duty. This was expressly approved by the Court of Appeal in **R (W) v London Borough of Lambeth [2002]**, one of the three 'housing' cases considered below. The possible application to the situation in Case Study (3) of this tentative development of the law is considered below: the question is whether it could have the effect of turning the mere target duty in s. 17 Children Act 1989 into a duty to provide more suitable accommodation for Anne and Martin together with Elin.

The problem of accommodation

Three typical cases fell to be considered in: *R (G) v Barnet London Borough Council*; *R (W) v Lambeth London Borough Council*; *R (A) v Lambeth London Borough Council* [2003]. Each of the cases provides an example of children and families in need and the application of s. 17 to their circumstances. The common factor was that the parenting of the children was not criticised: the parents simply lacked accommodation suitable for the children's needs. In W's case the mother was classified as intentionally homeless and had a background of domestic abuse leading to rent arrears and eviction. A's case involved disabled children who were assessed as in urgent need of re-housing with their mother but the local authority had failed to supply that need. G's case involved a mother and child who were homeless where the mother's illegal immigration status meant she did not qualify for housing support.

In all of the cases, the House of Lords held by a majority that s. 17 imposed no duty to provide accommodation. Section 17(1) was broadly expressed with a view to giving the authority the greatest possible scope as to what it chose to do. Although the authority may provide accommodation under s. 17(6), provision of residential accommodation to enable a child to live with his or her family was not the principal or primary purpose of the legislation. Housing was the function of the local housing authority (often, in practice, a separate department of the same local authority) and was governed by separate legislation. Section 17(1) should not be interpreted by the courts in such a way as to make the social services department another kind of housing authority. It was also emphasised that the courts should be mindful that insisting on the use of s. 17(1) to provide accommodation would mean there was less available resource for other kinds of services for children in need.

However, this was not the end of the matter. Section 17 Children Act 1989 confers discretion; s. 20, on the other hand, imposes a duty to provide accommodation for a child in need who requires it (Box 5.6). This contributes to the position where local authorities may feel compelled to offer accommodation to the children but not the parents of destitute families. Some, like Lambeth and Barnet (in *G* and *W*), had adopted this as a policy. This could result in the separation of the children from their parents, even though the local authority's assessment was that it was in the child's best interests for the family to continue to live together. In practice, the local authorities had found that in many cases, parents faced with the prospect of separation had managed somehow to find accommodation, thereby relieving the local authority of the burden of accommodating the children. In cases where this remained impossible, the local authority's duty to the child alone, under s. 20, would 'kick in'.

Application of 'positive obligation' under the ECHR

Clearly, this situation engaged the rights of the children and their mothers under Article 8 ECHR. Could it be argued that the State's positive obligation required that provision be made to enable the family to stay together? Lord Nicholls (in his dissenting opinion) addressed this question. He did not accept the proposition that choosing to accommodate a child alone would necessarily be in breach of Article 8 and therefore unlawful under s. 6 Human Rights Act 1998, but approached the matter in a more nuanced way.

He said that a blanket policy of not accommodating families under s. 17 was not consistent with the State's positive duty under Article 8: each case must be considered on its own merits. But, he thought,

> without detracting from this overriding principle, a recognisable distinction is discernible here between two broad types of cases: (1) cases where a child is old enough to understand what is happening and is not likely to be significantly upset by being accommodated away from his parent, and (2) cases where this is not so. In the former type of cases the policy adopted by Lambeth Council is, in principle, reasonable. The social services authority is not under a duty to accommodate the parent of a child in need although it has power to do so. In this type of case, where the only need of the child is for short term accommodation, accommodating the child alone will safeguard the child's immediate welfare. It would be preferable if accommodation were provided for the parent as well. But this would have ... seriously adverse financial repercussions ... This is a factor the council may properly take into account.

Matters stand differently where the child is not old enough to understand what is going on or, if he is, he would be likely to be significantly upset at being separated from his parent. Providing accommodation for the child alone in this type of case may satisfy the authority's duty under section 20 of the Children Act 1989. But in this type of case the child's immediate need is for accommodation with his parent. This is a basic need. It is difficult to see how the local authority can be said to fulfil its duty under section 17(1) of the Children Act 1989 by accommodating the child alone in such circumstances. It cannot be reasonable in this type of case to give greater weight to the wider financial repercussions than to the adverse consequences to the individual child in the particular case. Parliament cannot have intended that the latitude afforded to local authorities by section 17(1) should embrace such a highly unsatisfactory result regarding the accommodation needs of a child in need.

He went on to point out that s. 213A Housing Act 1996 (inserted by the Homelessness Act 2002), provides a mechanism for joining up the exercise of statutory functions of the local authority as housing authority and as social services authority; where a local housing authority is aware that a person living with a child may be ineligible for housing, it requires the housing authority to ensure the local social services authority is made aware of the case, if the applicant agrees. Then, if the social services authority requests the housing authority to provide advice and assistance in exercise of its functions under Pt. III Children Act 1989, the housing authority is obliged to provide the social services authority 'with such advice and assistance as is reasonable in the circumstances'. So, Lord Nicholls concluded, where necessary a social services authority should now exercise its power under s. 213A of the 1996 Act to request assistance from the local housing authority. If such assistance was not forthcoming the court would scrutinise the housing authority's reasons with rigour if the consequence was that a homeless dependent child, not old enough to understand what is going on or likely to be significantly upset by being separated from his/her parent, would be accommodated separately from the parent.

Thus it would be wrong for a local authority to threaten a parent that the most it would do was to accommodate the child alone: to that extent a general policy such as Lambeth's needed adjustment: it went outside the latitude afforded by s. 17(1).

Lord Nicholls' views on the general policy were *obiter dicta*, and he was in a minority: Lord Scott, the only other law lord to consider the general policy, disagreed with the suggested distinction between cases involving older and younger children, and thought the general policy was acceptable. Lord Hope referred to the ECHR but appears to have considered the State's margin of appreciation sufficient to justify the local authorities' position.

A's case involved a slightly different point: the argument here was about whether the making of an assessment identifying the need for a specific type of accommodation for children with learning difficulties 'crystallised' the general duty and fixed the local authority with a duty to provide the services assessed as necessary. The majority held that it did not. Again, Lord Nicholls, with whom Lord Steyn agreed, took a different view: he thought the local authority should have requested assistance from the housing authority and that the case should be remitted for reconsideration on that basis.

These cases demonstrate the relationship between the Children Act 1989 and ECHR obligations, and how there is scope for judicial disagreement about what it means in practice. Arguably, Lord Nicholls' approach is more child-centred than the others, in the sense that it attempts to view the impact of the decision primarily from the standpoint of the child. On a practical note, the cases illustrate the predicament of the local authority, the ubiquitous problem of resources and how partnership working may be more or less helped by separate statutory schemes for different types of provision – here the housing legislation and s. 17 Children Act 1989 – and express connections between the two.

Applying all of this to Case Study (3), there may well be a difficulty in rela-tion to the direct provision of accommodation under s.17 Children Act 1989, but the help of the housing department could be formally requested, follow-ing Lord Nicholls' suggestion. Although the housing department could not be compelled to offer accommodation, they would need to be able to give a rational explanation for a decision not to do so.

Partnership working, accommodation and domestic violence

There is a suggestion in the Case Study that the relationship between Elin and James may be an abusive one: she says he has been threatening her and that in the past he has withheld money from her. Recent developments in multi-agency working come into play here. Borrowing from and expanding on the 'MAPPA' (multi-agency public protection arrangements) which have statutory force under criminal justice legislation in relation to certain categories of offenders, a non-statutory model known as the 'MARAC' (multi-agency risk assessment conferencing) has been developed, starting in South Wales and then being taken up by many local authorities across the UK. MARAC is designed to improve and co-ordinate all the facets of responses to domestic violence from criminal investigation, prosecution and non-molestation injunc-tions through to housing, victim support and child protection. The system is predicated on the wide definition of domestic violence now accepted by both UK and Welsh Assembly Governments (see Chapter 3) encompassing emo-tional and financial abuse as well as direct physical or sexual abuse. The idea is to share information across all statutory and voluntary agencies who may be involved to produce the best possible risk assessment and response. Early eval-uation suggests the approach has achieved positive results (Robinson, 2004). In Case Study (2) and (3) this is something that should be considered if local arrangements are in place.

Accountability

All of the actions discussed here – the referral, the assessment, decisions as to what services to provide and the drawing up of the children in need plan – are carried out within administrative processes. Judicial authority is not required. Yet there is always the possibility of judicial scrutiny in addition to other mechanisms for accountability such as a complaint under the Children Act 1989 itself (see Chapter 3). As Murphy (2004) has argued, when applied to decisions under Pt. III Children Act 1989, these accountability mechanisms may be less effective in practice than they appear at first sight. It is, however, worth noting certain aspects of judicial review that are particularly pertinent to assessment and provision of services.

As seen in Chapter 3, judicial review does not operate as an appeal against a substantive decision: it is a means of challenging the way in which the decision was made. That being the case, it might appear that provided a proper process is followed, and the decision is one which is within the scope of the discretion conferred on the decision-maker, there should be little prospect of a successful challenge, unless a rights-based argument such as those discussed above in relation to the cases of *G, W, A* or *J* can be maintained.

However, an application for judicial review may well succeed if an assessment has not been carried out, or carried out in accordance with the statutory guidance, before a decision is made as to what if any services to provide. Particular caution must also be exercised wherever it might be argued that an established policy or a particular course of dealing has given rise to a 'legitimate expectation' that certain services will be provided or maintained, or when a case has become so complex and long-running that the proper basis of a particular decision is obscured so that the decision itself may be viewed as 'irrational'. Box 5.8 and Box 5.9 provide examples. In both examples, the pervasive issue of resources can be seen to have contributed to the problems.

The first example (Box 5.8) is the well-known case of Pamela Coughlan which arose from a decision by a health authority to close a nursing home. The significance of the case in our context is that it established that a service user may be able to assert a right to continuation of a service if the authority providing the service commits itself in such a way that it would be an abuse of power for the authority to resile from the particular commitment. Such cases are likely to be rare, but *Coughlan* is a salutary reminder that careful attention must be paid to fairness to the service user when any decision is made to withdraw or substantially alter service provision – and that in this context, fairness has a particular, legal meaning.

The second example is the case of a severely disabled teenaged girl, C, for whom a local authority provided services under s. 17 Children Act 1989 and accommodation under s. 20. The dispute was about proposed changes in C's care. Dealing with the dispute required close scrutiny of the care plan and the local authority's thinking behind it. This kind of close scrutiny is the norm in care proceedings (see Chapter 7), but in C's case no care order was sought nor indeed would have been justified. Accordingly it fell to the High Court exercising its judicial review function to adjudicate on the legality and in particular the rationality of the plan.

Box 5.8   *R V NORTH AND EAST DEVON HEALTH AUTHORITY EX PARTE COUGHLAN* [2001]

Ms Coughlan suffered severe disabilities as a result of an accident and had been placed by the health authority in a particular residential facility. The authority had promised her that this would be a 'home for life' but subsequently financial considerations led to the authority proposing to close the home. It was proposed that Ms Coughlan's care needs would then become the responsibility of social services rather than the NHS – with significant implications as to payment for the cost of it. Ms Coughlan applied for a judicial review, relying on an argument which had been gradually emerging in case-law on procedural fairness, that the court should protect the interests of individuals whose expectation of a particular type of treatment has a legitimacy which in fairness 'out-tops' the policy choice which threatens to frustrate it. When Ms Coughlan brought her case this notion was highly controversial amongst public lawyers as it was argued that it could amount to the court imposing a particular policy choice on the decision-maker. But the Court of Appeal accepted her case and held that the authority had committed itself in such a way that it would be an abuse of power to resile from their commitment unless some overriding public interest could be shown, which was not the case here.

Box 5.9   *CD (A CHILD) V ISLE OF ANGLESEY COUNTY COUNCIL* [2004]

C, a 15-year-old girl, had multiple disabilities which meant that she needed constant and intensive physical support. Her mother suffered from chronic fatigue and was unable to cope with all C's needs full time. Over the years, C's package of support had come to include substantial support from Mr and Mrs R, who as local authority foster carers had become in effect a second family for C. C stayed at the home of Mr and Mrs R on average for five nights a week and with her mother for two nights, with substantial help from local authority support workers whilst C was at her mother's and rather less whilst C was at Mr and Mrs R's. However, everyone agreed that Mr and Mrs R's home was not adequately equipped to care for C with an acceptable degree of dignity, especially in relation to washing and

(Continued)

---

using the toilet. C attended a special school where boarding facilities were available and C had indicated she would like to board two nights a week during termtime, as did several other pupils. The local authority took the opportunity to review the totality of C's care. Their plan was to bring Mr and Mrs R's role to an end, for C to board four nights a week at the school and for C to spend the rest of her time with her mother with the help of local authority support workers and monthly respite weekends. No doubt this represented a rationalisation in terms of the substantial resources being applied to C's care. But the plan was opposed by C (who was dismayed that her family life with Mr and Mrs R was being taken away, and who did not want to be the only child boarding more than two nights a week at school), her mother (who was sure she could not cope with the additional days caring for C) and Mr and Mrs R (who regarded C as a member of their extended family and wished to continue as such). The local authority's plan was declared unlawful on the grounds that it failed:

- to provide for C's welfare by providing a range and level of services appropriate to her needs (s. 17(1) Children Act 1989);
- to provide her with services designed to minimise the effect on her of her disabilities (s. 17(2));
- to give due consideration to her wishes as to her accommodation, having regard to her age and understanding (s.20(6));
- to secure that the accommodation was not unsuitable to her particular needs (s.23(8)).

The judge acknowledged that the local authority had acted in good faith, but made the graphic comment that 'like a computer virus, some demon has, in my judgement, come to infect the local authority's decision-making referable to C in the course of the last two years'.

These two cases demonstrate that especially careful consideration needs to be paid to decisions to change or discontinue services. Competing priorities, financial and operational imperatives can easily obscure adequate consideration of the legitimate expectations of individuals who are in receipt of or have been promised services. A rights-based approach to decision-making is the best way of avoiding this. It tends to refocus minds on the child as a person with an entitlement to provision and with agency in the decision-making process, rather than on the needs of the local authority most efficiently to procure or provide certain services.

Conclusion

The idea of provision is closely linked to prevention in the Children Act 1989, Children Act 2004 and the associated guidance. The Laming Report criticised a recognised tendency in practice to concentrate on child protection at the expense of assessment of need and provision of support, when in reality the two are not separate. A failure to address need at an early stage on a basis of voluntary engagement may allow problems to escalate, leading to the need for compulsory measures later on. It is easy to see how, in a situation like that of Anne, Martin and Elin, targeted support given promptly might help prevent such a sequence of events and conversely how a failure to give support could contribute to its occurrence. The refocusing of children's services in England and Wales under the Children Act 2004, and the associated increase in bureaucratic prescription, does seek to improve matters in this regard. It would do better if based on the UNCRC concept of children's rights to provision or, as paraphrased at the beginning of this chapter, their entitlement to nurture. Social workers are professionally obliged to think in those terms, and if they do so, may help to import and maintain in local processes the values to which they are professionally committed. It may also help to develop a focus on the ubiquitous issue of resources as a matter of human rights compliance, because of Article 4 UNCRC.

Further Reading

A good analysis of the way in which positive obligations under the ECHR may impact on the exercise of s. 17 Children Act 1989 functions is E Palmer's 'Courts, resources and the HRA: reading section 17 of the Children Act 1989 compatibly with Article 8 ECHR', 3 (2003), *European Human Rights Law Review*, (2003) pp. 308–324.

John Murphy's article 'Children in need: the limits of local authority accountability', *Legal Studies*, 23 (2004), pp. 103–134, listed as Further Reading for Chapter 3, should be revisited here. It points to the weakness of administrative mechanisms and the limited impact of accountability to the courts.

M. Millar and B. Corby's research-based article 'The framework for the assessment of children in need and their families – a basis for a therapeutic encounter?', *British Journal of Social Work*, 36 (3) (2006), pp. 887–899 offers evidence of some positive effects of 'bureaucratised' assessment methods generated by current government guidance. A further critique of the use of current assessment frameworks, including the Framework for the Assessment of Children in Need and their Families, can be found in an article by B. Crisp, M. Anderson, J. Orme and P. Lister: 'Assessment frameworks: a critical reflection', *British Journal of Social Work*, 37 (6) (2007), pp. 1059–1077.

A good, independent source of critique of current provision of services to children in need and their families against the standards of the UNCRC is the documentation generated by the UN reporting process itself, especially the NGO alternative reports for Wales: (2007) *Stop, Look, Listen: The Road to Realising Children's Rights in Wales*, Cardiff: Save the Children and for England: (2007) *State of Children's Rights in England*. London: Children's Rights Alliance for England.

6

Compulsory Measures to Safeguard Children and Promote Their Welfare

- **Introduction**
- **Rights, powers and duties**
  The UNCRC
  The ECHR
  Domestic provisions
  Key criteria and thresholds
- **Satisfying Article 8.2 ECHR**
- **Process, purpose and proportionality in the use of compulsory measures**
  Immediate safeguarding steps: the options
  Domestic violence
  Emergency powers
  The child protection conference
  The child protection plan

Introduction

This chapter is concerned with action that may be taken under the authority provided by Pts. IV and V Children Act 1989 when there is reason to believe that a child is at risk of, or is already suffering, significant harm due to want of parental care or control. Where this is the case, a range of compulsory measures is available. Some are designed to secure the child's immediate safety in an emergency or to hold a position while further assessment is undertaken. Others are designed for the provision of longer-term support, supervision or substitute care. Compulsory measures do not depend upon the consent or voluntary engagement of parent or child. Most carry judicial authority and all are enforceable by law. To illustrate their application in practice, we continue the story of Anne and Martin from Chapter 5.

CASE STUDY (4)

The children in need plan includes provision of a day nursery place for Anne, for Adi to continue to work with Elin, liaising with the health visitor, nursery and other agencies, and for a request to be made to the housing authority for help in finding accommodation for Elin and the children. Arriving early at the flat for an arranged visit, Adi finds the children in the care of Naomi, a 10-year-old neighbour. He begins to suspect Elin is abusing drugs, prescribed or otherwise. He has still not managed to see James when, following a neighbour's report, the police are called to an incident at the flat. James had gone by the time the police arrived but both children had witnessed him hitting Elin's head against the floor. Because of this the police consider there are 'child protection concerns'. A case conference is called for the following day but just before it is due to take place, a communication is received from the A&E paediatrician at Blankshire Hospital. Martin has been admitted having sustained a subdural haemorrhage: the paediatrician suspects the injury was inflicted non-accidentally. The circumstances are not clear, but there is an allegation that it happened when the children were alone with Naomi.

Clearly, a fresh appraisal of the children's position is required in the light of these developments. Blankshire will inevitably consider using compulsory measures although, as will be discussed below, it is by no means inevitable that they will actually use them. They must follow a course which best promotes the rights of the children while also respecting the rights of others involved. Blankshire must act within their specific statutory powers, in a manner consistent with relevant statutory guidance. It may be necessary to act fast. Sound knowledge and careful adherence to the relevant powers, principles and process are essential in this situation. Social work professionals within the local authority need to work at a high level of competence and integrity, collaborating with other professionals and agencies but ultimately taking responsibility for ensuring that decisions and actions are within lawful authority, reflect child-centred principles and are carried out not only in accordance with prescribed process but with full understanding of the requirements of due process.

Rights, powers and duties

Box 6.1 shows the relevant UNCRC and ECHR requirements, together with the domestic provisions that can be seen broadly to satisfy them. There is some tension concerning the application of the paramountcy of welfare principle (s. 1 Children Act 1989), since it gives precedence to the interests of children over others whose rights may be engaged, although the ECtHR has accepted that the child's best interests must prevail where otherwise the child's well-being would be undermined. In comparison to the ECHR, the UNCRC contains many more specific provisions directed at protection of vulnerable children. As in the case of voluntary engagement, the pervasive themes of the UNCRC – non-discrimination, the right to survival and development, the best interests principle and the child's right to express views and have them taken into account – are also relevant to any decisions taken and the associated processes.

Box 6.1   CONVENTION RIGHTS AND DOMESTIC LAW

UNCRC	ECHR	Law in England and Wales
The 'four pervasive themes':		
1. Protection from discrimination (Art. 2)	Non-discrimination in enjoyment of Convention rights (Art. 14)	Protection from discrimination: Equality Act 2006 and anti-discrimination statutes
2. Best interests of the child a primary consideration in all actions concerning children (Art. 3)	The ECtHR has accepted that the child's best interests may take priority over the rights of adult family members: *Johansen v Norway [1996]*	The child's welfare is paramount in most compulsory measures authorised by the court under the Children Act 1989
3. Right to survival and development (Art. 6)	Right to life (Art. 2) and right to private life (incorporating the notion of personal development) (Art. 8): generate positive obligations on the State: *Z v United Kingdom [2001]* (Chapter 1, 3)	Compulsory measures under Pts. IV and V Children Act 1989 – these powers may generate a common law duty of care to child thought to be at risk: *JD (FC) v East Berkshire [2005]* (Chapter 3)
4. Right to have views taken into account (Art. 12)	Right to fair hearing (Art. 6); procedural guarantees implied by Art. 8	Automatic representation of child in 'specified proceedings' (includes proceedings under Pts. IV and V): s. 41 Children Act 1989
Protection from all forms of abuse (Art. 19);	Right not to suffer torture, inhuman or	Compulsory measures under Pts. IV and V

UNCRC	ECHR	Law in England and Wales
protection of liberty and from torture, cruel, inhuman or degrading treatment or punishment (Art. 37); protection from economic exploitation, drug abuse, trafficking and all other forms of exploitation (Arts. 31–36)	degrading treatment (Art. 3): generates positive obligations on the State: **Z v United Kingdom [2001]** Right to liberty (Art. 5)	Children Act 1989. Local safeguarding structures under Children Act 2004. Common law duty of care in negligence. Trespass to the person (assault, etc.). Protection of Children Act 1999. Child-specific criminal offences: e.g. child neglect; sexual offences
Special protection where deprived of family environment (Art. 20)		Duties in respect of looked after children: Pt. III Children Act 1989 (Chapter 8)
Right to familial relations and contact (Arts. 9 and 10)	Right to family life (Art. 8). A care order does not sever the rights of child *and* parents to familial contact. The State has a positive obligation to work towards family reunification unless contrary to the child's interest. Action interfering with familial contact must be proportionate to the aim of securing the child's interests. **K and T v Finland [2001]**	Parental contact with child in care: s. 34 Children Act 1989
Measures to promote physical and	Right to private and family life (Art. 8)	A plan for the child must be put before the *(Continued)*

149

UNCRC	ECHR	Law in England and Wales
psychological recovery where abuse has occurred (Art. 39)	includes right to develop relationships, etc. (see Chapter 5): **Re S**, **Re W** **[2002]** (Chapter 8) shows importance of effective review of children in care to satisfy Art. 8	court: s. 31A Children Act 1989; and monitored and reviewed for all looked after children: s. 26 Children Act 1989

The UNCRC

The UNCRC contains many provisions aimed at protection of children. The most obviously relevant to compulsory measures is Article 19:

19.1 States Parties shall take all appropriate legislative, administrative, social and educational measures to protect the child from all forms of physical or mental violence, injury or abuse, neglect or negligent treatment, maltreatment or exploitation, including sexual abuse, while in the care of parent(s), legal guardian(s) or any other person who has the care of the child.

19.2 Such protective measures should, as appropriate, include effective procedures for the establishment of social programmes to provide necessary support for the child and for those who have the care of the child, as well as for other forms of prevention and identification, treatment and follow-up of instances of child maltreatment described heretofore, and, as appropriate, judicial involvement.

The idea of a 'right' to protection is not conceptually problematic in the law of England and Wales. This is because the law has long endorsed the sovereign's (= State's) basic duty to ensure the subject's right to personal safety and peaceful enjoyment of possessions: some of the earliest forms of legal action, such as the law of trespass, were designed precisely to protect people in this way. As shown in the third column of the table in Box 6.1, modern child protection law in England and Wales comprises a collection of powers, duties, criminal offences and procedures.

Yet the UK has been criticised for its performance on implementation of the UNCRC's protection provisions. In its Concluding Observations on the UK's second periodic report, the UN Committee noted various initiatives that had been taken in the area of child abuse, but stated that it was:

deeply concerned that one or two children die every week as a result of violence and neglect in the home. It is also concerned at the prevalence of violence, including sexual violence, throughout the State party against children within families, schools, in institutions, in the care system and in detention. It also notes with deep concern the growing levels of child neglect. The Committee is alarmed at the lack of a coordinated strategy to limit the extent of these phenomena. (UN, 2002a: para. 39)

The Committee's recommendations included new or further measures to receive and monitor, investigate and prosecute instances of abuse, to provide for care, recovery and reintegration of victims and to support and protect children received into substitute care. Although not based on the Committee's recommendations, some of the structural changes introduced by the Children Act 2004 are clearly directed at better co-ordination of action to prevent abuse and neglect of children. Article 19 UNCRC clearly envisages the taking of compulsory measures to protect children, but also emphasises the need to support whoever 'has the care of the child'. When considering what action to take in respect of the incidents in Case Study (4), Blankshire must maintain a focus on Anne's and Martin's rights to support for their longer-term development, including their rights to maintain their familial relationships, as well as to ensure their immediate safety.

The ECHR

The ECHR requires a delicate balance to be struck between competing rights. Where compulsory measures are under consideration, typically these will include:

- the child's right to protection from harm (Arts. 2, 3 and 8);
- the child's right to personal development (Art. 8);
- the child's right to private and family life (Art. 8);
- the parent's right to private and family life (Art 8);
- the child's right to a fair process (Arts. 8.2 and 6);
- the parent's right to a fair process (Arts. 8.2 and 6).

We have seen that issues may arise under Article 8 ECHR in relation to the provision of support and services in the context of voluntary engagement, where it is argued that a failure to provide or continue support or services constitutes a violation of the child's right to respect for private and family life. In contrast, compulsory measures always engage Article 8. They can only be justified if they can be shown to be authorised by law, necessary in a democratic society to achieve a legitimate aim and proportionate to the end to be achieved (Article 8.2 ECHR: see discussion of Article 8 as a qualified right in Chapter 2).

With the exception of the police power to remove and accommodate a child in an emergency (s. 46 Children Act 1989), and the local authority's duty to investigate (s. 47), a court order is required before any compulsory measures can be used. The court order confers clear legal authority and ensures that there is a forum in which the rights of those involved and the question of what is necessary to protect the child can be judicially considered. For this reason, compulsory measures will not normally breach Article 8 ECHR. Where problems arise they are most often about:

- process: failing to give or obtain adequate information or failing to ensure that the people affected have the chance to be heard: examples are ***W v United Kingdom* [1988]**, ***TP and KM v United Kingdom* [2001]**, ***P, C and S v United Kingdom* [2002]**, ***Re M (Care: Challenging Local Authority Decisions)* [2001]**, ***Re L (Care: Assessment: Fair Trial)* [2002]**, ***Re G (Care: Challenge to Local Authority's Decisions)* [2003]** and ***Re M (interim care order: removal)* [2005]**;
- proportionality: interfering more or for longer than is necessary in order to safeguard the child or promote the child's welfare: examples are ***Johansen v Norway* [1996]** and ***P, C and S v United Kingdom* [2002]**; or
- purpose: care planning that does not strike an appropriate balance between the child's interest in stability and permanence on the one hand and the preservation of family ties on the other: examples are ***Olsson v Sweden* [1988]** and ***Eriksson v Sweden* [1989]**.

It will be remembered that, as shown in *Z v United Kingdom* [2001] (see Chapter 1), inaction or insufficient action as well as unwarranted or over-zealous action may breach children's ECHR rights. This is consistent with Article 19 UNCRC which makes crystal clear that children who are at risk of neglect or abuse in the home have a right to State interference in their private lives. In Case Study (4), Blankshire's task is to assess the risk to Anne and Martin and to act to safeguard them and protect their welfare in a manner which satisfies the requirements of due process, proportionality and purpose.

Domestic provisions

The statutory provisions are mainly in Pts. IV and V Children Act 1989. Part IV deals with the making of care and supervision orders on the application of a local authority or authorised person (in practice, only the NSPCC). Part V provides a range of powers and duties relating to child protection, including the power for a court to make an emergency protection order (EPO). The Children Act 2004 left the Children Act 1989 provisions basically unchanged but created statutory partnerships (Local Safeguarding Children Boards, LSCBs) aimed at improving the effectiveness of their use. These partnerships are responsible for ensuring local protocols, policies and procedures are in place to improve inter-agency working, to review performance and to conduct investigative reviews where things go wrong.

Key criteria and thresholds

Justification for the measures available under Pts. IV and V Children Act 1989 is built around the key concept of significant harm. This is a welfare-oriented criterion, focusing on the prevention of harm or further harm to the child concerned. It is partially defined in s. 31(9) Children Act 1989 in that there it is stated that 'harm' means 'ill-treatment or the impairment of health or development' (further, see Chapter 7). There is another route through which a child and/or parents may be the subject of compulsory measures aimed at improving outcomes for the child. This forms part of the new youth justice system introduced by the Crime and Disorder Act 1998 and is predicated primarily on community safety rather than child welfare. The rationale for these latter measures gives greater prominence to the notion of protection from children rather than protection of children. They may run in parallel to welfare-oriented interventions under the Children Act 1989. They are discussed in Chapter 9.

Satisfying Article 8.2 ECHR

The table in Box 6.2 shows how the domestic provisions authorising compulsory measures can be seen to satisfy the requirements of Article 8.2 ECHR. Column 1 lists the domestic statutory provisions. These confer lawful authority, so that it can be said the measure taken is clearly in accordance with the law. Columns 2 and 3 identify in bold print the key statutory criteria which are the starting point for establishing that interference is for a legitimate aim and is proportionate to that aim. As these criteria are only the starting point, the issues of process, proportionality and purpose need to be considered in each individual case according to its facts.

Box 6.2   COMPLIANCE OF COMPULSORY MEASURES UNDER PTS. IV AND V CHILDREN ACT 1989 WITH ARTICLE 8.2 ECHR

'in accordance with the law' (lawful authority is conferred by ...)	'legitimate aim' (the 'pressing social need' is ...)	proportionality (the proposed degree of interference is necessary because ...)
Local authority's duty to investigate: s.47 Children Act 1989	Enquiries are necessary to decide whether action should be taken to **safeguard or promote the child's welfare**	Emergency protection or police protection powers have been triggered, a child curfew has been breached, a court has ordered an investigation or a local authority has **reasonable cause**

(Continued)

'in accordance with the law' (lawful authority is conferred by ...)	'legitimate aim' (the 'pressing social need' is ...)	proportionality (the proposed degree of interference is necessary because ...)
		to suspect a child is suffering, or is likely to suffer, **significant harm**
Child assessment order: s. 43 Children Act 1989	Assessment is required to determine whether a child is suffering or likely to suffer **significant harm**	**Reasonable cause to suspect** a child is suffering or is likely to suffer **significant harm**, and satisfactory assessment unlikely in the absence of an order
Police protection in cases of emergency: s. 46 Children Act 1989	Prevention of likely **significant harm** if the child is not removed, or if removal (e.g. from a hospital) is not prevented	**Reasonable cause to believe** a child is likely to suffer **significant harm**
Emergency protection order: s. 44 Children Act 1989	Prevention of likely **significant harm** if the child is not removed, or if removal (e.g. from a hospital) is not prevented	**Reasonable cause to believe** a child is likely to suffer **significant harm**
Child recovery order: s. 50 Children Act 1989	**Law enforcement**: a child subject to a care order, emergency protection order or in police protection has been abducted, has run away or has gone missing	**Lawful authority has been undermined**, where that authority was triggered by likelihood of **significant harm** (care, emergency protection or police protection)
Care order: s. 31 Children Act 1989	Prevention of likely **significant harm**, attributable to lack of reasonable parental	**The court is satisfied** that the child is suffering or likely to suffer

'in accordance with the law' (lawful authority is conferred by ...)	'legitimate aim' (the 'pressing social need' is ...)	proportionality (the proposed degree of interference is necessary because ...)
	care or the child being beyond parental control	**significant harm** and the child's welfare is best served by making a care order
Supervision order: s. 31 Children Act 1989	Prevention of likely **significant harm**, attributable to lack of reasonable parental care or the child being beyond parental control	**The court is satisfied** that the child is suffering or likely to suffer **significant harm** and the child's welfare is best served by making a supervision order
Educational supervision order: s. 36 Children Act 1989	Ensuring that a child is **properly educated**: receiving full-time education suitable to age, ability, aptitude and any special educational needs	**The court is satisfied** that the child is of **compulsory school age and not being properly educated**
Interim care/supervision order: s. 38 Children Act 1989	Need to make interim order, which may include further assessment, pending final decision on care or supervision order, turning on criterion of **significant harm**	**The court is satisfied** that there are reasonable grounds for believing that the child is suffering or likely to suffer **significant harm**

Process, purpose and proportionality in the use of compulsory measures

In Case Study (4), there are four incidents, of escalating seriousness, which could trigger compulsory measures justified on the significant harm criterion:

(a) Anne and Martin, aged just three years and 18 months, have been left in the care of a 10-year-old;

(b)   their mother may be abusing drugs;

(c)   Anne and Martin have witnessed a violent assault by their father on their mother;

(d)   Martin has suffered a suspected non-accidental injury (n.a.i.).

In relation to (a) and (b), a classic dilemma arises: there is an accumulation of small(ish) concerns, none of which may be sufficient alone to trigger reasonable suspicion of significant harm but which taken together may suggest the need for compulsory measures. Weighing up the effect on the children and, critically, the future risk to them, is at the core of the social work process. It requires a multi-agency approach, but ultimately the local authority must decide which of a range of actions should be taken and must ensure that whatever action is decided upon is carried out lawfully and effectively. The local authority must be ready to change course if circumstances change or if action fails to achieve the intended outcomes.

With regard to (c) and (d), there is less room for doubt: under s. 47(1)(b) Children Act 1989, Blankshire 'shall make, or cause to be made' enquiries to decide whether they should take action if they have 'reasonable cause to suspect that a child ... is suffering, or is likely to suffer, significant harm'. Children suffer harm through witnessing domestic violence even where they are not themselves the object of an assault: this was officially recognised by the addition of the words 'including, for example, impairment suffered from seeing or hearing the ill-treatment of another', to the definition of 'harm' in s. 31(9) Children Act 1989 (the amendment was made by the Adoption and Children Act 2002). This applies to the assault on Elin, witnessed by both children, and may also be relevant if Anne witnessed an injury being inflicted deliberately on Martin. In any case, a n.a.i. to Martin, inflicted by a carer (notwithstanding the doubt as to precisely which one), would in itself constitute reasonable cause to suspect not only that he had suffered, but that he and Anne are likely to suffer, significant harm. An example of a case where the likelihood of significant harm rested on alleged abuse suffered by a sibling is *Re H and R (Child Sexual Abuse: Standard of Proof)* [1996], discussed further in Chapter 7.

Blankshire must, therefore, conduct a s. 47 assessment once they have knowledge of (c) or (d). Key decisions as to the conduct of and action consequent upon this assessment will be taken at a child protection conference. However, given the seriousness of the incidents reported, Blankshire are also bound to consider whether immediate action needs to be taken in order to safeguard the children. Again, the fact that only one child, Martin, has sustained a suspected n.a.i. does not mean that any such action should be confined to him. *Working Together* states that wherever an agency is considering whether safeguarding action is necessary, they should always consider whether action is also necessary to safeguard and promote the welfare of other children in the same household (DfES, 2006 / WAG, 2006: para. 5.49 and para. 8.72 respectively).

Under the process set out in *Working Together,* the decision whether immediate compulsory measures (and if so, what) are necessary will be taken by Blankshire following an immediate strategy discussion between the local authority, the police and other agencies as appropriate (DfES, 2006 / WAG, 2006: para. 5.50 and para. 8.73 respectively). In the particular scenario of Case Study (4), the fact that a case conference was already scheduled to take place may mean that some of the relevant persons are on hand. Where, as in this case, a child is receiving hospital treatment, the strategy discussion must include the relevant medical consultant – in this case the A&E paediatrician who referred the suspicion of n.a.i.. The senior ward nurse should also be involved if Martin has been admitted as an inpatient. The discussion should include steps to secure the safe discharge of the child from hospital in due course (DfES, 2006 / WAG, 2006: paras. 5.54, 55 and paras. 8.81, 82 respectively). Legal advice should always be obtained before initiating any legal action (para. 5.50 and para. 8.73 respectively).

The options available to Blankshire include:

- removal of the children with parental agreement (accommodation under s. 20 Children Act 1989): the effect is that they enter 'voluntary care' and can be removed at any time by either parent;
- application to court for an Emergency Protection Order (EPO) under s. 44 Children Act 1989: the effect is to authorise Blankshire to remove and accommodate the children without parental consent for up to 8 days, with a possible extension for a further 7 days by a second court order;
- carrying out the s. 47 assessment whilst leaving Anne and Martin in the care of their parents: in this event, a 'child protection agreement' might be entered into, setting out a basis for co-operation between social services and the parents;
- in addition to or instead of any of the above, an application for an interim care order under s. 38 Children Act 1989 and/or an application for a child assessment order under s. 43 Children Act 1989;
- if an application is made for an EPO or interim care order, Blankshire could ask the court also to make an exclusion order under s. 44A or 38A Children Act 1989 respectively: this might be thought appropriate if Blankshire were satisfied that the children's safety could be secured for the time being if James were excluded from the home.

The local authority bears a heavy responsibility at this point. A poorly judged decision may have a seriously detrimental effect on the children and other persons involved. Where an apparent emergency has arisen (as with the suspected n.a.i. to Martin) it is vital to think clearly about the legal requirements for any compulsory measure. 'Feeling' is not enough: there must be hard evidence which can be presented to a court and tested. A case study in how not to proceed is to be found in **Re X, Emergency Protection Orders** [2006]. In **Re X**, an EPO was obtained without notice being given to X or her parents, on the basis of the oral evidence of a social work team manager. This manager had not been personally involved with the case and the evidence given to the court turned out to be almost completely wrong. There were multiple failures in the use and recording of information and in communication. Key decisions were made on the basis of 'gut feeling' which turned out to be uninformed or seriously misjudged. The EPO application began a chain of events in which X was separated from her parents for 14 months resulting in what was described in the court's judgment as 'the destruction of this family's ordinary life'. The judgment was severely critical of those responsible for these failures, but also gave extensive directions as to how such failures should be avoided in the future. The trial judge did, however, acknowledge the exceptional nature of the case and paid tribute to the role played by professional social workers in the many successful interventions which do not, in the nature of things, attract the notice of the courts or the public. The following extract from Mcfarlane J's judgment eloquently describes the position of the social worker in relation to critical child protection decisions:

The child protection system depends upon the skill, insight and sheer hard work of front-line social workers. Underlying those key features, there is a need for social workers to feel supported and valued by the courts, the state and the general populace to a far greater degree than is normally the case. Working in overstretched teams with limited resources, social workers frequently have to make crucial decisions, with important implications, on issues of child protection; often of necessity these decisions must be based upon the available information which may be inchoate or partial. There are often risks to a child flowing from every available option (risk of harm if the child stays at home, risk of emotional harm at least if the child is removed). It is said that in these situations, social workers are 'damned if they do, and damned if they don't' take action. Despite these difficulties, it is my experience that very frequently social workers 'get it right' and take the right action, for the right reasons, based upon a professional and wise evaluation of the available information.

Domestic violeFnce

The report of an assault on Elin means that the case should be treated as one in which domestic violence is an issue. The model approach to this is by means of a MARAC, already mentioned in Chapter 5, as a possible route to securing support for Elin in protecting herself and the children. One advantage is potentially to enhance the package of support that Elin may be able to access, especially from non-statutory agencies. However, it is very important that the children's social worker remains focused on the children. Their interests may well be best served by provision of support to Elin in dealing with domestic violence through the criminal route, perhaps with a prosecution taking place in a specialist domestic violence court which has a specialist 'IDVA' (Independent Domestic Violence Advocate), or through a civil justice route seeking an injunction under the Family Law Act 1996. But this is not necessarily the case, nor is it necessarily enough so far as the children are concerned. There are other features here which require thorough examination. In order to safeguard the children it may be necessary at least temporarily to find alternative care for them, whether or not any action is taken with regard to the domestic violence as such. If this is so, a crucial immediate decision is whether the need is so urgent as to justify the use of emergency powers.

Emergency powers

Section 46 Children Act 1989 provides a police power to remove and accommodate a child. This is relevant if it is thought that the position is so urgent that it cannot even await an application for an EPO. *Working Together* states that police powers should only be used in exceptional circumstances where there is insufficient time to seek an EPO or for reasons relating to the immediate safety of the child (DfES, 2006 / WAG, 2006: para. 5.51 and para. 8.74 respectively). However, an EPO is itself a draconian measure, which the courts have stated must be used only with extreme care. The courts have held that an EPO should not be sought or made unless it is necessary and proportionate and no less radical form of order will achieve the essential end of promoting the welfare of the child.

In *X Council v B (Emergency Protection Orders)* **[2004]**, Munby J set out 14 points that must be followed by social workers, their legal advisers and the court to which an application for an EPO is made. In *Re X, Emergency Protection Orders* **[2006]** (above), Macfarlane J said it was the duty of the local authority to place these 14 points before the court whenever an application was made. They emphasise the need for due process, proportionality and clear purpose, essential for compliance with the ECHR. Box 6.3 restates the points under those headings.

In *Re X, Emergency Protection Orders* **[2006]**, Mcfarlane J added further requirements including that the applicant (that is, the local authority) should ensure that a copy of Munby J's judgment in *X Council v B (Emergency Protection Orders)* should be available at every hearing of an application for an EPO, that evidence should come from a social worker with direct knowledge of the case, that case conference minutes should be produced and that the court should give detailed reasons and findings. Blankshire must follow these guidelines if it is decided that an EPO should be sought in relation to Anne and Martin in Case Study (4).

This means that while the suspicion that Martin has suffered a n.a.i. make it imperative to investigate, and quickly, there is not necessarily adequate evidence to justify the use of emergency powers. Often, expert medical evidence will be essential, and this may involve obtaining a view from more than one clinician (for example, the view of an orthopaedic specialist in addition to that of the paediatrician). Expert evidence is considered in some detail in Chapter 7, but here it should be noted that while the opinion of a social worker is properly to be regarded as expert evidence in relation to matters on which the social worker's training and experience gives them special expertise, this does not extend to essentially clinical diagnoses. For example, in **Re X, Emergency Protection Orders**, one of the problems was that the family proceedings court had accepted social work opinion, in the absence of qualified medical opinion, that X's mother's behaviour was consistent with Munchhausen's Syndrome by Proxy. This was not a matter on which social workers had adequate expertise to be regarded by the court as experts. In fact, in the absence of direct factual evidence (such as might be given by a reliable witness to an assault), both the clinical diagnosis and the proof of n.a.i. can be a notoriously complex business.

Box 6.3   PROCESS, PROPORTIONALITY AND PURPOSE IN THE USE OF EPOS: (FROM MUNBY J'S 14 POINTS IN *X COUNCIL V B (EMERGENCY PROTECTION ORDERS)* [2004])

Process:

- Both the local authority which seeks and the court which makes an EPO must pay 'scrupulous regard' for the ECHR rights of both the child and the parents. Evidence must be full, detailed, precise and compelling: unparticularised generalities will not suffice, sources of hearsay evidence must be identified and expressions of opinion must be supported by detailed evidence and properly articulated reasoning.
- Save in wholly exceptional cases, parents must be given adequate prior notice of the date, time and place of any application by a local authority for an EPO and of the evidence the local authority is relying upon. An application should be made without notice only if the case is genuinely one of emergency. Even then it should normally be possible to give some kind of (albeit informal) notice to the parents. Where an application is made without notice there is an even heavier evidential burden on the local authority. They must make the fullest, most candid and frank disclosure of all the relevant circumstances known to them and must present the court with all relevant matters both of fact and law.
- Where oral evidence is given both the court and the local authority must keep a note of the substance of it. Reasons for the court's decision and any findings of fact must be recorded in writing. These records must be available on request to the parents. Parents are also entitled to be given, on request, proper information as to what happened at the hearing (if they were not present) and to be told exactly what evidence was before the court and what legal argument was made.

Proportionality:

- An EPO requires exceptional justification and extraordinarily compelling reasons. Such an order should not be made unless the court is satisfied that it is both necessary and proportionate and that no other less radical form of order will achieve the essential end of promoting the welfare of the child. Any order must provide for the least interventionist solution consistent with the preservation of the child's immediate safety. No EPO should be made for any longer than is absolutely necessary to protect the child.
- Separation is only to be contemplated if immediate separation is essential to secure the child's safety: imminent danger must be actually established: even when an EPO has been made the local authority should not physically separate the child and parents unless, in the words of s. 44 Children Act 1989, it is necessary 'to safeguard the welfare of the child'. The local authority should consider less drastic alternatives to emergency removal and should ensure that its reasoning is documented.
- Both s. 44 Children Act 1989 and Article 8.2 ECHR require the local authority to keep the necessity of separation under review: if it becomes safe for the child to be returned, this should be done. In this, as in other respects, the local authority is under a duty to exercise 'exceptional diligence'.

Purpose:

- If the real purpose of the local authority's application is to enable it to have the child assessed then consideration should be given to whether that objective cannot equally effectively, and more proportionately, be achieved by an application for, or by the making of, a child assessment order under s. 43 Children Act 1989.
- Although the EPO may form part of a process in which ultimately a child will be the subject of a plan for permanent alternative placement, the purpose of family reunification must not be suppressed, nor should outcomes be prejudged. Section 44 Children Act 1989 requires the local authority to allow a child who is subject to an EPO 'reasonable contact' with his parents, unless the court otherwise directs. Arrangements for contact must be driven by the needs of the family, not stunted by lack of resources.

In Case Study (4) Blankshire will need to consider carefully the totality of evidence in relation to all the concerns, including but not limited to the suspected n.a.i. In relation to (a) (the children being left alone or under the supervision of a 10-year-old), Adi's own evidence can be given as to the facts. In relation to (b) (suspicions of drug abuse) Adi can also give factual evidence and could give his professional opinion about the impact on the family, although expert opinion based on medical examination of Elin would be desirable. As to (c) (the assault on Elin) there will be a police report but direct evidence may prove difficult to obtain: the children are very young and through fear Elin may not be willing to give the necessary evidence. This is a problem which the MARAC process and associated changes in the approach of the courts and prosecuting authorities are designed to address by ensuring support for victims of domestic violence through court processes: this may be effective if available in this case. If the decision is to go for an EPO, the totality of evidence must be presented to the court.

The child protection conference

Key decisions as to further action will be made at an initial child protection conference. *Working Together* sets out in considerable detail the process and the decisions and actions that have to be taken (DfES, 2006 / WAG, 2006: paras. 5.80–106 and paras. 8.110–142 respectively). The initial child protection conference is designed to bring together the child (where appropriate, depending on age and understanding), family members and those professionals most involved with the child and family, following s. 47 Children Act 1989 enquiries. The conference must be held within 15 working days of the last strategy discussion (above, 'Immediate safeguarding steps: the options'). It should be chaired by a professional who is independent of operational or line management responsibilities for the case. The purpose of the conference is to:

- bring together and analyse all the information so far gathered;
- make a judgement about risk of significant harm to the child;
- decide on future action to safeguard and promote the welfare of the child, how it is to be taken forward and with what intended outcomes.

The matters the conference must consider and decide upon are:

- Is the child at continuing risk of significant harm?
- If so, what category (this must be recorded for entry on the Integrated Children's System, see below).
- Child in need plan (if appropriate).
- Child protection plan (if appropriate).
- Plan(s) to include a lead body and key worker, a core group of professionals, involvement of the family, agreed timescales and plan for reviews, further assessments (if appropriate), targets for change/outcomes with associated aims, objectives, monitoring and evaluation, contingency plans and clear role allocation: who is responsible for what, when and for checking it is done.

The initial child protection conference should be presented with a report prepared by the local authority's children's social care department (England) or children's social services department (Wales). This report and, wherever possible, reports contributed by other attendees should be distributed in advance and discussed with the child (if appropriate) and relevant family members.

Sources of information should be given and it should be made clear whether statements are of fact, observation, allegation or opinion. Rigorous discipline as to these matters at this stage will help to avoid problems later, especially if the case proceeds to court, and will help to avoid the failures highlighted in cases falling foul of ECHR requirements as to due process (see *ECHR* above). In particular, parents against whom allegations are being investigated should be informed of what is alleged against them and given an opportunity to respond. This is essential in order to comply with the procedural guarantees implied by Article 8.2 ECHR. According to the ECtHR in *W v United Kingdom* [1988]: what is required is that

> having regard to the particular circumstances of the case and notably the serious nature of the decisions to be taken, the parents have been involved in the decision-making process, seen as a whole, to a degree sufficient to provide them with the requisite protection of their interests.

Parents should normally be invited to attend the child protection conference but *Working Together* acknowledges that there are some cases where this is not possible for one or more of a variety of reasons. Procedures established locally by the LSCB should set out criteria for excluding a parent or caregiver. Guidance as to the implications for disclosure of information where parents were excluded was also given in *Re X (Emergency Protection Orders)* [2006]. Amongst the catalogue of failures in that case, there had been misunderstanding or misinterpretation of the need to treat some of the matters discussed at the case conference as confidential and this may have contributed to a failure fully to record what was said. The court held that a full minute should be taken of everything discussed and that where circumstances were such as to warrant exclusion of parents from all or part of the conference, the full minute should be given to and approved by the professionals in attendance and the parents should be given a copy of the agreed minute excluding only that part containing confidential information. Furthermore, the need to retain confidentiality should be kept under review by the chair of the conference, and if the need ceases, the parents should be given full disclosure of the whole minute.

In Case Study (4), the children themselves are too young to be involved directly, but older children should be given the opportunity to attend 'subject to consideration about age and understanding', with a friend/supporter or advocate if they wish.

A common theme in cases that run into problems over process is the difficulty for social workers of dealing with parents once adversarial positions are, or appear to have been, taken. As discussed in Chapter 7, this becomes increasingly hard to avoid once a decision has been taken to apply for a court order. From that point on, however, procedural requirements about disclosure and other matters should in practice be rigorously policed by the courts themselves. Furthermore, independent representation of the child's interests should follow from the appointment by the court of a children's guardian. Prior to deciding to apply to court, it is up to the local authority as an administrative body to police its own process, ensuring fairness to the child and other family members. *X Council v B (Emergency Protection Orders)*, *Re X (Emergency Protection Orders)*, *P, C and S v United Kingdom* [2002] and a host of other reported cases provide examples of failure to manage the admittedly very difficult job of ensuring procedural fairness within the local authority's administrative processes when parents have come to be perceived by the social workers as hostile or 'unco-operative'.

In this situation it may help if the professionals are able consistently to remind themselves of the principles underlying the process rather than focus on the letter of the law. *P, C and S v United Kingdom* was a difficult, distressing case where a baby was removed from a mother whilst she was still in hospital following a caesarean delivery. The parents had come to be perceived as unco-operative. Through their solicitors they had sought involvement in the instruction of an expert to assess future risk to the unborn baby. The local authority responded that the conduct of the s. 47 investigation was a matter for their own discretion and that the rules governing instruction of experts for court proceedings (see Chapter 7) did not apply. Whilst this response was technically correct, with hindsight it was unnecessary and unfair in the circumstances of the particular case to take such a rigid stance. Perhaps crucially, it also had the effect of further entrenching the parents' growing suspicion of, and hostility to, the professionals. In turn this rendered achievement of the principle of family unity very much less likely in this case where there were, certainly, grounds to fear for the safety of the baby if collaboration between the professionals and the parents could not be achieved.

A specific issue to be discussed at the child protection conference is what information about the case should be entered on to the Integrated Children's System (ICS). This system replaces the child protection registers formerly kept by all local authorities in England and Wales. It is essentially an information management tool and *Working Together* requires each local authority to designate an experienced social worker to manage the records, notifications and disclosures (DfES, 2006 / WAG, 2006: paras. 5.141–148 and paras. 8.181–187 respectively). Information in the register is, of course, intended to be used by professionals having a legitimate interest in it. This has consequences for suspected child abusers, especially if their occupations are such that their employers may have reference to the register. Litigation in relation to child protection registers established the following important principles, which should be taken to be equally applicable to the ICS:

- a decision to place a child on the child protection register is amenable to judicial review: *R v Norfolk County Council ex parte M* [1989], although usually there should first be recourse to the complaints procedure under s. 26 Children Act 1989: *R v Hampshire County Council ex parte H* [1999];

- such a decision should be taken only after careful consideration and must be supported by evidence: **R v Hampshire** (above);
- careful consideration means looking at the adults' as well as the child's interests, although in balancing the two, the interests of the adult may have to be placed second to the needs of the child: **R v Harrow LBC ex parte D [1990]**.

The necessary 'careful consideration' could not normally be carried out without having the parents' side of the story properly articulated at the key decision-taking meetings – a further reason for ensuring the *Working Together* requirements in this regard are complied with in practice.

The child protection plan

The child protection conference should result in agreement of a child protection plan which will identify a key social worker to ensure its implementation. The plan must strike a balance between securing the child's safety and well-being and respecting the principle of family unity. In Case Study (4) it may yet be that the children's rights, interests and well-being can be secured in Elin's care, but events and/or further investigation may prove this not to be the case. In this situation, the preferred approach is 'twin-tracking', whereby Blankshire would continue to assess the possibility of Anne and Martin's rehabilitation with their parent(s) but would simultaneously prepare the case for a permanent alternative placement. There is clear judicial support for this, for example in **Re D and K (Care Plan: Twin Track Planning) [1999]**. Twin-track planning supports the 'no delay' principle (s. 1(2) Children Act 1989) and is consistent with the policy underlying the Adoption and Children Act 2002, promoting increased use of adoption/special guardianship to provide permanence for looked after children. It is discussed further in Chapter 8.

Whatever the plan for the child, process, purpose and proportionality are the key concepts that will keep it reconciled with Article 8 ECHR. There must be clear reasons and a carefully recorded, transparent process. In Case Study (4), if the decision is to apply for a care order, a court-oriented and court-directed process is now engaged, up to the point where the court will make a final decision whether to make the order. This process is the subject of the next chapter.

Further Reading

Students and practitioners will find the Journal of the British Association for the Prevention and Study of Child Abuse and Neglect (BAPSCAN), *Child Abuse Review*, a valuable source of current and recent research findings, practice developments, training initiatives and policy issues in safeguarding children. It is published by Wiley & Sons and is free to BAPSCAN members.

An excellent, detailed account of emergency protection procedures is J. Masson,

D. McGovern, K. Pick and M. Winn-Oakley, *Protecting Powers: Emergency Intervention for Children's Protection*. Wiley (2007).

Judith Masson has also written a number of research-based articles on emergency procedures and child protection. These include 'Fair trials in child protection', *Journal of Social Welfare and Family Law*, 28 (2006), pp. 15–30, which discusses the impact of courts' awareness of Articles 6 and 8 ECHR on the use of emergency protection powers and 'Emergency intervention to protect children: using and avoiding legal controls', *Child and Family Law Quarterly*, 17 (2005), pp. 75–96.

The core government guidance, *Working Together,* Department for Education and skills, London/Welsh Assembly Government, Carditt, 2006, should be read, re-read, thoroughly absorbed and operationalised by all practitioners with safeguarding responsibilities.

7

Preparing a Case for Court

Introduction

At the end of Chapter 6, our discussion of the story of Anne and Martin had reached the point where the local authority would, inevitably, consider whether an application should be made to the court to authorise compulsory measures to safeguard the children (Case Study (4)). Various options would be considered, one of which would be an application under s. 31 Children Act 1989 for a care or supervision order. This chapter is concerned with the preparation and conduct of such an application.

Control of the process: the Protocol for Judicial Case Management

The process is governed by the Protocol for Judicial Case Management in Public Law Children Act Cases ('the Protocol'), which came into force in November 2003 (HMCS, 2003). The purpose of the Protocol is to ensure consistency in the application of best practice by all courts hearing applications under Pt. IV Children Act 1989, in particular by reducing delay and in ensuring the achievement of the 'overriding objective'. The Protocol drew on judicial guidance in decided cases so that it represented not a radical new departure but a synthesis of the experience of the courts and a recognition of the need to prevent 'drift' and consequent additional, avoidable harm to the child.

The 'overriding objective'

The overriding objective of the Protocol is to enable the court to deal with every care case

(a) justly, expeditiously, fairly and with the minimum of delay;
(b) in ways which ensure, so far as is practicable, that
    (i) the parties are on an equal footing;
    (ii) the welfare of the children involved is safeguarded;
    (iii) distress to all parties is minimised;
(c) so far as is practicable, in ways which are proportionate
    (i) to the gravity and complexity of the issues; and
    (ii) to the nature and extent of the intervention proposed in the private and family life of the children and adults involved.

The influence of the ECHR can clearly be seen in this language, with its emphasis on fairness/due process and proportionality. Equally important, however, is the principle, enshrined in s. 1(2) Children Act 1989, that any delay in determining the application is likely to prejudice the welfare of the child. The problem of delay was examined in a number of reports and studies prior to the introduction of the Protocol (LCD, 1996; LCD, 2002b; LCD, 2002c). Active judicial case management of the process, wherever possible by the same judge throughout all the stages, was seen as a means of ameliorating the problem. It is recognised, however, that other factors, not addressed by the Protocol, also play a part: for example, inadequate or patchy access to advice for families, a shortage in specialists across all the professions involved (including the judges) and a lack of specialised court facilities (DfES, 2004).

The Protocol has a strong modernising flavour, with a requirement for each Care Centre and Family Proceedings Court (see Chapter 3) to have a Care Plan and to allocate responsibility for monitoring implementation of the Protocol. Implementation has been subjected to early review and evaluation by a review team of senior family court judges, whose Thematic Review report was published in December 2005 (JRT, 2005) and fed into the

UK and Welsh Assembly Governments' Care Proceedings Review (DfES/
DCA/WAG, 2006).

Effect of the Protocol on social work and the case for purposeful delay

The Protocol sets target times for the completion of various steps in the
process, starting with the date of the application to the court. The overall
target time for completion of the whole case (that is, the point at which the
court makes a final order on the application) is 40 weeks. Appendices to the
Protocol contain forms, questionnaires, check lists, codes of guidance and
directions for various purposes. Of particular relevance to social work are
Appendix F (Social Services Assessment and Case Planning Aide-Memoire)
and Appendix C (Experts Code of Guidance), but any child care social worker
likely to be involved in an application to court will also require a thorough
understanding of the objectives and requirements of the Protocol as a whole.

Clearly, one effect of the Protocol is to exert pressure on social workers to
adhere to the court's timetable for the case, ensure reports and other documents are available and generally comply with the court's requirements. In
addition to the court's directions in the individual case, national and local targets for increasing the proportion of cases dealt with within the 40-week
target time help to sustain this pressure. It may be felt especially keenly in
relation to the completion of assessments and the question whether additional, specialist assessments should be commissioned. Prolonging a case to
obtain further parental assessment (as opposed to assessment of the child)
came in for particular criticism in the House of Lords in *Kent County Council
v G* [2005], and research into lengthy care cases suggests that a proliferation
of assessments is sometimes the result of 'pursuit of an unattainable level of
certainty', contributing to delay (Beckett & McKeigue (2003), quoted in the
Care Proceedings Review (DfES/DCA/WAG, 2006: para. 3.5)).

In the midst of this zeal to avoid delay, it should not be forgotten, as the
court stated in *Re G (Protocol for Judicial Case Management in Public Law
Children Act Cases: Application to become a Party in Family Proceedings)*
[2004], that the Protocol is a tool designed to improve the quality of family
justice and not, in pursuit of speed and consistency, to impair it. In *Re G*, the
rigid application of local arrangements pursuant to the Protocol had led to the
exclusion of the child's grandparents, with whom G was living at the time of
the application, from the interim care hearing in the family proceedings court.
On appeal against the magistrates' refusal to allow the grandparents to be
joined as parties (because the local arrangements were that such applications
would be heard only by the care centre after the case was transferred) the
High Court rightly criticised this result. The Protocol, said Hedley J, was
'a practical tool to be used in furtherance of the securing of what is best for children within the family justice system' and must always be read subject to the
relevant primary and subordinate legislation (that is, the Children Act 1989

and Rules of Court). Social workers may need to be robust in arguing the case for purposeful delay, for example to assess the impact of a genuinely new aspect of the case.

Tension between process and principle

Hedley J's remarks in *Re G* reiterate a point of general application, that adherence to process should not be allowed to frustrate underlying principles. Giving practical effect to this point calls for careful, informed judgement to which both legal and social work expertise has been applied. In *P, C and S v United Kingdom* [2002] (discussed in Chapter 6) part of the problem for the local authority was that its own policy based on expertise in child development led to the assumption that baby S had to be in a permanent adoptive placement before reaching the age of one. This contributed to the local authority's desire to encounter no delay in bringing the court proceedings to fruition. It also influenced the court's decision, taking into account the 'no delay' principle in s. 1(2) Children Act 1989, not to adjourn the care and freeing proceedings when the mother, P, ceased to be legally represented. When eventually the case reached the ECtHR this was deplored since the result was that P was not able to conduct her case effectively on matters of critical importance to herself and S. This was in breach of Article 6 ECHR and also of the procedural requirements imported into Article 8.2 ECHR. In fairness to both the court and the local authority in *P, C and S v United Kingdom*, at the time when the critical decisions were made the Human Rights Act 1998, with its s. 3 requirement for compatible interpretation and its s. 6 requirement for Convention-compliant practice, was not yet in force. Nowadays, such a case would surely be 'twin tracked' (see Chapters 6 and 8), allowing of a more proportionate method of protecting the baby's immediate and long-term interests whilst also respecting the parents' rights.

It is important to bear in mind that the requirements of due process, reinforced by the need to comply with Articles 6 and 8 ECHR, and research evidence about the beneficial effect of participation pull in precisely the same direction. Research on children in the care system (Marshall, 1997) and on decision-making in the family courts (James, James and Macnamee, 2004; Ruegger, 2001) suggests that even where the eventual decision is not what the participant hoped for, the fact that their point of view was properly presented and considered before the decision was made, and reasons given, increases the likelihood of the decision being accepted rather than perpetually resented.

'Route Map' through the Protocol

The Protocol gives a step by step guide through a care case, and a 'Route Map' identifying six key steps. This is summarised in Box 7.1

Box 7.1   THE SIX KEY STEPS IN THE PROTOCOL FOR JUDICIAL CASE MANAGEMENT

Step and objective	Tasks to be completed	Target time	Local authority (social work) role
Step 1. The Application. Objective: to provide sufficient information about the local authority's case to enable the parties and the court to identify the issues, and the court to make early welfare and case management decisions	Application (Form C1) and Reasons (Form C3) filed with court Fix date for first hearing (Form C6) Appoint guardian/refer to CAFCASS (who must allocate and inform court by day 3)	By day 3	Work with local authority solicitors to prepare application and comprehensive statement of reasons and to file and serve Prepare local authority documents including social work statement (Appdx. B/3), chronology (Appdx. B/2) and assessment(s) (Appdx. F)
2. First Hearing in the FPC Objective: to decide what immediate steps are necessary to safeguard the welfare of the child by determining interim care application/ deciding with whom the child will live, identifying how to prevent	Consider who should be a party, arrange for interim care hearing (if necessary), decide whether to transfer to Care Centre If remaining in family proceedings court give directions and fix date for case management conference, pre-hearing review and final hearing	By day 6	Communicate a clear position on the issues to be decided by the court If case transferred to Care Centre, work with local authority solicitors to prepare case synopsis to be filed within 2 days (by day 8)

(Continued)

Step and objective	Tasks to be completed	Target time	Local authority (social work) role
delay, identifying the appropriate court and transferring to the appropriate court (where applicable)			
3. Allocation Hearing and Directions. **Objective:** to make provision for continuous and consistent case management	Allocation of case to judge(s)/ family proceedings court. Standard Directions (Form at Appdx. A/1) concern parties, representation, expert evidence and refining issues	By day 11	Communicate a clear position on core assessment, interim care, additional assessment and any special features (ethnicity, special facilities etc.)
4. Case Management Conference. **Objective:** to consider what case management directions are necessary to ensure a fair hearing and that the final hearing takes place within or before the recommended hearing window	Case management documents and case management questionnaire filed at court 5 days before case management conference	Between days 15 and 60	Work with local authority solicitors to ensure case management documents are ready and questionnaire complete – including position statement and guardian's comments on local authority plans
5. Pre-hearing Review. **Objective:**	Before the pre-hearing review, update case	By week 37	Work with local authority solicitors to ensure documents are ready and

Step and objective	Tasks to be completed	Target time	Local authority (social work) role
to identify and narrow the issues between the parties and ensure the final hearing is effective	management documents and hold advocates' meeting. A pre-hearing review checklist is at Appdx. A/5		local authority position refined and agreed
6. Final Hearing Objective: to determine the remaining issues between the parties	Case management documents filed at court in accordance with earlier court directions at least two days before hearing	By week 40	Work with local authority solicitors to ensure documents are ready to file
			Prepare to give oral evidence in court.
	Judgment to give clear reasons and set out the threshold criteria and care plan. At end of case court must consider any question of disclosure of documents		Give oral evidence
			Communicate and explain decisions to child and family

The application

An application for a care or supervision order under s. 31 Children Act 1989 may be made by a local authority or some other authorised person (in practice only the NSPCC). The automatic respondents are the child and every person whom the applicant believes has parental responsibility for the child (see Introduction to Part Two above). The application must be served on these persons and they then have a right to play a full part in the proceedings, subject always to the court's direction. Other persons may apply to be joined as a party (such as the grandparents in *Re G*, above), and certain persons are required to be notified without automatically becoming a party. This latter group comprises any person or authority accommodating the child, any parent without parental responsibility (e.g. some unmarried fathers) and any person believed to be a party to any other proceedings in respect of the same child. The detailed rules as to parties, service and notification are laid down in rules of court (the Family Proceedings Court (Children Act 1989) Rules 1991 and the Family Proceedings Rules 1991).

The making of an application formalises the respective positions of the social worker, child and family members. In some 70% of s. 31 applications, families have been known to social services for some time and around the same proportion of applications include allegations that parents are not co-operating with child welfare professionals (Brophy, 2006). Often, the child concerned will already have been entered on the child protection register/integrated children's system under one or more categories of risk. If the social work process has been properly followed, the child (depending on age and understanding) and family members will know what the local authority's concerns are and will be aware of the local authority's powers and duties to intervene if a certain threshold is reached. But the making of an application changes the relationship. Now, the local authority must allege facts and put forward opinions to justify the order sought. The child becomes formally represented by a court-appointed children's guardian. The parents must formally respond, representing their own version of facts and their own views. Although sometimes the court's function in care proceedings is described as inquisitorial, and indeed the court does have powers to instigate inquiries and assessments (for example under ss. 37 and 38 Children Act 1989), it is inevitable that in most cases the making of the application puts the local authority and the other parties into adversarial positions. This may make it particularly difficult for a social worker to sustain collaborative work with the family, even though eventual family rehabilitation may be a clear part of, or option within, the local authority's plan for the child. It is evident that such efforts do succeed in a significant minority of cases, since some 30% of care orders do not result in permanent removal of a child from the family home (Brophy, 2006).

Representation

The local authority

The local authority will be represented by its own legal team, who may instruct a solicitor and/or barrister from the private sector to act on their behalf. The local authority is in a position of relative strength at this point: its team includes the relevant social workers and lawyers, acting on their own assessments, supported by such specialist reports as they may have commissioned. A collective view has crystallised, has been formally adopted by the local authority and is now being pursued by persons skilled and experienced in using the court process.

The child

Under s. 41 Children Act 1989, the appointment of a children's guardian is the norm. Since the creation by the Criminal Justice and Courts Services Act 2000 of the Child and Family Court Advisory and Support Service (CAFCASS), this will normally be an officer employed or engaged by CAFCASS.

It is common for the children's guardian to instruct a solicitor. This means that the child is often formally represented in the proceedings by two professionals. Because of this the system is sometimes described as the tandem system.

The tandem system is generally thought to be fully compliant with Articles 6 and 8.2 ECHR and with Article 12 UNCRC (for example, Fortin, 2003: 233). Certainly, it provides formal machinery within which the child's right to be heard can be ensured.

One of the tasks of the guardian is to elicit and represent the child's wishes and feelings, which are amongst the range of matters that the court must take into account under s. 1(3) Children Act 1989. However, the guardian also reports to the court on the welfare question as a whole, so it is not the case that the guardian simply represents the child's own position. Guardians have been described by one judge (Charles J in *Re R*, discussed under *Expert evidence* below) as 'in many ways the eyes and ears of the court'. Research suggests that in practice the guardian's role as adviser to the court is more prominent than their role as advocate for the child's views and that despite having party status, children's own concerns and wishes are rarely either raised or resolved in court proceedings (Masson and Winn Oakley, 1999). It has also been suggested that guardians' own professional and personal understandings of childhood tend to suppress recognition of the child as a potential 'actor' in the process (James et al., 2004). Very occasionally a child may be permitted to have separate representation, typically where an older child's clearly held view differs from the guardian's view. Even then, it remains in the court's discretion whether the child may be physically present during the hearing.

The operation in practice of the 'tandem' system therefore merits careful scrutiny, despite its formal compliance with human rights obligations, bearing in mind that one of the most frequently reported experiences of children in the care system is of not feeling that anyone listened to them or that their views were taken seriously. A useful comparison can be drawn between the position of children in relation to medical decisions under the notion of 'Gillick competence' (*Gillick v West Norfolk and Wisbech Area Health Authority and the DHSS* [1986]) and the approach taken to the separate representation of their own views in care proceedings. Under 'Gillick' principles, it may well be that, for example, a 13-year-old child could expect to be asked directly and to be able to contribute directly to decisions about her medical care, without the mediation of an adult whose main focus is on delivering a professional opinion to the decision-maker about what is in the child's best interests. We should question what makes the child's direct participation the norm in the medical case and the exception in the legal case; it is surely not that the child's developmental capacity is different in the different settings.

Parents

Parents can be quite vulnerable, especially in the period from the local authority's decision to go for a s. 31 application to the point where they can access effective legal representation. Relations between the parents and the social work team may already have become strained and may now be polarised because the local authority is seen to be seeking to 'take the children away'. Parents may rightly be advised that this will not necessarily be the result, but it is the result in more than 70% of cases. The Care Proceedings Review (DfES/DCA/WAG, 2006: para 1.8) recognised these problems and recommended the adoption generally of steps already taken by some authorities to ameliorate them. These include routine provision to parents of pre-court guidance together with a list of local Law Society Children Panel solicitors/family law firms.

Such advice and information should therefore be given to parents, but that is not the end of the story. Most families involved in care proceedings are dependent on publicly funded legal services through the legal aid system. This system has come under intense scrutiny because of what the UK Government has described as an 'unsustainable' increase in spending on it – from £1.5 billion in 1997 to £2 billion in 2006. In the consultation paper Legal Aid Reform: The Way Ahead (DCA, 2006: 3), legal aid was aptly described as 'one of the cornerstones of the post-war welfare state, yet ... unique as a public service in that it is provided almost entirely by thousands of private and third-sector practitioners, running their own businesses'. Legal aid policy strives to balance the interests of the private practitioner, the client and the taxpayer. It is not necessary here to go into detail, but it should be noted that the Government's proposals for reform include a change in the way legal aid work is remunerated and concerns have been expressed (for example, Macdonald, 2007) that this may impact on provision by law firms to the extent that more parents in care cases will find it difficult to access appropriate legal advice and representation.

Pre-court diversion: 'alternative dispute resolution' for care proceedings?

Current trends suggest that numbers of children becoming looked after under care orders will continue to increase. Government concern about the costs and other implications are generating a focus on pre-court diversionary mechanisms such as family group conferences and improved preventive work (DfES / DCA / WAG, 2006: paras. 4.9–4.13). The Care Proceedings Review recommended that guidance should be issued covering all the activities that the courts can reasonably expect a local authority to have completed before the decision is taken to apply to court. These are issues on which the local authority must expect to have to give an account of itself to the court, and the Review suggests that they should be systematically considered at a 'gateway' meeting within the local authority, involving the legal team as well as the social work/child care team, before an application is made. The list of issues is set out in Box 7.2.

Box 7.2   ISSUES TO BE CHECKED AT GATEWAY MEETING BEFORE MAKING A S. 31 APPLICATION

- appropriate provision of support and services to families prior to proceedings;
- completion of core assessments;
- rigorous examination of kinship-care opportunities;
- preparation of an interim care plan;
- proper provision of information to parents and children, including that relating to the local authority's concerns and a list of local Children's Panel solicitors and/or family law firms.

(DfES / DCA / WAG, 2006: para. 5.15)

While the Government's desire to avoid cases brought before the courts is understandable, it must be said that the notion of alternative dispute resolution does not fit as comfortably in care proceedings as in many legal disputes. Care proceedings are a mechanism whereby the State may discharge its obligations to ensure children's rights to protection by interfering as far as necessary in the private sphere of family life. This is reflected in the fact that the rules of court require that once an application for a care order has been made, it cannot be withdrawn without the court's leave (Family Proceedings Court (Children Act 1989) Rules 1991 r. 5, and the Family Proceedings Rules 1991 r. 4.5) and that the child's guardian must have an opportunity to be heard as to whether leave should be given. It has been held that it is not sufficient for the guardian simply to be represented by a lawyer when an application for leave to withdraw is made: ***Re F (A Minor) (Care Order: Withdrawal of Application)* [1993]**. Once proceedings have been started, the children's guardian has the job of ensuring that the child's standpoint is properly represented. The fact that the local authority and the parents may reach a compromise as to some allegation or other aspect of the case does not necessarily mean that the case will proceed on the basis of that compromise: it may be appropriate in the interests of the child for the court to make a finding. If necessary the court can even call witnesses itself in order to allow for cross-examination: ***Re F***, above, and also ***Re N (Leave to Withdraw Care Proceedings)* [2000]**.

At the pre-court stage there is no such formal representation for the child, nor is the child's welfare formally the paramount consideration as it is when the court makes a decision. If, for example, some agreement were reached in Case Study (4) (Chapter 6) between Elin and the local authority, or even between Elin, James and the local authority, under which no court application will for the time being be made, the question arises whether and how the children's separate interests can be adequately protected. There will be no children's guardian at this stage and the social workers may find it difficult to maintain a focus on the children as they engage more with the parents in trying

---

to address their own problems. A very heavy onus rests on the local authority to ensure that the child's position is not suppressed when discussions take place between adults aimed at avoiding recourse to a s. 31 application.

What has to be proved?

In dealing with an application for a care or supervision order the court has to consider:

(a) whether the 'threshold' or trigger for the court's power to make an order has been reached (the 'threshold question'); and
(b) whether it is in the child's best interests that an order be made (the 'welfare question').

The local authority has to prove both of these matters by producing relevant evidence. The facts and opinions which will be relied on as evidence must be set out in the statement of reasons accompanying the application (Protocol, Step 1, see Box 7.1). In each case, behind that statement lies a combination of assessments, records of meetings, contacts, decisions and actions. Some of these may have occurred before a court application seemed likely. Yet all now become a part of a narrative that has to be related to the court in the manner and form prescribed by the legal system. Initially this means they must be transposed into a case synopsis, social work chronology and social work statement (Protocol, Appendix B). The wider functions and objectives of the assessments and other actions (for example, as a basis of procuring specialist support or treatment or as part of ongoing therapeutic work) are not extinguished, but for the purposes of the court application their relevance is confined to the questions that the court is called upon to decide: the threshold question and the welfare question.

The threshold question

Section 31(2) Children Act 1989 provides:

(2) A court may only make a care order or supervision order if it is satisfied:
   (a) that the child concerned is suffering, or is likely to suffer, significant harm, and
   (b) that the harm, or likelihood of harm, is attributable to:
      (i) the care given to the child, or likely to be given to the child if the order is not made, not being what it would be reasonable to expect a parent to give to the child; or
      (ii) the child's being beyond parental control.

'Harm', according to s. 31(9) Children Act 1989 means 'ill-treatment or the impairment of health or development'. 'Health or development' is to be judged by comparing it 'with that which could reasonably be expected of a similar child'.

'Significant' is not defined in the Act but the courts have accepted that it should be construed according to its dictionary meaning which is 'considerable, noteworthy or important' (**Humberside County Council v B** [1993]).

'Likely to' in this context means that there is a 'real possibility', not necessarily that it is 'more likely than not': **Re H and R (Child Sexual Abuse: Standard of Proof)** [1996]. However, as explained below (under 'Burden and standard of proof'), the courts require that facts relied upon to establish likelihood must be proved to be more likely than not to be true. Equally, the facts supporting an assertion that a child has suffered significant harm must be proved to be more likely than not to be true.

Where the court is satisfied that a child has suffered significant harm at the hands of one or more of several carers, but cannot be certain which one, the threshold test may nonetheless be satisfied because the court interprets the attributable condition in s. 31(2)(b)(i) as embracing the care given by any of the child's carers. This was made clear in the House of Lords decision in **Lancashire County Council v B** [2000], in a case where there was uncertainty as to whether (and which) one of the child's parents or the child-minder inflicted injuries. The House of Lords recognised that a more restrictive interpretation might arguably be fairer to the possibly innocent parents, but stated that it would represent a 'dangerously irresponsible' approach to protection of the child from risk of future harm.

Whether a child is suffering or likely to suffer significant harm is a matter that must be judged at the time immediately before the initial statutory intervention: **Re M (A Minor) (Care Order: Threshold Conditions)** [1994]. This means, for example, that the fact that immediate danger has been averted by the child being safely placed for the time being in kinship-care does not preclude the court from making a finding of significant harm. Matters occurring or coming to light after the initial intervention may, however, be taken into account **Re G (Children) (Care Order: Evidence)** [2001].

The welfare question

If the court is satisfied that the threshold test has been met, then it will proceed to consider whether it is in the best interests of the child that a care or supervision order, or no order, be made. The 'no order' principle in s. 1(5) Children Act 1989 applies. Thus it is not necessarily the case that a care or supervision order will follow a finding that the threshold test is satisfied. At the welfare or 'disposal' stage, the task of the local authority is to adduce evidence to satisfy the court that, on the balance of probabilities, it will be better for the child if the order sought is made. In making this decision the court is required by s. 1(3) Children Act 1989 to have regard in particular to certain matters, commonly called the welfare checklist:

(a) the ascertainable wishes and feelings of the child concerned (considered in the light of age and understanding);
(b) the child's physical, emotional and educational needs;
(c) the likely effect on the child of any change in circumstances;
(d) the child's age, sex, background and any relevant characteristics;

(e)   any harm which the child has suffered or is at risk of suffering;

(f)   the capability of the child's parents or relevant others to meet the child's needs;

(g)   the range of powers available to the court.

The key document in relation to the welfare question is the care plan. Under s. 31(3A) Children Act 1989 (as amended by the Adoption and Children Act 2002) the court is not allowed to make a care or supervision order without first considering a care plan submitted by the local authority in accordance with s. 31A (also inserted by the 2002 Act). This provision forms part of the legislative response to judicial criticism, on ECHR grounds, of the system for preparing, implementing and reviewing care plans in *Re S, Re W* [2002] (discussed further in Chapter 8). The court will consider the care plan carefully, together with the report and recommendations of the children's guardian and evidence that may be adduced on behalf of the parents and/or other parties. The better the preparation of the care plan, the better the chances of the court making the best decision for the child and the easier the task of implementation in the event that a care order is made. To quote Munby J:

Too often one is presented with care plans that are as long on rhetorical platitudes as they are short on specific detail. We all know that Johnny needs a safe and secure environment where his emotional, psychological and educational needs are met. What we need to be told, and too often are not, is, for example, that Johnny has certain identified mental health needs, that they are going to be addressed by Dr X, that the local authority has arranged that Dr X will be starting a 6-month course of therapy starting on some specified date, and that funding for this therapy is in place, having been authorised by the appropriate officer with decision-making powers. A care plan which contains clear and specific detail of this sort minimises the risk of the child drifting in care, for it sets out a clear programme whose performance can be monitored and checked. (2004: 431–2)

Burden and standard of proof

The burden of proof, generally in any legal proceedings, lies on the person making an allegation. This means that it is for this person to prove, to the requisite standard, that the allegation is true. Conversely, it is not for the person against whom an allegation is made to prove that it is untrue. In care and supervision proceedings, the burden of proof therefore lies on the local authority to prove its assertion that the threshold and welfare criteria are met. The process cannot accurately be cast as an inquisition in search of the truth. It is a matter of adjudicating on whether the person making the assertion (here, the local authority) has discharged the burden of proof. As Hedley J said in *A Local Authority v S and W and T by his Guardian* [2004]:

Truth is an absolute but elusive concept and the law, in recognising that, deals with it in terms of what can be proved. The fact that something cannot be proved does not mean it did not happen but that it cannot be proved to the requisite standard that it did. That is the price society has to pay for human fallibility in the quest for truth.

Accordingly, there must be a factual basis for each assertion made and the facts must be established to the requisite standard of proof. The practical implication for social work is that the information gathered from the various sources must be analysed and presented in a way that will facilitate the findings of fact that in turn will enable the court to make the order sought.

The civil standard of proof

The standard of proof is the civil standard: the balance of probabilities. This is a lower standard than that required in criminal proceedings where the prosecution must prove the material facts 'beyond a reasonable doubt'. It means that the local authority must prove that each factual allegation made is 'more likely than not' to be true.

Whilst maintaining the difference between the criminal and civil standards of proof, the courts adopt the approach that the more serious the allegation, the more cogent the evidence has to be. Where, for example, what is alleged as ill treatment would, if accepted, mean that a parent or carer was guilty of a serious criminal offence, the court requires more to be convinced that the burden of proof has been discharged. The rationale is, as Lord Nicholls put it in the leading case *Re H and R (Child Sexual Abuse: Standard of Proof)* [1996]:

> The more improbable the event, the stronger must be the evidence that it did occur before, on the balance of probability, its occurrence will be established.

This rule has been criticised (Hayes, 2004) because it may under-protect a child from some instances of really serious abuse. The problem is compounded because of the requirement that *each* allegation be proved to the requisite standard. This means that where there are several allegations, only some of which can be satisfactorily proved, the court is required to ignore those which cannot be proved. This creates an artificial approach to future risk assessment – the very task with which s. 31 Children Act 1989 clearly entrusts the court. In his minority opinion in *Re H and R (Child Sexual Abuse: Standard of Proof)* [1996], Lord Browne-Wilkinson recognised that

> the combined effect of a number of factors which suggest that a state of affairs, though not proved to exist, may well exist is the normal basis for the assessment of future risk.

He argued that this ought to be reflected in the approach taken to risk assessment under s. 31. Under that approach, evidence which is insufficient to establish the truth of an allegation to the required standard of proof would nevertheless remain evidence in the case for the purpose of assessing future risk. However, it is the approach of the majority in *Re H and R* which has been followed in subsequent court decisions: each allegation must be proved to the civil standard and the worse the behaviour alleged, the more cogent must be the evidence to prove it. If it cannot be proved, it must be left out of account.

The courts have insisted that this does not mean that in cases where a particularly grave allegation is made, the difference between the civil and criminal standards of proof is 'merely illusory'. Accordingly, an acquittal on criminal charges (where, for example, there is disagreement amongst medical experts leaving 'reasonable doubt' as to causation of injuries) will not necessarily mean that a court dealing with a care application must find the threshold question unproven. In *Re LU (a child) and Re LB (a child)* **[2004]** the Court of Appeal contrasted the roles and functions of criminal and care proceedings, the former focused on responsibility for past events and the latter ultimately on assessment of and protection from future risk. In care proceedings, the Court said:

the Judge invariably surveys a wide canvas, including a detailed history of the parents' lives, their relationship and their inter-action with professionals. There will be many contributions to this context, family members, neighbours, health records, as well as the observation of professionals such as social workers, health visitors and children's guardian.

In the end the judge must make clear findings on the issues of fact before the Court, resting on the evidence led by the parties and such additional evidence as the Judge may have required in the exercise of his quasi-inquisitorial function. All this is the prelude to a further and fuller investigation of a range of choices in search of the protection and welfare of the children. A positive finding against a parent or both parents does not in itself preclude the possibility of rehabilitation. All depends on the facts and circumstances of the individual case. In that context the consequences of a false positive finding in care proceedings may not be as dire as the consequence of the conviction of an innocent in criminal proceedings.

Applying all of this to Case Study (4), the Blankshire social work team and their legal advisers must review all the information the authority has collected about Anne and Martin and their family and consider it afresh as potential evidence supporting an application under a s. 31. The authority must consider alternatives, but if it is decided that an application will be made it is likely that the facts alleged will include that Martin's subdural haemorrhage was the result of deliberately inflicted injury and that at the very least this is evidence of want of parental care. Blankshire must establish, by adducing evidence of facts and expert opinion, that this is more likely than not to be the case. The allegations are grave and the case as a whole has become quite complex both in terms of its factual basis and assessment of future risk. Expert evidence is likely to be essential as to the cause of injury and probably other aspects as well. A further complication is that the assault on Elin and the suspected n.a.i. to Martin may well trigger separate criminal investigations which will be ongoing as the s. 31 application progresses.

Two important considerations arise: first, what use can be made of expert evidence to help determine the cause of Martin's injuries and assess the risk of future harm to him and Anne, and second, what is the likely impact of concurrent criminal proceedings against the alleged perpetrator(s) of Martin's injuries. The remainder of this chapter addresses these two issues.

Expert evidence in this context means evidence additional to the social work assessment, commissioned expressly for the purpose of the court application. The social work assessment itself constitutes expert evidence but it is rare for local authorities to rely on this alone: additional expert evidence is used in 80–90% of s. 31 applications (Brophy, 2006). Expert evidence is covered by an exception to the normal rule that only facts, not opinions, may be given in evidence. Most expert evidence is filed by the local authority making the application, but it may also be filed by parents and by children's guardians.

Expert evidence is often procured in relation to the threshold question, for example as to the cause of injury, but it is also common for the evidence of an expert or of several experts to be sought on the welfare question. Child and adolescent and family psychiatric reports are the most commonly commissioned in care proceedings, followed by adult psychiatric and paediatric reports (Brophy, 2006). The courts recognise that expert evidence is often indispensable in enabling them to make the complex decisions required in cases under the Children Act 1989, but equally emphasise that it is essential that all involved – the court, the experts themselves, the parties and their advisers – understand and adhere to the respective proper roles of the court and the expert. As Butler Sloss LJ said in *Re M and R (Child Abuse: Evidence)* [1996]:

> Many if not all family cases involving children feature expert opinion evidence ... In cases involving children, expert medical and psychiatric evidence from paediatricians and allied disciplines is often quite indispensable to the Court ... when dealing with children, the court needs 'all the help it can get'. But that dependence in no way compromises the fact that the final decision in the case is the judge's and his alone.

The general point

The general point being made by Butler Sloss LJ in the above quotation is that it is for the court to decide the facts and to determine the question of the welfare of the child. An expert should address identified issues, rather than seek to give an opinion on those matters which the court has to decide. This requires not only a high level of understanding in a particular area of expertise, but also understanding of the forensic process. The role of the expert in court is in clear contrast to the expert's role at the investigative stage. At the investigative stage, it may be not only appropriate, but also indispensable in the interests of child protection, that expert opinion is acted on even though it is founded on nothing more than a feeling that 'something is not quite right' (in the words of Lord Brown, making this point in *JD v East Berkshire Community Health NHS Trust* [2005]). In court, the expert's feeling that 'something is not quite right' proves nothing. Instead, the expert must give his or her opinion on the basis of the same 'factual matrix' as that of the court (a term used by the Court of Appeal in *GW and PW v Oldham Metropolitan Borough Council* [2005], see below).

This can be quite a complex exercise, requiring rigorous self-discipline both by those giving and those receiving instructions for expert opinion. In *A County Council v K, D and L* [2005], the local authority's case was founded on an assertion that the child's mother caused the death of one of her children. The opinion of six medical experts was that it was more likely than not that this was so. This was also the view of the judge on the totality of the evidence, but he took the opportunity to give some guidelines as to the way in which expert evidence ought to be presented (Box 7.3).

The judge accepted that there may be overlap between these matters, but considered it important to separate them out: it was not, for example, necessarily the case that the cause identified as 'most likely' under (iv) would also be identified as 'more likely than not to be the cause' under (v).

Box 7.3   GUIDANCE ON INSTRUCTION OF EXPERTS: *A COUNTY COUNCIL V K, D AND L* [2005]

(I)t might (a) assist all involved, (b) better reflect the roles of the expert and the judge, and (c) demonstrate that the expert is not the decision-maker as to whether the relevant death, injuries or harm is the result of non-accidental human agency and whether the threshold is satisfied, and does not have all the relevant information, if the medical experts were not asked to express a view as to the cause of the relevant death, injuries or harm on the balance of probabilities but were asked

(i) to identify possible causes of the death, injuries or harm, setting out in respect of each of the reasons why it might be a cause and thus why it should be considered;

(ii) state their views as to the likelihood of each possibility being the cause of the relevant death, injuries or harm and the reasons why they include it or reject it as a reasonable (as opposed to a fanciful or merely theoretical) possible cause;

(iii) compare the likelihood of the cause (or causes) identified as reasonable possibilities being the actual cause of the relevant death, injuries or harm;

(iv) state whether they consider a cause (or causes) is (are) the most likely cause (or causes) of the relevant death, injuries or harm; and

(v) state whether they consider that a cause (or causes) is (are) more likely than not to be the cause (or causes) of the relevant death, injuries or harm and their reasons for that view.

The general point applies equally to the welfare question as to the threshold question. The welfare of the child, to which the court must give paramount importance in deciding whether to make an order, is a legal concept which imports certain policy considerations. Some of the policy considerations are reflected in the Children Act 1989 itself, some in relevant international law and some in judicial interpretation of both. It was noted in Chapter 2 that all these sources reflect common principles, which in turn inform and direct policy: respect for the agency of the child, support for family unity and the best interests and development of the child. In some cases the need to adhere to policy may mean that experts' views on what the welfare of a particular child demands will not be followed. For example, an appraisal based wholly on research evidence from the medical and social sciences might well suggest that leaving a child in the care of the birth family or kinship group would be less good, in terms of measurable outcomes for the child, than a stable, long-term alternative placement. Respect for the agency of the child and support for family unity may nonetheless counter-balance this. An example can be seen in the Court of Appeal decision in *Re L (Children)* [2006], where reliance placed on a single psychologist's assessment was heavily criticised. The parents both had a relatively low IQ and the psychologist had relied mainly on two psychometric tests apparently showing tendencies adverse to the future welfare of the children. However, the Court of Appeal described the present relationship between each parent and the children as 'positive and deeply loving'. The fact that greater intellectual stimulus might be available in substitute care was irrelevant. The court must decide what the legal concept of welfare requires, weighing up all the evidence and applying its own judgement.

Case-handling and case-preparation

The appropriate use of experts requires careful case-handling from the outset. In *Re R (Care: Disclosure: Nature of Proceedings)* [2002], Charles J gave some sound and detailed guidance, some of which has since been taken up by the Protocol. He said that the local authority should identify the facts they need to establish (i) to satisfy the threshold test and (ii) to show why the proposed care plan best promotes the welfare of the child. (These two criteria should be separately addressed: another poor feature of the local authority's case preparation in *Re L (Children)* [2006], above, was that they had elided the two and thereby failed to deal adequately with the threshold question.) The local authority should then focus on the oral and documentary evidence they will need to adduce to establish these matters. This can only properly be done, Charles J said, with an 'understanding of the relevant legal principles, the issues in the case and the procedures of the court'. Effective working partnerships between local authority social work teams and their litigation lawyers are therefore essential at an early stage, since 'If this work is done properly, it would also mean or lead to ... experts being instructed on a properly informed basis ...'.

PREPARING A CASE FOR COURT

It is worth noting that responsibility for effective case management is shared by all involved, under the overall direction of the case management judge. In *GW and PW v Oldham Metropolitan Borough Council* [2005], the Court of Appeal stressed that even though the children's guardian may wish to remain neutral in a finding of fact hearing, the guardian and the child's solicitor (as well as the local authority, parents and their lawyers) should nonetheless play a proactive role in ensuring that the case is ready for hearing. They should examine the 'factual sub-stratum' of the case and be ready to advise the judge what evidence is required in order for the court to reach a just conclusion.

Disclosure: how much, to whom?

The judgment in *Re R* gives guidance on many aspects of case management and preparation, but the main issue in the case was disclosure. Greater concern to provide full and frank disclosure, and greater appreciation of the extremely limited scope of public interest grounds for non-disclosure – both in part the result of the influence of the ECHR – may contribute to an overload of information, with associated delays as experts and other professionals have to deal with voluminous documentation. However, in *Re R*, it was a failure to give full disclosure of all relevant notes of interviews and discussions concerning allegations of sexual abuse that led to the experts being instructed on incomplete information and to a withdrawal of the allegations at a late stage in the trial once the extent and implications of the failure became apparent. This resulted in considerable consequent wasted time, expense and complexity. An early request by the lawyers for the child's father for disclosure of all the notes had not been complied with and had not been pursued at later pre-trial stages in the court. The judge was at pains to emphasise that responsibility for disclosure was shared by all the parties and gave guidance of general application. This repays careful study and is summarised in Box 7.4.

Current issues: future solutions?

The supply and quality of expert evidence has been the subject of intense and anxious scrutiny following the overturning of the criminal convictions of Angela Cannings (the subject of *R v Cannings*, [2004]), Sally Clark and Trupti Patel for causing the deaths of their children, and subsequent reviews of child care decisions based on disputed medical evidence. Those cases clearly had implications for the use of medical evidence in care proceedings, and guidance was given on this by the Court of Appeal in *Re LU (a Child) and Re LB (a Child)* [2004]. The crux of the matter is the approach the court must take where there is medical uncertainty as to causation of injuries. A summary is set out in Box 7.5.

Box 7.4 LESSONS FROM *RE R (CARE: DISCLOSURE: NATURE OF PROCEEDINGS) [2002]*

- In putting together the factual basis of the case, it is essential that as full as possible an examination is carried out of all the information available to the local authority, including proper and full discussion with relevant witnesses, examination of all the background and circumstances and proper consideration of what further material or information should be obtained.
- Where allegations of instances of abuse have been made, the details should be checked so far as possible. If there has been a police investigation leading to a decision not to prosecute, information from that source may well be relevant, for example as to credibility of persons involved.
- It is essential that the local authority involves its lawyers in the initial preparation of evidence as well as at later stages, 'because social workers do not have the requisite training, experience or expertise' to carry out the essential tasks in preparing evidence, disclosure and instruction of experts.
- Contemporaneous notes of relevant conversations and events should be appended to witness statements, and witness statements should be prepared by someone who is trained and experienced in litigation. Such a person should also examine all relevant files. In this way matters requiring further investigation or clarification are more likely to be identified and dealt with.
- As a general rule, all contemporaneous notes should be collated in chronological order and disclosed. The guardian's notes are likely to be particularly helpful and relevant.
- The local authority has the primary responsibility for collating the relevant information, but all parties share responsibility for ensuring that all relevant matters are before the court. This means that respondents should pursue applications for disclosure if they think that relevant evidence is being withheld, and it is inappropriate for parents to adopt a position focused only on isolated allegations. It is also wrong for parents to adopt a 'you prove it' approach. They should give a full account of what is accepted and what is denied at as early a stage as possible. Guardians share the general responsibility to ensure that all relevant material is before the court: they are 'in many respects the eyes and ears of the court'.
- Letters of instruction to experts require the utmost care. They must focus on the issues in the individual case. Precedents should not simply be reproduced although they may be used as a basis and to check that all matters are covered. Where experts are jointly instructed all the parties should consider the letter and agree it.
- On receipt of the expert's report, all parties to a joint instruction should raise points as quickly as possible, for example as to the approach taken by the

(Continued)

PREPARING A CASE FOR COURT

expert, facts that the parties wish the expert to take into account and the evidential basis for the expert's views.

- Even where an expert is not jointly instructed, those who do not join in the instructions should also consider carefully how the expert should be instructed, and should raise questions about the report as soon as possible.
- If an expert videos interviews this should be stated in the report and the videos made available unless the expert wants to make a particularised point as to why they should not be seen. The general rule is that they should be disclosed. Videos should be disclosed as early as possible so that any points arising from them can be raised by the parties as early as possible.

There were wider ramifications to the Cannings, Clark and Patel cases. They stimulated concern about the quality and availability of expert evidence in cases concerning children. The UK Government's Chief Medical Officer was commissioned to examine and make recommendations for reform of the delivery of medical expert evidence in family law cases. The resultant report, *Bearing Good Witness* (DoH, 2006) identified a number of 'serious difficulties':

- identifying a suitable medical expert;
- securing a report on time;
- insufficient experts in some specialisms;
- lack of organisation, no succession planning and no collective responsibility for supply of expert evidence;
- lack of training and inter-disciplinary understanding.

Box 7.5   MEDICAL UNCERTAINTY AND N.A.I.: LESSONS FOR CARE PROCEEDINGS FROM *R V CANNINGS*, ACCORDING TO THE COURT OF APPEAL IN *RE LU, LB*

- The cause of an injury or an episode that cannot be explained scientifically remains equivocal.
- Recurrence is not in itself probative.
- Particular caution is necessary in any case where the medical experts disagree, one opinion declining to exclude a reasonable possibility of natural cause.
- The Court must always be on guard against the over-dogmatic expert, the expert whose reputation or *amour propre* is at stake, or the expert who has developed a scientific prejudice.
- The judge in care proceedings must never forget that today's medical certainty may be discarded by the next generation of experts or that scientific research will throw light into corners that are at present dark.

The Report recommends that the provision of expert evidence should be commissioned and delivered as a public service, consistent with the duty of the NHS to safeguard and promote the welfare of children under the Children Act 2004, and on a collective, multi-disciplinary, team basis rather than by individual, named clinicians.

A multi-disciplinary approach may result in the production of a single report for the court representing a consensus reached by experts from various disciplines. This may have the advantage of savings in cost and reduction of delay, but is not free from difficulty, especially if it leads to resistance by the court to the commissioning of a second opinion independent of the multi-disciplinary team. In *GW and PW v Oldham Metropolitan Borough Council*, above, the Court of Appeal found that it was the insistence on a single expert's report, based on a medical consensus between four experts, which under-mined what would otherwise have been an unassailable decision by the trial judge. The medical consensus was belied by the fact that the crucial opinion was that of a single radiologist, to whom, the Court found, the other doctors clearly deferred. The Court noted that while a true medical consensus, which might well be the result of the appointment of a second expert if the second expert's report substantially confirmed the first, can have the effect of radi-cally reducing or eliminating the issues in a case, it is self-evident that any medical consensus must be genuine and not based on deference. This is an issue that will need to be borne in mind in any implementation of the *Bearing Good Witness* recommendations.

Concurrent criminal and civil proceedings: police/social work collaboration

Where the local authority's evidence on the threshold question includes an allegation of deliberate or reckless infliction of injury, it is very likely that there will be a police investigation and possibly a prosecution proceeding at the same time as the s. 31 application. This presents a number of challenges for inter-disciplinary working, not least in relation to disclosure of information.

The respective processes have very different objectives: the criminal process follows a pattern of

arrest → charge → trial → sentence

geared towards providing a response on behalf of society to proven past crim-inal conduct, whereas the civil process started by a s. 31 application follows a route through

initial protective action→assessment of future risk→care
order→rehabilitation/permanent alternative placement

In the early stages, the sharing of information between the child protection system and the criminal justice system is supported by the *Working Together* process, bolstered by the formalisation of safeguarding procedures pursuant to

PREPARING A CASE FOR COURT

the Children Act 2004. The police are likely to be actively involved in initial child protection conferences and at that stage there may be quite free exchange of information between police and social services. As the case proceeds, however, research suggests that joint working tends to diminish and exchange of information becomes more fragmented (Cobley, 2003).

Once court proceedings under Pt. IV or V Children Act 1989 have begun, s. 98(2) of the Act ensures that any admission made in care proceedings will be inadmissible in evidence in criminal proceedings. This covers admissions made to a children's guardian or expert preparing a report as well as admissions made in court but does not generally extend to admissions to a social worker, whether in the course of assessment or otherwise, prior to commencement of court proceedings. The underlying aim of s. 98(2) is to encourage frankness and co-operation by parents in care proceedings so that the best possible assessment of future rehabilitation prospects can be made, in accordance with the partnership spirit of the 1989 Act and the principle of support for family unity.

The dilemma for carers is that co-operation (which may involve an admission) decreases the prospect of a care order and increases the chances of rehabilitation, but that an admission of abuse renders a criminal prosecution more likely. Protection from use of an admission as evidence in criminal proceedings removes an obvious disincentive to confess. In the past the courts have taken this into account in deciding how to exercise their discretion to allow disclosure. For example, in **Re AB (Care Proceedings: Disclosure of Medical Evidence to Police)** [2003] Wall J said:

Depending on the seriousness of the abuse, and the practicality of rehabilitation, the court is more likely to refuse an application for disclosure to the police in a case involving child abuse where there is a frank acknowledgement of responsibility by the abusing parent. This is often perceived as a vitally important first step towards rehabilitation between parent and child, particularly when coupled with a recognition of the harm caused and a genuine desire for help to avoid repetition.

Consistent with this approach, in **Re AB**, a court medical report indicating a mother's responsibility for child deaths was allowed to be disclosed to the police since there was no prospect of rehabilitation of the mother with the surviving child. By contrast, in **Re M (Care Proceedings: Disclosure: Human Rights)** [2001], where the return of a child home remained a possibility, the court refused to permit disclosure to the police of the mother's admission in care proceedings.

Changes introduced by the Family Proceedings (Amendment No. 4) Rules 2005 now mean that more information relating to care proceedings can be disclosed for certain purposes, including the investigation and prosecution of offences, without the court's permission. This may help to relieve a sense of frustration felt in the past by police and prosecuting authorities. However, s. 98(2) Children Act 1989 remains in force, so that even though an admission may be disclosed for the purpose of investigating and preparing a case for prosecution, it still cannot be used in evidence in criminal proceedings.

It has been suggested (Cobley, 2004) that the approach to investigation and prosecution should change to accommodate more clearly the notion of the child's best interests and that this would help further to reduce the tensions between the child care and criminal systems. A child-centred approach to the exercise of discretion to prosecute would put first the question of how, if at all, a criminal prosecution would benefit the child and how, if at all, a decision not to prosecute would be detrimental to the child. It might give precedence to this factor over the standard tests of sufficiency of evidence and the public interest applied by the Crown Prosecution Service (CPS, 2004). The practical consequences might be a greater use of discontinuance of criminal proceedings where the care proceedings route is leading towards rehabilitation, or a greater emphasis on rehabilitation as part of a disposal following a criminal conviction. The latter has been hinted at in criminal case-law, for example *R v W* [2001], in which it was suggested that the public interest in encouraging parents involved in family proceedings to make confessions about abuse of their children might result in a reduction in sentence in some cases. The difficulty with this proposition is in overcoming the perception that an offender is being 'let off' too lightly, and it would be rash to suggest that the tension between criminal and care proceedings can be easily resolved.

Conclusion

This chapter has examined law and practice relating to the preparation of an application under s. 31 Children Act 1989. Hopefully it is clear that the process should be characterised by intellectual rigour, a proper understanding of the tests to be satisfied and, above all, fairness. Where, at the end of the court hearing, a care order is made, the likely immediate effect is the removal or continued retention of the child away from the family home. By virtue of the order, the local authority shares parental responsibility and can exercise it to the exclusion of others in important respects. The local authority then bears the responsibility of 'corporate parenting': the responsibility for fulfilling the State's positive obligation to replicate, so far as possible, a missing family environment. The next chapter considers the way in which the law directs and regulates the discharge of this responsibility.

Further Reading

On the question of delay, discussed at the beginning of this chapter, interesting research findings are discussed by D. McSherry, E. Larkin and D. Iwaniec in 'Care Proceedings: Exploring the relationship between case duration and achieving permanency for the child', 36 (6) (2005) *British Journal of Social Work*, (2005) pp. 901–919. In particular, the authors found that the quality of interim decisions and contact arrangements could be just as significant, or even more significant, than case duration alone.

Parts 4 and 5 of the government's *Care Proceedings Review* (DfES / DCA / WAG, 2006) set out areas for improvement and immediate recommendations, and are worth reading carefully to further understand the government's perception of the issues of cost and delay, and likely future government-driven developments in the court process.

Working in the Family Justice System, the Official Handbook of the Family Justice Council (2nd edition), by E. Walsh (Jordan Publishing, 2006), gives a good overview of the organisation of the court system, the responsibilities of the respective professionals and how they interact in connection with care proceedings and other family proceedings.

8
Looked After Children

Introduction

This chapter is concerned with the contribution made by social workers to the carrying out of the local authority's role as corporate parent once a child becomes looked after. Just as in the case of voluntary engagement (Chapter 5) and compulsory measures (Chapter 6) it is necessary to consider rights and obligations flowing from international law as well as the domestic legal framework of specific powers and duties. Again, there is a large amount of supplementary provision in the form of statutory and non-statutory guidance. Again, the requirement imposed by the Children Act 2004 that children's services be directed towards the five 'aspects of well-being' applies.

'Looked after' children in this context means:

- children in the care of a local authority pursuant to a care order under s. 31 Children Act 1989 or an interim care order under s. 38 Children Act 1989;
- children who are the subject of an emergency protection order under s. 44 Children Act 1989;

- children who are provided with accommodation by a local authority under s. 20 Children Act 1989; and
- children compulsorily accommodated under s. 21 Children Act 1989 (this category comprises children referred via the criminal justice system, see Chapter 9).

Although they get there by different routes, children falling within these categories have one thing in common: while they are 'looked after' the local authority exercises, to a greater or lesser extent, the role of parent, assuming responsibility for their accommodation and basic welfare and ensuring that provision is made to ensure their education, health and general well-being. In relation to all looked after children other than those accommodated under s. 20 Children Act 1989, the local authority may exercise aspects of parental responsibility to the exclusion of others also having parental responsibility (see Introduction to Part Two above).

The social work role

Each looked after child must have a key social worker or case manager. Other social workers within the same local authority may also be involved, or social workers from another authority having had dealings with the child or family members, and sometimes an independent social worker from whom additional assessment may be sought. Core areas of knowledge include:

- the rights of looked after children;
- local authorities' powers and duties;
- legal considerations in carrying out the core social work role: application of the principles of family unity, best interests and development, respect for agency of the child;
- the process for planning, placement and support;
- mechanisms for accountability and review.

Some facts about looked after children

In the year ending 31 March 2006, some 60,300 children were looked after in England and some 4,500 in Wales. With some variation between England and Wales, the majority (70–75%) were accommodated in foster homes. Of the rest, 9–12% were living with their parents or family and around 5% were placed for adoption.

Statistics about looked after children are published annually by the Department for Children, Schools and Families and the Welsh Assembly Government. This is a statutory requirement under s. 83 Children Act 1989. A classified abstract of the information so gathered is published as the annual Children Act Report. The information is contributed by local authorities at the request of the respective central governments, together with information relating to the performance of local authorities against indicators and targets also set centrally. From the Children Act Reports and from a substantial body of independent research evidence we can learn that:

- the quality of care for looked after children is variable, but often unsatisfactory;
- outcomes are often grim: looked after children are at least three times more likely than children generally to be involved in the criminal justice system, girls leaving care are more likely to become single mothers before the age of 20 and both boys and girls leaving care (and in some cases whilst in care) are more likely to be sexually exploited and become involved in prostitution;
- the scale of abuse of children in children's homes and other institutional settings is not fully known but is a serious and persistent problem;
- instability and lack of permanence in placements is common, especially for older children and those with complex needs, and this is detrimental to their welfare;
- educational achievement of looked after children is unacceptably low.

These problems raise issues about compliance with the UK's obligations under the UNCRC and to a lesser extent the ECHR. In response to the research evidence about poor outcomes for looked after children and many problems faced by them, there has been a flurry of governmental activity in recent years in England and Wales. In particular, the government's response to the Utting Report, *People Like Us* (TSO, 1997) was the *Quality Protects* programme in England and *Children First* in Wales. Common features of these policies were greater central direction as to the targeting, provision, evaluation and accountability of children's services and recognition that enabling looked after children to have a voice is critical to improving care quality and outcomes.

Policy initiatives in England and Wales

Building on the government's *Modernising Social Services* agenda (TSO, 1998b), the *Quality Protects* programme was introduced for England in 1999 (DfES, 1998, now absorbed within the *Every Child Matters* programme). It was intended to ensure effective protection, better quality care and improved life chances for looked after children. It involved central government allocating specific grant to local authorities for specific activities intended to improve management and information sharing, increase quality and permanence of placement for looked after children and support children's participation and advocacy. Associated with it were government objectives for children's services, and programmes such as *Choice Protects* (directed at improving quality of placement of looked after children), and the development of national service frameworks.

In Wales, *Children First* (originally, Welsh Office, 1999) operates in a similar fashion but is controlled by the Welsh Assembly Government rather than a UK government department. There are some differences in approach. Like *Quality Protects*, *Children First* involves payment of a grant for specified activities and is associated with centrally set targets and objectives. In Wales, these are linked to *Children and Young People: A Framework for Partnership* (the Welsh Assembly's strategy for partnership with local authorities in Wales) and *Extending Entitlement* (the Welsh Assembly's direction under s. 123 Learning and Skills Act 2000), both of which make explicit links to implementation of the UNCRC (see the discussion of both these strategies in Chapter 3). The UNCRC is clear about children's entitlement to family life and to substitute care in the event this is not available from the birth family, and also about their entitlement to special protection and provision when they are in that particularly vulnerable position. The Welsh Assembly Government's most recent consultation document, *Towards a Stable Life and a Brighter Future* (WAG, 2006b), continues this approach.

The establishment of a children's commissioner who could act on behalf of children was the first recommendation of the Waterhouse Report, *Lost in Care* (TSO, 2000). Effective complaints and advocacy services for all looked after children and for those in NHS care were recommended respectively by the Waterhouse Report and by the Carlile Report, *Too Serious a Thing* (NAW, 2002). These recommendations, arising out of inquiries into serious abuses of children in institutional care, influenced government policy for the establishment of the Children's Commissioner for Wales, Children's Rights Director for England and the English Children's Commissioner (see Chapter 4). They also influenced the introduction of statutory advocacy services for children under ss. 26 and 26A Children Act 1989 as amended by the Adoption and Children Act 2002. A report and recommendations on complaints, advocacy and whistle-blowing procedures by the Children's Commissioner for Wales, *Telling Concerns* (CCfW, 2003), identified continuing problems in the implementation of adequate protection for children in this regard. The following extract eloquently encapsulates the problem that any system for corporate parenting must struggle to address:

there seems to be a significant difference between how a parent is able to respond to a child or young person raising concerns, and how the corporate parent responds to children who are looked after. A reasonable parent would be able to give an immediate response and explanation of what will happen or how the issue will be resolved so that the child or young person knows that they have been heard. The experience is very different for a child who is looked after. The current process can be extremely bureaucratic and remote with certain decisions only able to be made by the Director of Social Services or even by full council. (CCfW, 2003: 12)

Clearly, seeking to replicate parental care by means of bureaucratic processes is inherently difficult. This has contributed to a policy preference on the part of the UK Government for greater use of adoption or, failing adoption, some other form of 'forever family' as the permanency choice for children unable to live with their birth families. In 2000, the Prime Minister commissioned a review of adoption. This led to a White Paper, *Adoption, A New Approach* (DoH, 2000), followed by legislative changes in the Adoption and Children Act 2002. This Act replaced the former scheme for adoption under the Adoption Act 1976. The main underlying policy aims are to:

- substantially increase the number of children adopted from the looked after system;
- simplify and streamline the adoption process;
- provide more, targeted and continuous support for adoptive families;
- apply the paramountcy of welfare principle to decisions to place children for adoption and for adoption itself;
- introduce a new type of order – 'special guardianship' – to provide permanence and stability for looked after children who cannot return to their birth family but for whom adoption is not the most suitable option.

It remains the case that adoption is an option in practice mainly for younger children. In the year ending 31 March 2006, 64% (63% in Wales) of children adopted were in the age group one to four and 26% (27% in Wales) were between five and nine. Thus in both England and Wales only 10% were aged under one or over nine.

Rights, powers and duties

Box 8.1 shows the relevant UNCRC and ECHR requirements, and the domestic provisions most consonant with them.

Box 8.1   CONVENTION RIGHTS AND DOMESTIC LAW

UNCRC: rights and obligations	ECHR: rights and obligations	Law in England and Wales
The 'four pervasive themes':		
1. Protection from discrimination (Art. 2)	Non-discrimination in enjoyment of convention rights (Art. 14)	Protection from discrimination: Equality Act 2006 and anti-discrimination Acts (Chapter 2) Children Act 2004: 'outcomes' aimed at reducing social exclusion
		Duty to give due consideration to child's racial origin, cultural and linguistic background: s. 22(5) Children Act 1989

(Continued)

197

UNCRC: rights and obligations	ECHR: rights and obligations	Law in England and Wales
2. Best interests to be a primary consideration in all matters concerning children (Art. 3) 3. Right to survival and development (Art. 6)	Right to life (Art. 2)	Duty to safeguard and promote welfare of looked after child: s. 22(3) Children Act 1989 Statutory requirements to assess and provide for education and health services for looked after children: Children Act 1989
4. Right to have views taken into account (Art. 12)	Right to fair hearing in determination of civil rights and obligations (Art. 6); implied procedural requirements in Art.8.2 to justify continuing interference with Art. 8.1	Duty to ascertain and give due consideration to views of child and family members: s. 22(4), (5) Children Act 1989. Advocacy arrangements: ss. 26, 26A Children Act 1989
Right to familial relations and contact (Arts. 9 and 10)	Right to respect for home, family and private life (Art. 8)	s. 34 Children Act 1989: duty to facilitate familial contact
Protection from all forms of abuse (Art. 19) Special protection where deprived of family environment (Art. 20)	Arts. 2 and 3 generate positive obligation: *Z v United Kingdom* (see Chapter 1)	s. 22 Children Act 1989: general duty to looked after children; other child protection provisions (see Chapter 6)
Paramountcy for adoption (Art. 21)	*Pini and Bertani v Romania [2004]*: the best interests of the children outweigh the rights of prospective adopters even where an adoption order has been made	s. 1 Adoption and Children Act 2002: the welfare of the child, throughout the child's life, is the paramount consideration, both for the court and for adoption agencies making decisions in relation to an adopted child

UNCRC: rights and obligations	ECHR: rights and obligations	Law in England and Wales
Special protection for children seeking asylum (Art. 22)		
Periodic review of looked after children (Art. 25)	Justification under Art 8.2 needs to continue – lack of adequate review of children in care may lead to breach: **Re S, Re W**	s. 26 Children Act 1989: statutory reviews of looked after children Care Standards Act 2000: systematic standard-setting and inspection of residential care
Protection of liberty and from torture, cruel, inhuman or degrading treatment or punishment (Art. 37)	Right to liberty (Art. 5) Right not to suffer torture, inhuman or degrading treatment (Art. 3)	s. 25 Children Act 1989 requires court authority for secure accommodation: full due process rights apply: **Re K (Secure Accommodation: right to liberty) [2002]**
Measures to promote physical and psychological recovery where abuse has occurred (Art. 39)		s. 22 Children Act 1989 and Children (Leaving Care) Act 2000, which extends duties to looked after children beyond 16

The UNCRC

Column 1 of the table in Box 8.1 shows a number of UNCRC provisions of particular relevance to looked after children. The basic propositions are set out in Article 20 which provides that a child temporarily or permanently deprived of his or her family environment, or in whose own best interests cannot be allowed to remain in that environment, is entitled to special protection and assistance provided by the State. National laws must ensure alternative care, whether by foster placement, adoption or placement in a suitable institution. In considering solutions, the authorities must pay due regard to a child's ethnic, religious, cultural and linguistic background. Other UNCRC articles deal in more detail with aspects of care such as periodic review, familial contact and the need for rehabilitative services.

In its Concluding Observations on the UK's Second Periodic Report under the UNCRC (UN, 2002a), the UN Committee welcomed some developments in provision for children living away from home, including the extension of duties to children leaving care in the Children (Leaving Care) Act 2000. However, the Committee expressed concerns about:

- discrimination, both against children in the care system and those leaving care in the 16–18 age group;
- the prevalence of violence against children in the care system;
- the relative lack of basic educational attainment of children in the care system and inequality in access to education for looked after children;
- the particularly vulnerable position of asylum-seeking children and the failure in many cases properly to assess and provide accommodation and support for them as children in need.

On the last point concerning asylum-seeking children, the UN Committee has issued a General Comment (UN, 2005), drawing attention to and elaborating upon the requirement in Article 22.2 UNCRC. Article 22.2 requires that such children must be accorded the same protection under Article 20 as any other child permanently or temporarily deprived of his or her family environment. The UN Committee's General Comment sets out basic expectations of alternative care applicable to all looked after children, which must equally be applied to those seeking asylum:

- children should not, as a general rule, be deprived of liberty;
- changes in residence should be limited to where this is in the best interests of the child;
- family contact should be maintained;
- siblings should be kept together;
- arrangements should be made for regular supervision and assessment;
- interim care arrangements should provide not only for the child's security and physical and emotional care but also the child's general development;
- children should be kept informed of all care decisions and their opinions must be taken into consideration;
- access to formal and informal educational facilities should be ensured including for children with special needs and/or disability. (UN, 2005: para. 40)

Pre-dating the UNCRC, the UN had adopted in 1986 the Declaration on Social and Legal Principles relating to the Protection and Welfare of Children with special reference to foster placement and adoption nationally and internationally (UN, 1986). This Declaration placed the best interests of the child as the 'paramount' consideration in any decision as to placement outside the care of the child's own parents. This is the position taken in Article 21 UNCRC in relation to adoption, and has been the formal position in the law of England and Wales since commencement of s.1 Adoption and Children Act 2002.

We have seen in Chapter 6 that compulsory measures (which will have been used in the case of many looked after children) always engage children's rights under Article 8 ECHR, and normally also those of related adults. Any interference with Article 8 rights by a public authority must be justifiable under Article 8.2. As Munby J said in *Re L (Care Proceedings: Human Rights Claims)* [2004]:

> the substantive and procedural guarantees afforded to parents by Article 8 of the European Convention apply at all stages of child protection ... not merely when the care proceedings are on foot but also after the care proceedings have come to an end ...

In other words, there is a need for continuing justification, for review and evaluation against human rights standards. Once a care order has been made, this falls to be done largely within administrative rather than judicial processes – that is, by the local authority not by the courts. However, since s. 6 Human Rights Act 1998 makes it unlawful for the local authority carrying out its role to act incompatibly with the Convention rights, a failure so to act has the potential to generate a challenge in the courts.

It is important to note that the notion of 'private life' and possibly 'family life' may extend not only to a child's birth and kinship ties but also to those established pursuant to placement of looked after children. A number of cases in the ECtHR and in the UK courts have illustrated that the concept of 'family life' is an elastic one and much depends on the facts of the individual case (this is the way that Scott Baker J put it in *R (L) v Secretary of State for Health* [2001]). A foster placement *might* provide the basis of a 'family life' claim, so that a decision to change to another placement would constitute an interference with family life – although the ECtHR's comments in *Eriksson v Sweden* [1989] suggest that this would not extinguish the birth parents' claim to family life. Even if not sufficient to establish 'family life', a relationship between foster parent and child is certainly an aspect of a child's 'private life' under Article 8. In fact, any decision about the placement or treatment of a looked after child has the potential to give rise to a successful Article 8 claim, unless justified under Article 8.2. Process, purpose and proportionality are therefore watchwords for decision-making in relation to looked after children just as much as when considering and applying for compulsory measures.

Process, purpose, proportionality

Process
The ECHR's concept of fairness requires the provision of information to parents and enabling them to make their views known before decisions

are made. In *Re G (Care: Challenge to Local Authority's Decision)* [2003], Munby J said:

The fact that a local authority has parental responsibility for children pursuant to section 33(3)(a) of the Children Act 1989 does not entitle it to take decisions about those children without reference to, or over the heads of, the children's parents. A local authority, even if clothed with the authority of a care order, is not entitled to make significant changes in the care plan, or to change the arrangements under which the children are living, let alone to remove the children from home if they are living with their parents, without properly involving the parents in the decision-making process and without giving the parents a proper opportunity to make their case before a decision is made. After all, the fact that the local authority also has parental responsibility does not deprive the parents of their parental responsibility.

Re G is one of a number of cases in which a lack of openness and fairness towards the parents of children subject to care orders was exposed as a violation of Article 8 ECHR. It is only in recent years that attention has also turned to the need for openness and fairness towards the children themselves. In *Re S, Re W* [2002] both the Court of Appeal and the House of Lords noted the particularly vulnerable position of looked after children in terms of protection of the procedural aspect of their Article 8 rights. In one of these cases, a care order was made in respect of two children on the basis of a care plan which included family therapy and other support with a view to the children's rehabilitation with the mother. After the care order was made, the local authority failed to implement these aspects of the plan. The Court of Appeal considered that there was a risk in this situation that the Article 8 ECHR rights of children and their families could be breached without any effective means of redress, especially where there was in practice no one to pursue the case on behalf of a young child. Applying the interpretive duty in s. 3 Human Rights Act 1998, the Court of Appeal created a new system of 'starred milestones' which would enable a case to be brought back to court after a care order had been made. The House of Lords rejected this initiative, holding that it went too far against the clear policy of the Children Act 1989 and that any change in the law needed to come from Parliament, not the courts. But the lack of effective protection for looked after children had been signposted, and this influenced the government's decision to introduce, in the Adoption and Children Act 2002, statutory reviews by an Independent Reviewing Officer and provision of advocacy services for looked after children. These measures are explained further under *Domestic provisions* later in this chapter.

The due process rights of the looked after child are especially significant in relation to the imposition of additional restrictions. We have already noted (Chapter 1 and Box 8.1) that secure accommodation authorised under s. 25 Children Act 1989 has been held to be compatible with Article 5 ECHR, thanks to a generous interpretation by the Court of Appeal of the notion of 'educational supervision' for the purposes of Article 5 in

Re K (Secure Accommodation: right to liberty) [2001]. However, in another case, *Re M (A Child) (Secure Accommodation)* [2001] the court acknowledged the severity of the restriction on a child's liberty when placed in secure accommodation and held that even though an application for the court's authority to place a child in secure accommodation is not a criminal procedure, the child is entitled to the full protection required by Article 6.2 ECHR (which sets out minimum standards of protection for persons accused of criminal offences). This means that a child facing an application for a secure accommodation order must be informed promptly of the application, be given adequate time and facilities for the preparation of a defence, the opportunity to participate and be legally represented, to have the free assistance of an interpreter if required and to examine witnesses.

Purpose

The ECtHR has repeatedly made clear that the taking of a child into public care 'should normally be regarded as a temporary measure, to be discontinued as soon as circumstances permit, and that any measures implementing such care should be consistent with the ultimate aim of reuniting the natural parent and the child' (*KA v Finland* [2003]). The ECtHR has acknowledged that reunification may not always be possible or consistent with the best interests of the child, but calls for strict scrutiny of any additional restrictions on parental contact and for regular review of the necessity for the steps taken (*K and T v Finland* [2001]; *Eriksson v Sweden* [1989]). It is therefore inappropriate to adopt a 'single track' approach in which it is assumed that a looked after child is destined for permanent alternative care unless it is crystal clear at the point of the child's reception into care that a return home is not going to be possible at a later stage. What the ECtHR expects is not reunification at all costs but (as the ECtHR put it in *KA v Finland*) 'serious and sustained effort on the part of the social welfare authority directed towards facilitating a possible family reunification'. Of course, while such effort is taking place, the child's long-term future remains uncertain and this brings into play the 'no delay' principle in s. 1(2) Children Act 1989. The development of 'twin tracking', discussed under *Domestic provisions* below, was therefore an essential tool to ensure compliance with the ECtHR's interpretation of Article 8 while avoiding unnecessary delay in finding a permanent alternative placement if efforts towards rehabilitation fail.

Proportionality

The aim must be family reunification unless this would be contrary to the child's best interests. Proportionality requires that steps taken must be proportionate to the aim underlying the interference – typically, securing the child's safety. *Eriksson v Sweden* [1989] demonstrates that if the required 'serious and sustained effort' towards reunification is not made but that with it, family reunification could reasonably be expected to be achieved, the continuance of the interference (i.e. the child continuing to be in care) is likely to be considered disproportionate to the aim which justified the initial interference. *Olsson v Sweden* **[1988]** demonstrates that geographical placement may attract criticism as being disproportionate if, for example, as in that case, it restricts familial contact between siblings or between children and their parents by placing too great a geographical distance for regular contact to take place.

Domestic provisions

Part III of, and Pts, II and III, Sched. 2, Children Act 1989, and associated Regulations, set out the general principles and regulatory framework. The main regulations governing reception into care and placement are the Placement of Children (Wales) Regulations 2007 and the Arrangements for Placement of Children (General) Regulations 1991. References to 'the Placement Regulations' in this chapter are to both sets of Regulations. A process for decision-making and review is provided by the Review of Children's Cases Regulations 1991. These Regulations cover both England and Wales but important amendments made in 2004, introducing the IRO (independent reviewing offices) system, are contained in separate amending regulations for England and Wales. References in this chapter to 'the Review Regulations' are to the composite regulations for both England and Wales.

There are further regulations made principally under the Children Act 1989 and Care Standards Act 2000 governing arrangements for fostering and for children's homes. Following implementation of the Adoption and Children Act 2002 there are regulations governing the process for adoption, special guardianship, provision of post-placement support services and the constitution, role and functions of adoption panels. A useful point of reference for the English and the Welsh regulations and associated guidance is the website maintained by the British Association for Adoption and Fostering (www.baaf.org.uk).

General principles

The general principles can be summarised by reference to the three pervasive themes of child care law and policy (see Chapter 2) – the best interests and development of the child, support for family unity and respect for the agency of the child. The following illustrations include some examples of tensions as well as consonance with these principles.

Best interests and development
Section 22(3)(a) Children Act 1989 imposes on the local authority the duty to safeguard and promote the welfare of children looked after by it. This is subject to a power to do what seems necessary to protect the public (s.22(6)), so that in practice community safety considerations may take precedence over the child's interests (*R (M (A child)) v Sheffield Magistrates Court* **[2004]**,

discussed in Chapters 1 and 9). Section 23(1) imposes a specific duty to provide accommodation and other aspects of maintenance and the Placement Regulations require a local authority to consider specified factors about the child's health and education when making arrangements. In respect of disabled children, there is a rather half-hearted duty to ensure that the accommodation is 'not unsuitable' to the child's particular needs (s. 22(8) Children Act 1989). The tensions that arise in relation to these 'provision' duties predominantly concern availability of appropriate placements and support services and competing demands for resources.

Support for family unity

Section 22(3)(b) Children Act 1989 requires a local authority to make such use as appears reasonable of services available for children cared for by their own parents. Section 23(6) goes further and requires that a child be placed in what is often termed 'family and friends care' unless this is not reasonably practicable or is inconsistent with the child's welfare. Of course, private kinship care predates the modern welfare state and is thought to account for a greater number of children cared for other than by birth parents than the statutory looked after children system (Hunt, 2001: 4). Such arrangements attract no regulatory control unless the child is placed with someone who neither has parental responsibility nor is a close relative. In that case, s. 67 Children Act 1989 as amended by the Children Act 2004, and associated regulations and standards (DfES, 2005 / WAG, 2006) requires that the local authority be notified and that the authority takes steps to satisfy itself that the welfare of the child is being satisfactorily safeguarded and promoted. The dangers inherent in unregulated private fostering were brought starkly to public attention by the Victoria Climbié Inquiry (Laming, 2003). Some argue that it remains doubtful whether this particular instance of deference to the private sphere of family life adequately protects children and that a compulsory system of prior registration is required, rather than the enhanced notification scheme under s. 67 of the 1989 Act (Stuart and Baines, 2004: 73–75).

Whether or not a looked after child is placed in the care of family and friends, section 23(6) and (7) Children Act 1989 require that the child be placed at a geographical location near to home and with siblings, unless this is not reasonably practicable or is inconsistent with the child's welfare. Familial contact is supported by s. 34 Children Act 1989 which imposes a duty on the local authority to make arrangements for contact in relation to any child subject to a care order and by a requirement in the Placement Regulations that the local authority must not only consider arrangements for contact but must actively promote it so far as consistent with the child's welfare.

Respect for agency of child

Under s. 22(4) Children Act 1989 a local authority is required to ascertain the wishes and feelings of child, family and other relevant persons. Under s. 22(5) the authority must take these into account before making any decision with respect to the child. Under the Placement Regulations the local authority has a duty to agree arrangements for accommodation etc. with a child over 16 who is voluntarily accommodated and with parents or most recent carers of other children. Under s. 22(5)(c) Children Act 1989, in making any decision with respect to a current or potential looked after child, the authority must take into account the child's religious persuasion, racial origin and cultural and linguistic background.

Types of placement for looked after children

If a child is accommodated under s. 20 Children Act 1989 it is essential to secure consensus with the child's parents, if available, as to placement. The arrangements should reflect the fact that accommodation under section 20 does not restrict the exercise of the parents of their parental responsibility. The arrangements should also reflect active acknowledgement of the agency of the child, in a manner appropriate to the child's age and understanding. Where it is not possible to reach agreement the local authority must consider whether there is a risk of significant harm to the child if the authority's view does not prevail. If there is such a risk, compulsory measures should be considered as a means of safeguarding the child. If there is not such a risk, then the authority does not have the power to insist on a particular placement and must strive to find a compromise in order to discharge its duty under s. 20.

Wherever a child is looked after pursuant to a court order, the demarcation of parental responsibility between the parents, other carers and the local authority varies according to the type of order or combination of orders the court has made. In deciding which order or combination of orders is appropriate, the court must apply the paramountcy of welfare principle (s. 1 Children Act 1989 and s. 1 Adoption and Children Act 2002) and will consider carefully all the evidence and arguments about the child's current and future care. The court order determines the child's status and determines the degree of 'protection' from outside interference enjoyed by the child's carer. Box 8.2 shows the different orders the court can make, the effect of each one on the status of the child and the way each type of order allocates parental responsibility between the private and the public sphere. A residence order, special guardianship order or adoption order specifies a private person who will care for the child. A care order leaves the child in the looked after system with the local authority as corporate parent. A placement order is effectively a half-way house, putting the child on a route to a permanent home in the private sphere but in the meantime remaining looked after by the local authority. Once a child is adopted, the adoptive parents acquire all aspects of parental responsibility to the exclusion of all others. Even pre-agreed contact with birth parents cannot be enforced by law once the adoption order has been made, the child's care and all decisions about the child's upbringing having transferred to the private sphere of the adoptive family. After adoption, the birth parents are not precluded from applying to the court for leave to seek a contact or other order under s. 8 Children Act

Box 8.2   COURT ORDERS: EFFECT ON PARENTAL RESPONSIBILITY

Court order	Statutory provision/ regulation	Effect on child's status and on parental responsibility
Residence order Can be applied for by private person seeking residence order, e.g. a family member or foster carer (after one year of fostering the child), or may be imposed by court	s. 8 Children Act 1989 s. 10 Children Act 1989 as amended by Adoption and Children Act 2002 (governs who may apply)	The order determines with whom the child should live. The person in whose favour the order is made gets parental responsibility but shares it with others having parental responsibility (e.g. birth parents). Can be made in relation to a child subject to a care order or a special guardianship order: in this case responsibility for the child's care is shared between the person with a residence order and the local authority
Residence order with supplementary provision Supplementary provision may be sought by private person, local authority or may be imposed by court	s. 8 Children Act 1989: contact, specific issue, prohibited steps s. 91(14) Children Act 1989: restriction on future applications	Residence order as above but supplementary provision can provide further protection and greater prescription about aspects of the child's upbringing
Care order Applied for only by local authority or NSPCC	s. 33 Children Act 1989	Local authority gets parental responsibility and can restrict the exercise of parental responsibility by others (e.g. birth parents) – but only where satisfied that this is necessary to safeguard or promote the child's welfare (s. 33(4) Children Act 1989). Child remains looked after and subject to the statutory system

(Continued)

Court order	Statutory provision/ regulation	Effect on child's status and on parental responsibility
Special guardianship order Applied for by prospective special guardian or imposed by court but must be a local authority report specifically directed to suitability of special guardianship	s. 14A Children Act 1989 (inserted by Adoption and Children Act 2002)	The special guardian gets parental responsibility and can restrict the exercise of parental responsibility by others (e.g. birth parents). Child no longer 'looked after' and statutory review systems do not apply, subject to any other order, e.g. a supervision order, made by the court
Placement order Applied for only by local authority	s. 21 Adoption and Children Act 2002	Empowers an adoption agency to place a child who is subject to a care order with a prospective adopter. Parental responsibility is shared between the local authority and the birth parents, and further shared with the prospective adopters once the child is placed. The child remains 'looked after' by the local authority (s. 18(2) Adoption and Children Act 2002)
Adoption order Applied for only by prospective adopter	s. 46 Adoption and Children Act 2002	Child treated in law as if born to adoptive parent (s. 67 Adoption and Children Act 2002). Accordingly adoptive parents get exclusive parental responsibility

1989, but they have no right to make such an application and in practice the courts are very reluctant to grant leave in the face of resistance from the adoptive family.

The Adoption and Children Act 2002 increased the potential for flexibility and creativity on the part of those involved in assessment and care planning and for the courts in identifying a formula that will best serve the interests of the child. The court can make a combination of orders to suit the individual case. In particular, special guardianship, introduced by the 2002 Act, provided a new option in the quite common situation where someone already in the child's life – often but not necessarily a relative – is willing and able to provide a permanent home, but adoption by that person seems inappropriate. This may be because it would 'skew' the reality of family relationships (for example where a child is adopted by an aunt or grandparent) or because it is simply a disproportionate interference with ongoing ties with the birth family (as for example in *Re B (Adoption Order)* [2001], where the child had a thriving relationship with his father whilst residing with a long-term foster mother who wished to adopt the child). In this situation, there may seem no reason for the child's care not to revert to the private sphere. One way of achieving this is for the court simply to make a residence order and discharge the care order but in some cases this will leave the carer inadequately protected from interference by others continuing to have parental responsibility. Sometimes it will be enough to make some supplementary order, for example restricting the possibility of future court applications (s. 91(14) Children Act 1989) or making one or more specific issue orders under s. 8 Children Act 1989. But if this is not enough, the position before the 2002 Act would normally have been that the child would remain in the looked after system under a care order, with all that that implies in terms of continued State interference in the private sphere of family life.

Special guardianship, introduced by the 2002 Act by way of adding ss. 14A–14G to the Children Act 1989, offers the looked after child in this situation a route back into the private sphere, short of adoption. A person appointed as a child's special guardian can restrict the exercise of parental responsibility by others, but the ties with the birth parents are not broken in the way that they are under an adoption order. The birth parent may have access to the court to determine contact or some specific issue concerning the child (unless restricted by an order under s. 91(14)) and may seek leave to apply to discharge the special guardianship if there has been a significant change in circumstances.

In some ways, the special guardian is in a similar position to a local authority with a care order, being able to exercise parental responsibility in a way which restricts the exercise of parental responsibility by others. In other ways, the special guardian is in a very different position to a local authority. The special guardian is a private individual operating in the private sphere of the family rather than a statutory body exercising public law functions. Accordingly, the special guardian is not subject to the public law constraints which apply to a local authority with a care order. This means that restrictions placed by a special guardian on the exercise of parental responsibility are not subject to the criterion of welfare (s. 33(4) Children Act 1989), the statutory system for complaints and reviews (s. 26 Children Act 1989) does not apply, the special guardian is not subject to the prohibition in s. 6 Human Rights Act 1998 against acting incompatibly with the child's ECHR rights and there can be no possibility of judicial review of the special guardian's decisions.

Three cases appealed separately to the Court of Appeal at the end of 2006 provided an opportunity for senior family court judges to consider the underlying principles of special guardianship and adoption and to give guidance on the approach to be taken by the courts. Each of the cases – *Re S (a child)*; *Re AJ* and *Re M-J* [2007] – concerned the question whether an adoption or special guardianship order was appropriate: in other words, the issue was what status the child, primary carer and birth parent should enjoy.

The Court noted that while the decision which order to make was governed by the paramountcy of welfare principle, special guardianship was a less intrusive order than adoption in terms of the child's link to the birth family and for that reason it may well better serve the principle of proportionality. Drawing on the White Paper *Adoption: A New Approach* (DOH, 2000), the Court noted that the purposes behind special guardianship were to:

- give the carer clear responsibility for all aspects of caring for the child or young person, and for making the decisions to do with their upbringing;
- provide a firm foundation on which to build a lifelong permanent relationship between the carer and the child or young person;
- preserve the legal link between the child or young person and their birth family;
- allow proper access to a full range of support services including, where appropriate, financial support;

and that examples of their use would include:

- older children who do not wish to be legally separated from their birth families;
- children being cared for on a permanent basis by members of their wider birth family;
- children in some minority ethnic communities, who have religious and cultural difficulties with adoption as it is set out in law;
- unaccompanied asylum-seeking children who need secure, permanent homes, but have strong attachments to their families abroad.

However, the Court emphasised that the decision was for the judge in the individual case, must turn on the particular facts and is certainly not limited to the above examples. The judge's decision must represent a careful balancing of all the factors and detailed written reasons must be given. The Court confirmed that a special guardianship order can be made without anyone having applied for it but that no order should be made unless a report directed specifically at special guardianship has been prepared by the local authority looking after the child and submitted to the court. For example, the carer may seek an adoption order but the judge, as in the case of *Re S (a child)*, may take the view that special guardianship is more appropriate. In that situation, following consideration of a report which the court itself may have to request, the court may impose the status of special guardianship on the would-be adopter.

Box 8.3 provides an example based on a practitioner's description of a real case, showing imaginative use of a combination of special guardianship, residence and supervision in a case which previously would have been likely to have been dealt with either by the child continuing in local authority care or by adoption (Eddon, 2007).

Where none of the range of methods for transferring a looked after child back to the private sphere is available, the child will remain looked after with the local authority, as corporate parent making all major decisions about the child's upbringing, within a highly regulated system of individual case management.

Box 8.3   IMAGINATIVE USE OF SPECIAL GUARDIANSHIP

In the course of care proceedings it became clear that Aidan was not going to be able to live with either of his birth parents. He wanted to live with his grandmother Mari and she was willing to care for him, but Mari was of an age when she might well become unable to cope with Aidan's needs as he grew into adolescence. Aidan's aunt Jo was willing to take long-term responsibility for him. On the basis of careful assessment, the court made a residence order in favour of Mari and a special guardianship order in favour of Jo. A time-limited supervision order was made in favour of the local authority as an additional safeguard.

Reception into care and individual case management

Under the Placement Regulations the local authority is required to keep a register of all children in care and to notify key agencies of the child's reception into care. Parents and any person who has been consulted about the arrangements for placing the child must also be notified. Under Pt. III of Sched. 2 Children Act 1989, the local authority can recover financial contributions towards the child's maintenance from the parents or, where the child is 16 or over, the child.

A statutory process governs individual case management of all looked after children. Under the Review Regulations, there must be:

- a first review of the case within four weeks of the child becoming looked after;
- a second review within three months thereafter ('the four month review');
- subsequent reviews at no longer than six month intervals.

These reviews are referred to as looked after children LAC reviews. Each LAC review must include:

- updating of information about the child, the circumstances of the case and the persons whose views should be taken into account before decisions are made;
- explaining to the child (if of appropriate age and understanding) the steps that s/he can take, for example applying for discharge of a care order under s. 39 Children Act 1989 or for a residence or other order under s. 8;
- consideration of whether any change in the child's status should be sought;

- review of contact arrangements, especially whether further steps to promote contact should be taken;
- consideration of the educational arrangements for the child;
- consideration of the child's health, medical and dental care and any screening, vaccinations etc. that may be required.

Each LAC review meeting must be properly minuted and a written record must be made of the decisions taken. These written records must be disclosed to those whose views the LAC review must take into account: the child, parents, any other person with parental responsibility and any other person the authority thinks should be notified.

In addition to the Placement Regulations, Review Regulations and associated guidance and standards, all local authorities should also have their own practice manuals setting out more detail of local procedures to be followed. The statutory guidance requires that these should include a requirement that unless already under consideration or already clearly not appropriate, a referral to an adoption team should be made before the four month review. This is to ensure that if adoption is the ultimate plan there is no delay in preparation of the case for consideration by an adoption panel. Accordingly an adoption team social worker will attend the four month review unless it is clear that adoption will not be the plan for the child. Parents, guardians and the child should also be involved in this process.

The Review Regulations require a local authority to appoint a 'responsible officer' who co-ordinates LAC reviews. The authority must also appoint an independent reviewing officer or IRO. Under the *Quality Protects* and *Children First* programmes and further encouraged by the judgment in *Re S*; *Re W* (above), many local authorities had appointed IROs within a non-statutory system of internal 'independent' review. The Adoption and Children Act 2002 gave statutory force to these arrangements. Crucially, in terms of ECHR compliance, the statutory system includes a means of referring the case to court, or back to court, if necessary.

The IRO can be a person employed by the authority but must be outside the line management of any person involved in managing the case. The IRO must be a registered social worker with sufficient relevant social work experience to undertake the prescribed functions, which are:

- participating in periodic reviews (normally the IRO will convene and chair LAC review meetings);
- monitoring performance of the local authority's functions in respect of the review;
- deciding whether it is appropriate to refer the case to CAFCASS and if so, referring it;
- helping children who wish to do so to apply to the court in their own right, for example for a contact order or to discharge a care order.

The role of the IRO is to improve care-planning and decision-making for looked after children, thereby contributing to consistency in the local authority's approach. The IRO has a particular responsibility to ensure that care planning and reviews take proper account of the views of the child and those close to the child. If a child wishes to take any legal action, for example to apply to vary or discharge the care order, the IRO must ensure the child has access to legal advice or that there is a responsible adult who will pursue the case on the child's behalf. As chair of LAC review meetings the IRO must ensure that there is clear allocation of responsibility for implementing care plans and other agreed action.

As a last resort, if there are problems that cannot be resolved within this system, the IRO is empowered to refer a case to CAFCASS Legal. Although the emphasis is on mediation and negotiation, such a referral can lead to litigation under the Children Act 1989, Human Rights Act 1998 or some other form of action. Normally, CAFCASS lawyers will deal with any Children Act 1989 application (for example an application on behalf of the child to discharge the care order), but where other proceedings are indicated (for example, an application for judicial review, a freestanding human rights claim or a claim for compensation for negligence) will take steps to ensure the appointment of a litigation friend for the child to pursue the claim.

'Twin track planning'

This approach is driven by four main factors:

(a) the no delay principle in s. 1(2) Children Act 1989;
(b) the UK Government's commitment to adoption as the permanency choice for as many looked after children as possible;
(c) the 'market' reality that the chances of finding a 'forever family' diminish as children grow older and spend longer in care;
(d) the ECHR requirement that a 'serious and sustained effort' must be made at family reunification.

The idea of twin tracking is that the local authority and the same social worker/team, will simultaneously plan for and work towards both rehabilitation and permanent alternative placement in the form of long-term fostering, special guardianship or adoption. If rehabilitation proves not to be viable, excessive delay is thereby avoided because the process leading to alternative placement is well under way.

Thus a social worker may need simultaneously to prepare for consideration of the case by an Adoption Panel, to complete assessments of parents or other potential carers for the child and to work therapeutically with the child and family. It is likely that at least four processes are active in relation to a looked after child at this point, as shown in Box 8.4. Research suggests that, while social workers recognise the need to twin track, it can cause frustration and confusion and some feel it may damage their relationship with parents, thereby increasing the likelihood of eventual placement away from the birth family (for example, Addis, 2004). This tendency may increase the risk of creating grounds for ECHR challenge and means that twin tracking remains controversial. However, it is the approach necessarily generated by the Adoption and Children Act 2002, the underlying policy of which is to secure a 'forever family' for more looked after children, and there is consistent evidence that without twin-tracking there is unacceptable delay in achieving any kind of permanent placement (Ward et al., 2003).

Box 8.4   TWIN TRACK PLANNING WITHIN CARE PROCEEDINGS

LAC process	Rehabilitative work	Adoption planning	Court process
'Responsible officer' convenes reviews and IRO chairs reviews and supervises process in accordance with the Review Regulations	Field social worker dealing with the child and family working for local authority exercising functions under Pts. III and IV Children Act 1989	Adoption team/specialist social worker working for local authority as adoption agency under Adoption and Children Act 2002	Case management judge sets timetable and gives directions with target of making final order within 40 weeks from issue of application
One month review

Four month review: plan for permanency | Participation in all reviews. Completing needs assessment (may include specialist assessment, residential/ community assessment). Placement and support plan, time scales and timetables (may be interim and final care orders with child placed with parents or other carers) | Participation in four month LAC review – latest point for consideration of permanency Booking adoption panel | Application for placement order cannot be made until positive recommendation of Adoption Panel is endorsed by the local authority as adoption agency. This may result in application for placement order very late in the day, so - |

LAC process	Rehabilitative work	Adoption planning	Court process
Six month and subsequent reviews: if placement order made, reviews under Adoption Agencies Regulations 2005	Placement and support plan may result in eventual discharge of care order with/without another type of order, e.g. residence or special guardianship, and with/without a continuing children in need plan. Or placement and support plan may fail, in which case divert to adoption planning	Preparation of assessment and supporting material: obtaining court's leave to use reports in care Proceedings, e.g. children's guardian's report, other expert reports	Include directions for 'ghost' placement application to avoid delay pending adoption agency decision whilst also ensuring fairness
		Presentation of case to Adoption Panel* for recommendation whether adoption will best serve the best interests of this child? Following a positive recommendation, adoption agency decision	Placement order suspends care order. Impact on contact – if care order, s.34 Children Act 1989 applies, if placement order, contact only pursuant to s.26 Adoption and Children Act 2002
		Communicating decision and care plan	
		Preparation of child and family	

*Panel comprising a maximum of 10 members, convened by but independent from the local authority as adoption agency, with a remit to consider and make recommendations on whether adoption is the right plan for a particular child, whether prospective adopters should be approved to adopt and whether a proposed match of a child to prospective adopters is the right match. These panels may also consider and make recommendations on other permanency plans, and may then be referred to as 'adoption and permanency panels'.

There is clear judicial support for twin tracking. In *Re D and K (Care Plan: Twin Track Planning)* [1999] the court recommended its use instead of sequential planning which it said was rooted in an outmoded view of adoption 'only as a last resort when all else has been tried and not succeeded'. Where a child is looked after pursuant to compulsory measures and there is uncertainty whether rehabilitation will be possible, the court said that both the local authority and the court had responsibility for ensuring minimum delay in identifying a placement for the child's long-term settlement. The local authority must therefore make it clear to the natural family from the outset that it is considering two options and the court should be proactive in enquiring of the local authority at an early stage in the court proceedings whether twin track planning is suitable and giving appropriate directions. The Protocol Case Management Checklist (see Chapter 7) includes questions directed at ensuring consideration is given to twin tracking and the possible making of a placement order, that there is no delay in filing plans for these even before a care order has been made.

It is not unusual for the outcome to be that the court decides whether to make a care order and a placement order (allowing the child to be placed with prospective adopters) at the same hearing. This practice has been given judicial support by the Court of Appeal in *Re P-B* [2006] and by the Children in Safeguarding Proceedings Committee of the Family Justice Council (FJC, 2007). In practice, judges will strive, through active case management under the Protocol, to ensure that this happens, and that it happens within the overall target of 40 weeks for final disposal of the case (see Chapter 7). This can place great strain on the professionals, especially social workers, in completing all the necessary paperwork and assessments. It also produces tension between the twin imperatives of avoiding delay on the one hand and fairness on the other. An application for a placement order cannot be made until the local authority is satisfied that the child ought to be adopted (s. 22 Adoption and Children Act 2002). This decision must be informed by the assessment and recommendation of an Adoption Panel (Box 8.4 above, and Adoption Agencies Regulations 2005; Adoption Agencies (Wales) Regulations 2005), which in turn requires preparation and submission of various reports and assessments. In *Re P-B*, this process was happening whilst preparations for the care proceedings were also ongoing. The local authority ended up making the application for a placement order three days into the final care hearing. The court permitted this to proceed and made a placement order, treating the evidence filed in the care proceedings as evidence in the placement application. Despite the placement application being made so late, the Court of Appeal found that there had been no prejudice to the birth mother because she and her advisers had known for some time that the authority sought to place the child for adoption.

Because the adoption planning process requires information and the fullest possible involvement of the birth parents, it may often be the case that a placement application made late in care proceedings comes as no surprise, but there are dangers in the approach taken by the court in *Re P-B*. A placement order is qualitatively different from a care order and it may often be that parents and carers and indeed social workers would wish to have space to update their understanding of all the information, to reflect and reconsider their position before being required to respond to a placement application. Some judges dealing with care proceedings seek to mitigate potential unfairness by giving early directions on a 'ghost' placement application in cases where it seems likely that before the date scheduled for the final hearing in the care proceedings the local authority as adoption agency may decide to apply for a placement order. In such a case, the court's directions would be very specific and detailed, for instance giving the latest date by which a medical report would have to be completed by the medical adviser to the Adoption Panel and the latest date by which an Adoption Panel would have to be held. The court would also grant appropriate permissions for disclosure of documents filed in the care proceedings for the purposes of presentation of the local authority's case to the Adoption Panel.

Placement and familial contact

The Placement Regulations prescribe considerations to which the authority is to have regard (these include general welfare, contact, the long-term plan, whether there is a need for permanent care other than in the natural family, the child's health and educational needs). As already noted, there is a preference for placement with family or friends and if this is not possible, at least for accommodation to be provided near the child's home.

The ECtHR has made it clear that there is, effectively, a right to familial contact which is a civil right for the purposes of Article 6 ECHR (*W v United Kingdom* [1987]; *Eriksson v Sweden* [1989]). This means that a court must have power to determine disputes over contact between parents and their children in care: it cannot be left to mere administrative decision. The court's power to make a contact order under s. 34 Children Act 1989 (on an application for a care order or interim care order), under s. 26 Adoption and Children Act 2002 (on an application for a placement order) and under s. 8 Children Act 1989 (in other family proceedings) is consistent with this requirement.

Section 34 Children Act 1989 provides that where a child is in the care of a local authority the authority must allow the child reasonable contact with parents, guardians or any person who had care of the child before the care order was made. It also enables a court, either on making a care order or on a separate application made by such a person or by the authority itself, to determine what contact is to be allowed. The court must consider the authority's proposed contact arrangements and allow parties to comment on them before making a care order. A limited discretion is left to the local authority to refuse to allow contact for up to seven days in a case of urgency where the authority is satisfied that this is necessary to safeguard or promote the child's welfare.

LOOKED AFTER CHILDREN

No mention is made in s. 34 of other family members such as siblings, grand-parents and others, but 'any person' may seek the leave of the court to make an application for contact. The importance of maintaining these wider family relationships has been recognised by the ECtHR in *Olsson v Sweden* (1989), where the implementation of a care order (but not the care order itself) was found to constitute a violation of the parents' Article 8 rights, due not only to the restriction on the parents' access to their children whilst placed in foster homes but also to the fact that the three children were placed in separate homes at a distance from one another, thereby restricting the opportunities for them to maintain contact with each other. The authority argued that the spe-cial needs of one child justified the particular choice of foster home and that it would not have been 'psychologically appropriate' to place the other two sib-lings in one home (because of the inclination of one to seek to take too much responsibility for the other). The court found that neither of these reasons jus-tified the interference with family contact, and that interference had jeopar-dised the chances of family reunification. Consequently the action was not proportionate to the legitimate aim of safeguarding the children's welfare and was not 'necessary in a democratic society'.

Post-placement support and children leaving care

Where a child is adopted or a special guardianship order is made, the Adoption and Children Act 2002 places requirements on local authorities to assess the need for and to provide such support services as may be required (s. 3 of the 2002 Act and s. 14F Children Act 1989 as inserted by the 2002 Act). This requirement is supplemented by regulations (Adoption Support Services Regulations 2005; Adoption Support Services (Local Authorities) (Wales) Regulations 2005; Special Guardianship Regulations 2005; Special Guardianship (Wales) Regulations 2005). The child's transfer from the public to the private sphere does not therefore mean that the State, in the form of the local authority, is relieved of any obligation with regard to the child's nur-ture. The 2002 Act's requirements are in principle consonant with the State's positive obligation under Article 8 ECHR to ensure respect for the child's pri-vate life and with Article 18.2 UNCRC which requires provision of appro-priate assistance to parents and legal guardians in the performance of their child-rearing responsibilities.

For those children who remain in the looked after system, LAC reviews will continue as the main forum for ensuring that the well-being of the child is being promoted. The Children (Leaving Care) Act 2000 introduced a specific set of responsibilities in relation to older looked after children, aimed at improving sup-port for them in their transition to independent life. These duties, set out in ss. 23A–E and 24A–D Children Act 1989 as amended by the 2000 Act, encompass the appointment of a personal adviser for certain children aged 16 who are or have been looked after, the drawing up and implementation of a 'pathway plan', assistance including financial assistance with accommodation, education and training. The responsible local authority is the local authority which last looked after the child, even if the child subsequently moves elsewhere, and the responsibility may continue up to the child's 24th birthday in the event that s/he continues in education or training to that age.

Accountability

In a wide-ranging review published in 2004 on progress on the recommendations made in *People Like Us* (TSO, 1997), it was recognised that much greater emphasis is now placed on listening to children and taking their views into account as an integral part of the looked after children regime (Stuart and Baines, 2004). It was noted that provision for this in relation to social services placements, centred on the complaints and advocacy provisions in ss. 26 and 26A Children Act 1989, was now markedly better than in youth offender institutions, schools and health settings. Yet the research evidence suggested that there remained a common perception on the part of children in the looked after system and their families that complaints procedures were unlikely to be effective in changing decisions made by local authorities. Furthermore, the procedures were often not well understood or practically accessible to children. There was particular concern about the position of disabled children, black and ethnic minority children (Stuart and Baines, 2004: 61–64). It is perhaps too early to gauge the impact on this of the introduction of IROs into the LAC review process. It is suggested here that a key component of significant change is to entrench on the part of social workers, managers and all those responsible for operating the systems an understanding of accountability rooted in acceptance of the obligation to ensure the full entitlement of children in the especially vulnerable position of being without the protection normally provided by the private sphere of family life; in other words, consistent with the pervasive theme of this book, a central and permanent shift to rights-based thinking and practice.

Conclusion

Stuart and Baines' review (2004) noted that, since *People Like Us*, in general, much had been done to improve the legislative framework, develop policies and produce guidance. What was less clear was the extent to which these had been implemented, and attention now needed to focus on ensuring that policy aspirations are translated into improvements. The social work role in achieving this in dealings with individual cases of looked after children is clearly pivotal, but the extent to which social workers, through their assessments, recommendations and engagement with the children and their families, will succeed depends not only on their personal qualities and professional competence but also on the organisational and policy environment in which they carry out their work.

That environment is less favourable in relation to certain categories of children living away from home than others. The position of disabled and black and ethnic minority children was highlighted, but Stuart and Baines' review found the position of children living away from home in prison establishments to be 'the most worrying area of all' (2004: 91). It went on to note, as have others, that the numbers of children in this category had risen as a result of new policies under the ambit of criminal justice and community safety. The next chapter is concerned with social work with children who come into contact with the criminal justice system and explores some of these problems further.

Further Reading

Adoption and Fostering, the Journal of the British Association for Adoption and Fostering (BAAF), provides an excellent resource for new developments in child care practice and research. Available online to BAAF members and subscribers: www.baaf.org.uk.

Further discussion of the impact of special guardianship, including a judicial perspective by Munby J and a summary of research evidence by Professor June Thoburn, can be found in L. Jordan and B. Lindley, *Special Guardianship: What Does It Offer Children Who Cannot Live With Their Parents?* Family Rights Group (2006).

The position of children who remain in the looked after system and make the transition to adulthood from care is examined in Stuart and Baines' cited report *Progress on Safeguards for Children Living Away from Home. A Review of Actions since the People Like Us Report* (2004). Critical analysis of the impact of policy change and structural changes under the Children Act 2004 is included in M. Stein's article 'Missing years of abuse in children's homes', *Child and Family Social Work*, 11 (2006), pp 11–21. A research report by R. Barn, L. Andrew and N. Mantovani for the Joseph Rowntree Foundation provides further insights into the different experiences of young people from a variety of ethnic backgrounds and, amongst other things, identifies a low incidence of recognition, including by the young people themselves, of any notion of their entitlement during or after care: *Life After Care: The Experiences of Young People from Different Ethnic Groups*, Joseph Rowntree Foundation (2005).

9

Social Work with Children in the Youth Justice System

- **Introduction**
  Role of social workers in the youth justice system
  Some facts about youth offending
  Policy choices and post-devolution divergence
- **Rights, powers, duties**
  The UNCRC
  The ECHR
- **Domestic provisions**
  Organisation, guiding principles and direction
  Powers
- **Process, purpose, proportionality**
  Case Studies
- **Conclusion**

Introduction

This chapter is concerned with the role of a social worker where a child becomes involved in the criminal justice system. The principal organisational system here is youth justice rather than social services/children's services. Although many front-line services are delivered or substantially contributed to by local authorities, upward political accountability flows through the Youth Justice Board for England and Wales, the police, prison or probation services to the Home Office rather than through local authorities' social services/children's services departments to the Department for Children, Schools and Families or the Welsh Assembly. The various formal roles that may be carried out by a social worker in the youth justice system, and the likely organisational position of the social worker, is shown in Box 9.1.

Role of social workers in the youth justice system

In addition to the roles shown in Box 9.1 it should be remembered that a local authority's powers and duties under Pt. III Children Act 1989 continue where a child is detained in a penal establishment (*R (Howard League for Penal Reform)*

Box 9.1 SERVICES LISTED IN S. 38 CRIME AND DISORDER ACT 1998 ('YOUTH JUSTICE SERVICES'), AND LIKELY ORGANISATIONAL POSITION OF SOCIAL WORKER INVOLVED IN DELIVERY

Service	Legislation	Social worker
Provision of persons to act as appropriate adults in respect of children in police custody	PACE Codes of Practice (Code C governs interviews) s. 65 Crime and Disorder Act 1998 (reprimands warnings)	Any
Assessment for and provision of rehabilitation programmes following police warning	s. 66(2) Crime and Disorder Act 1998	YOT member
Provision of support for children bailed or remanded for trial or sentence	ss. 34 and 34A Children and Young Persons Act 1933; s. 5(8) Children and Young Persons Act 1969	YOT member
Provision of accommodation for children remanded to secure accommodation	s. 23 Children and Young Persons Act 1969	Social services
Provision of reports or other information for the court	s. 9 Children and Young Persons Act 1969	Any: principally YOT members
Provision of 'responsible officers' for parenting orders, child safety orders, reparation orders and action plan orders	ss. 8 and 11 Crime and Disorder Act 1998 Powers of Criminal Courts (Sentencing) Act 2000	Social services YOT member
Supervision for community sentences	ss. 63–67 Powers of Criminal Courts (Sentencing) Act 2000	YOT member
Supervision for detention and training and supervision orders	ss. 103(3) and (5) Powers of Criminal Courts (Sentencing) Act 2000	YOT member

Service	Legislation	Social worker
Post-release supervision of children	s. 65 Criminal Justice Act 1991	YOT member Social services
Provision of secure accommodation for children serving the detention period of a detention and training order	s. 102(1) Powers of Criminal Courts (Sentencing) Act 2000 Joint Home Office/Youth Justice Board Circular *The Detention and Training Order* 9 February 2000, paras. 2.100–2.112	Social services

PACE, Police and Criminal Evidence Act 1984; YOT, Youth Offending Team.

v Secretary of State for the Home Department and Department of Health [2002]). A local authority has the same supportive and protective duties in relation to a child in a penal establishment as it has in relation to other children in the local authority area. The issue for the local authority is how, not whether, to fulfil these obligations. Since the *Howard League* judgment, work has been undertaken by the government together with the Youth Justice Board, local authorities and the voluntary sector, to devise the best way of doing this, including by funding local authority social work posts within young offender institutions (YJB, 2003; Hart, 2006). The indications are that there are real difficulties over identification, assessment, planning and management of these cases as the respective services struggle to carry out their roles in a complementary manner (Hart, 2006: 4–11).

The youth justice roles listed in Box 9.1 embrace supportive or protective functions such as acting as 'responsible adult' where a child is in police custody. However, many of the youth justice functions that may be carried out by a social worker are directed at ensuring, by provision of supervision and other services, that court orders are carried out and that the risk of re-offending is reduced. The social worker's functions include preparation and presentation of information for court proceedings, making recommendations about placement and treatment, providing supervision pursuant to court orders on remand or sentence, assessing future need and risk, making plans for the child's release and support for the child and family during and after custody.

In addition to these formal roles in individual cases, local authority child care social work teams should be represented in crime and disorder reduction partnerships (England) or community safety partnerships (Wales) and in multi-agency risk assessment groups in relation to related cross-cutting issues such as domestic violence, substance and alcohol abuse (see Chapters 3 and 4).

A major challenge for the social worker is that once an issue is viewed from the perspective of criminal justice, particular policy priorities and underlying 'child views' come into play which may be at odds with those which predominate in other areas of child care practice. In youth justice policy there is a long-standing debate about the relative weight to be given to the aims of 'welfare' and of 'justice', of 'treatment' and of 'punishment/deterrence', and the inherent compatibility or otherwise of these notions (for example, Goldson, 2000). The current position in England and Wales is officially presented as a successful synthesis of these aims: 'tough on crime, tough on the causes of crime', but the rhetoric cannot disguise the complexity and contradictions of the system. The difficulties are compounded by uncertainty about the actual effects of measures, whether aimed at the individual, the family or the community (Ball, 2004).

Some facts about youth offending

Key data are collated periodically and published in the Youth Justice Survey by the Youth Justice Board. Evidence from official and independent sources presents a fairly consistent picture of the nature and scale of youth offending (Box 9.2).

In the light of this evidence it is widely accepted that the risk factors indicating the likelihood of a child becoming a young offender and of being a victim of crime can be identified from birth, even before birth, and that they are the very same indicators as for risk of neglect, under achievement, drug and alcohol abuse and mental illness.

Policy choices and post-devolution divergence

Thus all the research undertaken into young people 'in trouble' indicates that they are also 'in need' and typically will have been 'in need' for some time before coming to the attention of the criminal justice system. The question then is what, as a matter of policy, is to be done about it at that point: that is, when the problem surfaces as a criminal justice issue. The approach taken will vary according to many factors, not least the underlying ideology. An ideology which prioritises children's rights will produce a child-centred response which, whilst recognising the consequences of offending for the victims of offending behaviour, will take into account the developmental capacity of the child and the extent to which the offending child's entitlement (in the broad sense of the UNCRC) has been and may in the future be facilitated. An ideology which prioritises retribution and deterrence will produce a response designed to be seen as more victim-centred, allowing of 'no more excuses' for offending behaviour once a certain threshold is reached in terms of the consequences for others.

Box 9.2 THE NATURE AND SCALE OF YOUTH OFFENDING

- A disproportionate amount of crime is committed by young persons, with peak ages for offending being 19 for boys and 15 for girls. Youth offending is common, with about a quarter of 10–17-year-olds saying they have committed an offence in the past 12 months.

- However, it is not true that 'most' crime is committed by juveniles, nor do juveniles commit a disproportionate amount of *violent* crime. Over half of the indictable offences committed by juveniles are theft or handling offences, and over half the juveniles serving custodial sentences have been convicted of non-violent offences.

- Most youth crime is relatively minor. Although they attract much publicity, grave crimes committed by children are rare.

- There are links between truancy, school exclusion and youth crime. The children who are most likely to be excluded from school are male, black and (overwhelmingly) those with special educational needs.

- Young offenders are more likely to have displayed aggressive and hyperactive behaviour in early childhood, to have suffered from a childhood mental disorder, to have had poor relationships with family, friends and relatives and to have under-achieved in school.

- There are links between alcohol and drug abuse and youth crime: apart from substance abuse, common reasons given by young people for offending include boredom, to get money, peer pressure/trying to impress friends and immaturity.

- Young offenders are more likely to be from families with low socio-economic status, and from areas of high social exclusion.

- Significantly, the same is true of the victims of crimes committed by young people; *and*

- The victims of offences committed by young people are more likely to be other young people. There are links between youth offending and being a young victim.

- Young people in ethnic minority groups are particularly at risk at all stages in the criminal justice system; from the fact that black young people are more likely to be stopped and searched or moved on than white or Asian young people through to the disproportionate number of black youths serving custodial sentences.

Such differences in underlying ideology account for some of the ECHR and UNCRC compliance issues in relation to the youth justice system in England and Wales. The UNCRC approach, unsurprisingly, prioritises children's rights. Through its case-law the ECtHR has made it clear that the ECHR implies special consideration for children's vulnerability and lack of developmental capacity (for example, *V and T v* **United Kingdom [1999]**). By contrast, in England

and Wales from the early 1990s there has been a shift away from a 'welfare' to a 'justice' orientation in youth justice policy (Labour Party, 1996: 9).

For example, while neither the ECHR nor the UNCRC stipulates a particular minimum age of criminal responsibility, the relatively low age of 10 in England and Wales has been noted by the ECtHR as being out of step with most European comparators (*V and T v United Kingdom* [1999]) and has been criticised by the UN Committee as being inconsistent with other age thresholds based on notions of developmental capacity (UN, 2002a; Beijing Rules (1985), Rule 4.1). While detention of children pursuant to criminal process is not in itself prohibited by either Convention, the consequent interruption in provision for children's educational and health needs and the risk of exposure to ill-treatment has been noted both by the courts, in the *Howard League* case amongst others, and by the UN Committee (UN, 2002a: paras. 48, 59–62). The lack of separate processes for children charged with serious criminal offences gives rise to compliance issues both under Articles 6 and 8 ECHR (*V and T v UK* [1999]; *S.C. v United Kingdom* [2004]) and under Article 40 UNCRC (UN, 2002a: para. 62).

While the Welsh Assembly has few functions in relation to criminal justice as such, the delivery of youth justice services falls substantially to local agencies and partnerships involving health, education and welfare bodies over which the Assembly exercises substantial control. A more rights-oriented approach is discernible in the *All Wales Youth Offending Strategy* (WAG/YJB, 2004), which makes explicit connections with UNCRC obligations and emphasises the need to ensure that children who become or are at risk of being involved in the criminal justice system have access to their entitlement as set out in Extending Entitlement (see Chapter 3). Through regulation, guidance and other direction of those services, there may be more scope for the establishment of a Welsh direction in youth justice than appears at first sight, but this will only be measurable over time.

Rights, powers and duties

Box 9.3 sets out the relevant UNCRC and ECHR rights and obligations together with the domestic provisions which equate most nearly to them.

The UNCRC

In addition to the UNCRC provisions listed in Box 9.3, other UN texts are of particular relevance to the implementation of the UNCRC, containing principles which the UN Committee expects governments to adopt. The texts are:

- the United Nations Standard Minimum Rules for the Administration of Juvenile Justice (Beijing Rules), the United Nations Guidelines for the Prevention of Juvenile Delinquency (Riyadh Guidelines);
- the United Nations Rules for the Protection of Juveniles Deprived of their Liberty; and
- the Vienna Guidelines for Action on Children in the Criminal Justice System.

Box 9.3   CONVENTION RIGHTS AND DOMESTIC LAW

UNCRC: rights and obligations	ECHR: rights and obligations	Law in England and Wales
The 'four pervasive themes':		
1. Protection from discrimination (Art. 2)	Non-discrimination in enjoyment of convention rights (Art. 14)	Protection from discrimination: Equality Act 2006 and anti-discrimination legislation (Chapter 2)
2. Best interests of the child a primary consideration in all actions concerning children (Art. 3)	Restriction on publicity where in interests of juvenile (Art. 6)	Separate processes and sentencing powers. Courts required to have regard to welfare (s. 44 Children and Young Persons Act 1933) ss. 17 and 47 Children Act 1989 apply when children in custody and prison authorities obliged to make welfare and protection a primary consideration: ***Howard League [2002]***
3. Right to survival and development (Art. 6)	Right to life (Art. 2)	
4. Right to have views taken into account (Art. 12)	Minimum procedural guarantees in criminal matters (Art. 6.2)	Children can be prosecuted from age 10 and as suspects and defendants have most of the procedural rights enjoyed by adults. PACE Codes, Youth Court and adjustments in Crown Court procedures are intended to help children participate effectively
Guaranteed minimum standards of procedure for children accused of criminal offences (Art. 40)	Art 6.2 limited variation between children and adults but concern over effective participation in practice: ***V and T v United Kingdom [1999]; S.C. v United Kingdom [2004]***	

(Continued)

UNCRC: rights and obligations	ECHR: rights and obligations	Law in England and Wales
Right to familial relations and contact (Arts. 9 and 16). Protection of privacy, home, correspondence, honour and reputation (Art. 16)	Right to private and family life (Art. 8). Issues arise over e.g. babies born in prison and ASBO publicity measures	Discretionary, subject to statutory rules
Protection from all forms of abuse (Art. 19). Protection from inhuman or degrading treatment (Art. 37)	Prohibition on torture, inhuman or degrading treatment (Art. 3)	Protection of criminal law continues. Statutory rules govern conditions, supported by inspections
Restrictions on deprivation of liberty (Art. 37) Freedom of assembly and association (Art. 15)	Right to liberty and security (Art. 5) Freedom of assembly and association (Art. 11)	Restrictions authorised by court order but some (e.g. child curfews, ASBOs) may raise proportionality issues
Recovery and reintegration of child victims (Art. 37)		Continuing duties of local authorities under Children Act 1989

According to the UN Committee, the philosophy underlying these texts 'predicates a child-oriented system that recognises the child as a subject of fundamental rights and freedoms and ensures that all actions concerning him or her are guided by the best interests of the child as a primary consideration' (UN, 1995a). The UN Committee published a General Comment on Juvenile Justice in 2007 (UN, 2007), spelling out the implications: a higher minimum age of criminal responsibility; preventative and diversionary measures and greater protection for children who do end up in court or in custody. 'Compliant' systems would feature clear separation of children and adults at all stages of the process, provision of adequate support, information and services for children involved in the youth justice system, promotion of family contact and reintegration following any period of detention and special training for those involved in the administration of the system. The UN Committee has approved compliant aspects of the system in England and Wales, in particular the use of restorative justice and community-based measures and the use of multi-disciplinary YOTs. However, the UN Committee has declared to be non-compliant the following aspects:

- the relatively low age of criminal responsibility;
- detention of children in penal institutions, and the conditions of detention in many cases;
- lack of segregation of child and adult prisoners;
- trial of children in adult courts;
- lack of protection of children's privacy.

(UN, 2002a)

The ECHR

Some of these issues also raise questions of compatibility with the ECHR. In the ECHR only Article 6.2 makes express reference to children in criminal proceedings, by excepting restrictions on publicity intended to protect children from the general requirement that criminal proceedings be conducted in public. Nonetheless, the ECtHR has made it plain that special provision must be made to ensure overall fairness for children in criminal proceedings. The relatively low age of criminal responsibility in England and Wales and the incomplete provision of separate processes for children raise questions about whether they can participate effectively for the purposes of Article 6. Exposure of child defendants to media reporting may engage Article 8. The conditions of children deprived of their liberty may engage Article 8 and, if sufficiently severe, Article 3.

Domestic provisions

Since 1997 there has been a major restructuring of the youth justice system and a repositioning of youth justice policy, catalysed by the 1996 Audit Commission Report *Misspent Youth*. The main new features are:

- the creation of the Youth Justice Board for England and Wales;
- the imposition of a duty on all agencies having functions in relation to youth justice to have regard to the 'principal aim' of preventing offending by children and young people (s. 37 Crime and Disorder Act 1998);
- concentration of functions within multi-disciplinary teams (Youth Offending Teams, or YOTs);
- the introduction of a range of new powers and procedures for the courts and statutory bodies;
- a step change in efforts to achieve a scientific appraisal of both the nature of youth offending and the impact of youth justice measures; and
- a drive towards a highly managed and targeted approach at local and national level.

Organisation, guiding principles and direction

Section 39 Crime and Disorder Act 1998 requires every local authority in England and Wales to establish a YOT, comprising representatives from the police, probation service, social services, health, education, drugs and alcohol misuse and housing officers. The aim is to ensure a comprehensive response to the needs of young offenders and those at risk of offending. The YOT is responsible for identifying and supplying or procuring suitable programmes to address the needs of the child within the overall aim of preventing further offending.

YOTs are required to have a strong focus on preventive work and to work together with other agencies such as the police, the Youth Service, Connexions and Drug Action Teams. To support this wider collaboration, the duty under s. 37 of the 1998 Act (to have regard to its principal aim of preventing offending by children and young people) covers any person carrying out statutory functions in relation to the youth justice system, whether or not they happen to be a YOT member, and information sharing between relevant authorities is expressly authorised by s.115 Crime and Disorder Act 1998 'where necessary or expedient' for the purposes of the Act.

The Youth Justice Board (YJB) is established under s. 41 Crime and Disorder Act 1998 and has advisory, monitoring, procurement and resource allocation functions. It produces the *National Standards for Youth Justice Services* ('the National Standards') and a series of publications under the heading *Key Elements of Effective Practice*. The National Standards require local protocols to be established between YOTs and other relevant services on various subjects including anti-social behaviour, child safety orders, suitable accommodation, education and training provision and the provision of suitable preventive and rehabilitative schemes. The National Standards also require that local service agreements be drawn up between YOTs and the local magistrates, Youth Court and Crown Court administrators.

The YJB sponsors and requires the use of certain assessment tools: ASSET, for children who have come into contact with the criminal justice system because of offending behaviour; and Onset, used as a referral and assessment tool with a view to early intervention before that stage is reached. YOTs are required to ensure that ASSET is completed for all children subject to final warnings, community-based penalties and custodial sentences. It is used in relation to bail supervision and support, pre-sentence and specific sentence reports, in the assessment, review and closure stages of community disposals and in the assessment, transfer to the community and closure stages of custodial sentences. YJB guidance acknowledges the potential overlap between these assessment tools and the Common Assessment Framework (CAF) (see Chapter 5) and promotes the use of all three in a complementary fashion whilst maintaining the distinct purposes they are designed to serve (YJB, 2006: 13–14).

Once children's behaviour comes to be seen as a criminal justice issue, the available powers fall into four categories. The first is not concerned only with criminal offences but with the looser concept of 'anti-social behaviour'. The second comprises diversionary measures applicable where an offence is thought to have been committed for which a child could be successfully prosecuted. The third comprises measures available to the courts on conviction. The fourth comprises 'ancillary' measures that can be taken once a child has been convicted for an offence.

Regulating the behaviour of children

The Crime and Disorder Act 1998 introduced a suite of provisions designed to equip local authorities and their partners to reduce the incidence of anti-social behaviour. The aim was to avoid some of the evidential and procedural difficulties that prevented other action such as trespass, nuisance, statutory harassment (under the Protection from Harassment Act 1997) being seen as effective and also to enable central government to have greater control over the use of powers by local authorities and their partner agencies.

The best known and most widely used of these powers, the anti-social behaviour order or 'ASBO', was not originally promoted as a measure aimed at youth offending, or at children at all, but rather as a means of addressing persistent offending by adults, especially where this caused suffering to others in their neighbourhood (Labour Party, 1995). Yet by 2005 just under half of all ASBOs were being made against under-18-year-olds and of these some 40% were followed by a prosecution for breach, leading in some 15% of cases to a custodial sentence. The consequent 'widening of the custodial net' (Macdonald and Telford, 2007) is one of several serious concerns about the application of ASBOs to children.

Local authorities are expected to have in place strategies to use these measures in conjunction with non-statutory approaches such as acceptable behaviour contracts and in partnership with police and other relevant bodies. Box 9.4 shows the conditions and effects of the powers and the social work role in their use. The hallmarks are restrictions on children's movements in public places and on their association with others, requirements to participate in rehabilitative schemes and criminal sanctions for breach (for over 10-year-olds).

Clearly, restrictions such as those shown in the 'effect' column in Box 9.4 may constitute a substantial interference with the exercise of the ECHR rights of the person subject to an order – notably the right to respect for private and family life (Article 8) and freedom of assembly and association (Article 11). As such, the interference must be justified: it must be in accordance with law, necessary in a democratic society, it must serve a legitimate aim and must be proportionate to that aim. Such justification may be made by reference to the statutory conditions and effects but subject always to

Box 9.4   POWERS TO REGULATE CHILDREN'S BEHAVIOUR

Power	Conditions	Effect	Social work role
ASBO: s. 1 Crime and Disorder Act 1998, supplemented by Police Reform Act 2002, Anti-social Behaviour Act 2003, Criminal Justice Act 2003	Application only by local authority, police or social housing provider Proof of anti-social behaviour and necessary to protect other person(s) Where made in respect of a 10–18-year-old, the court must make an individual support order if satisfied this would help prevent recurrence	Imposes restrictions (two years to forever) the court thinks necessary to protect other person(s) e.g. restrictions on going to certain places or meeting certain people. A civil order, but breach of an ASBO or individual support order is a criminal offence Publicity often given to aid enforcement	Providing information for consideration before deciding to apply for ASBO Supervision pursuant to individual support order Reporting breach of ASBO or individual support order
Child safety order: ss. 11–13 Crime and Disorder Act 1998	Proof of behaviour that would amount to an offence if child were 10, breach of child curfew order or child behaving anti-socially	Places child under supervision of responsible officer Requires child to comply with specified conditions If breached, court can make care order if s. 31 Children Act 1989 conditions satisfied	May be the 'responsible officer' and as such a report breach, leading to possible care order

Power	Conditions	Effect	Social work role
Local child curfew scheme: ss. 14, 15 Crime and Disorder Act 1998; ss. 48, 49 Criminal Justice and Police Act 2001 Power exercised police or authorities (not by court order)	Scheme must be for the purpose of maintaining order Local authority scheme requires confirmation by Secretary of State	Children banned from specified places at specified times Police may take a child home if in breach of ban Breach reported to local authority, which must then investigate under s. 47 Children Act 1989	Social services should be consulted before scheme is introduced Investigation and assessment in case of breach
Dispersal order ss. 30, 32 Anti-social Behaviour Act 2003 Power exercised by police with agreement of local authority	1. Child under 16 in a public place not under effective control of an adult: police must notify local authority where this power is used 2. Where authorised by senior police officer, police power to require a group to disperse or non-residents to leave a locality: police must notify local authority where this power is used	1. Police power to take child home unless reasonable grounds to suspect child may be endangered 2. Failure to comply is a criminal offence	Dealing with referral: investigation/assessment

examination of purpose, process and proportionality in each case, as demonstrated in Case Study A (below).

Certain aspects have surfaced as legal challenges. Because of the potentially serious consequences of breach of an ASBO, the courts have held that although an application is technically a civil rather than criminal procedure, the criminal standard of proof applies to allegations of past anti-social behaviour. Whether an ASBO is necessary to protect others is a matter of judgement for the court, for the purpose of which relevant facts must be proved only to the civil standard (*Clingham v Royal Borough of Kensington and Chelsea; R(McCann) v Manchester Crown Court* [2002]).

Another issue is the forum for applications. Although an ASBO is available as an order the court can make in a range of civil and criminal proceedings, most ASBO applications in respect of children will be made in the magistrates' court, rather than the Youth Court. Normally, therefore, an ASBO application in respect of a child involves placing the child in an adult court environment where there are no automatic restrictions on publicity. Indeed, official guidance clearly favours publicity as an integral part of anti-social behaviour strategies. The 'wider community' is expected to take a part in enforcement and this cannot happen without publicity. Some local authorities publish details of ASBOs made and the persons against whom they are made, with photographs, even including maps of areas in which the subject is restricted, on their websites or in leaflets distributed in the relevant areas. The courts have, on the whole, supported this approach, rejecting the argument that publicity of this kind is a violation of Article 8 ECHR, and tending to favour the view that in many if not all cases the balance between privacy rights and the public interest in addressing anti-social behaviour (which impacts on the rights of others) is properly weighted in favour of publicity (*Stanley, Marshall and Kelly* (see Box 9.11); *R (T) v St Albans Crown Court* [2002]). Further confirmation of this preference for publicity is reflected in the lifting of reporting restrictions for orders made on conviction in the Youth Court (s. 86 Anti-social Behaviour Act 2003).

In contrast to ASBOs, child safety orders were designed from the outset for children. Unlike ASBOs, they have been rarely used. They were presented as a supplement to the child protection powers in the Children Act 1989. Technically they reintroduce criminal-type behaviour by young children as a trigger for the exercise of the care jurisdiction (this having been deliberately removed by the Children Act 1989). However, the criteria in s. 31 of the 1989 Act apply to the making of any care order where a child safety order is breached so that in practice it is difficult to see what they may add to local authorities' existing functions under the 1989 Act.

Diversion from criminal proceedings

Diversionary measures are those which can be used as an alternative to prosecution and conviction, 'diverting' the young offender from a path leading to criminal conviction. The aim of dealing with children accused of criminal behaviour without prosecuting them is supported by the UN texts. In particular, Article 40(3)(b) of the UNCRC urges States Parties to adopt 'measures for dealing with … children without resorting to judicial proceedings, providing that human rights and legal safeguards are fully respected'. The idea is rooted in both pragmatism and principle: pragmatism because it is well evidenced that the criminal justice system does not reform children, especially if they are sentenced to custody, and principle because diversionary measures serve the best interests of children and their right to development (Articles 3 and 6 UNCRC) and, where accompanied by an element of restorative justice, may also serve the interests of the victim. The UN texts acknowledge that there is scope for variation on the theme within different countries, and that local factors should be taken into account. All, however, also emphasise the requirement of due process and fairness in any procedures adopted.

In England and Wales, until the Crime and Disorder Act 1998, the main tool was police cautioning. In the early 1990s it was perceived that this did not work unless accompanied by other steps. The UK Government's response in 1994 was to issue guidance, in the form of Home Office Circular 18/94, discouraging the use of more than one caution before criminal proceedings were contemplated. The 1998 Act continued along this trajectory by abolishing police cautions for under 18s and replacing them with a highly prescribed system of reprimands and warnings. These are summarised in Box 9.5.

Box 9.5 DIVERSION FROM CRIMINAL PROCEEDINGS

Power	Condition	Effect	Social work role
Reprimand and warning: ss. 65, 66 Crime and Disorder Act 1998	Realistic prospect of conviction if prosecuted	No prosecution but can be cited as if a conviction in future prosecution and prevents use of conditional discharge if convicted of an offence in next two years	'Appropriate adult'
	Informed consent (child must fully understand the consequences)		Assessment for rehabilitative programme
	Reprimand only where no previous reprimand or warning		Supervision and support, needs assessment
	Warning for more serious first cases or where previous reprimand		Reporting for non-compliance with rehabilitative programme

---

Box 9.6   'REDEEMABLE' DISPOSALS

Power	Condition	Effect	Social work role
Absolute discharge: s. 12 Powers of Criminal Courts (Sentencing) Act 2000	'Inexpedient' to inflict punishment	Guilt with no punishment	Contribution to presentencing report
Conditional discharge s. 12 Powers of Criminal Courts (Sentencing) Act 2000	'Inexpedient' to inflict punishment	Guilt with no punishment but if there is a further conviction within a specified time (max three years) a different penalty can be imposed in addition to whatever is imposed for the later conviction	Contribution to presentencing report
Referral order Pt. I, Sched. 1 Youth Justice and Criminal Evidence Act 1999	First conviction Child pleads guilty	Child attends before youth offender panel (YOT member + two lay volunteers) which draws up and supervises a contract. This may include restorative action. If the child does not comply, the panel can refer back to court. for sentencing	May be 'appropriate person' for the child before the panel May be YOT appointed supervising officer

The system of reprimands and warnings has been criticised on several grounds (Goldson, 2000; Evans and Puech, 2001):

- placing the decision exclusively with the police undermines a multi-agency approach to dealing with children in trouble;
- there is a risk, evidenced in early research into the operation of the system, that in practice responses to relatively minor offending will be disproportionately harsh, with

children with no more than two minor criminal transgressions being placed on quite intrusive and punitive 'rehabilitative' schemes;

- citation of reprimands and warnings in subsequent criminal proceedings 'in the same circumstances as a conviction' may tend to dissuade the court from using rehabilitative community sentences, thereby increasing the likelihood of a custodial sentence;
- restriction on the use of conditional discharges in subsequent criminal proceedings will make it more likely that a more intrusive disposal will be used, which may be disproportionate to the seriousness of the offence and contrary to the interests of the child.

The Audit Commission Report, *Youth Justice 2004*, supported some of these criticisms, and found that more training was required for the police to improve consistency in properly applying the system. It also recommended greater scope for not referring young offenders to rehabilitative programmes where their offence was relatively minor.

Powers in criminal proceedings

Non-Custodial, 'Redeemable' disposals The word 'redeemable' reflects the fact that these disposals offer the offender the chance to 'wipe the slate clean', either by simply not re-offending or by making amends in some agreed way. The menu of orders is set out in Box 9.6.

The lack of legal representation before a youth offender panel raises potential conflict with Article 6 ECHR which has not, as yet, been tested in the courts. In practice it seems that early experience of the referral order is largely positive from the point of view of all involved, including young offenders and their parents (Audit Commission, 2004).

Other Non-Custodial Disposals If neither an absolute nor a conditional discharge is appropriate, and if the case is not one requiring to be dealt with by a referral order, the court has a wide range of other measures from which to choose, either in combination or alone. For example, a fine, compensation or reparation order can be imposed in addition to one of the 'youth community orders' aimed at controlling and improving the offender's behaviour. A summary of the orders available to the courts is in Box 9.7.

Custodial Disposals The UN texts stipulate that custody should be used as little as possible for children, and only as a measure of last resort. UK government policy supports this and s. 79 Powers of Criminal Courts (Sentencing) Act 2000 restricts the circumstances in which a custodial sentence can be imposed on any person. Yet in practice the UK has amongst the highest use of custody for children convicted of criminal offences in Europe. Children cannot be sentenced to imprisonment (s. 89 of the 2000 Act). The available custodial sentences are shown in Box 9.8.

As with all the powers described above, these powers to detain children are on their face justifiable interferences with the most obviously applicable ECHR rights: Article 5 (right to liberty) and Article 8 (right to respect for private and family life). They are authorised by law and serve the aims of public protection and crime reduction which are legitimate in any democratic society. But compliance issues relating to process, purpose and proportionality not infrequently arise in their application in practice, as illustrated in Case Study B (below).

Box 9.7   NON-CUSTODIAL DISPOSALS

Power	Condition	Effect	Social work role
Fine and compensation: Pt. VI Powers of Criminal Courts (Sentencing) Act 2000	For under 14-year-old, maximum fine is £250, and for 14–18-year-old, £1,000 Compensation-to maximum of £5,000. Person with parental responsibility (may include local authority) may be ordered to pay	Failure to pay attracts penal consequences	
Reparation order: ss. 67, 68, Sched. 5 Crime and Disorder Act 1998	Consent of victim	Failure to comply can lead to referral back to court to sentence afresh	May be 'responsible officer' supervising implementation of the order
Youth community orders: curfew, exclusion, attendance centre, supervision, action plans: s. 147 Criminal Justice Act 2003	Child assessed as suitable for a youth community order and a specific type of order is proposed	Failure to comply can lead to referral back to court to sentence afresh	Assessment or contribution to assessment of child as suitable

Supervision and support

Referral for non-compliance |

Ancillary Measures

These orders, summarised in Box 9.9, are aimed at changing the behaviour of those exercising parental responsibility or improving the effectiveness of their control over their children.

These orders reflect certain underlying assumptions about the exercise of parental responsibility, the agency of the child and the legitimacy of State interference in

Box 9.8   CUSTODIAL DISPOSALS

Power	Condition	Effect	Social work role
Detention during HM Pleasure: s. 90 Powers of Criminal Courts (Sentencing) Act 2000	Mandatory where person under 18 convicted of murder	Place of detention specified by Secretary of State	Assessment and support post sentence, pursuant to Children Act 1989
Detention for specified period: s. 91 Powers of Criminal Courts (Sentencing) Act 2000	Conviction for 'grave crime' other than murder Sentence cannot exceed maximum term of imprisonment that could be imposed for an adult	Place of detention specified by Secretary of State	
Detention and training order: ss. 100–107 Powers of Criminal Courts (Sentencing) Act 2000	Child convicted of offence that would be punishable by imprisonment in the case of an adult	Half of the time spent in secure accommodation, half under supervision	May be 'responsible officer' supervising second part of sentence
	If under 15, only if child is a persistent offender	Breach of supervision requirements can lead to return to secure accomm-odation or fine	
	Maximum duration two years		

private life. The power to bind over a parent is in the last resort a means of punishing parents for failing to exercise control over their child, demonstrating that the notion of parental responsibility has an outward (towards society) dimension as well as an inward (towards the child) one. The requirement of consent of a child of 14 or over before a drug treatment and testing order is imposed reflects assumptions about developmental capacity and can be compared to decisions relating to children's competence to consent to medical treatment (the notion of 'Gillick competence': *Gillick v West Norfolk and Wisbech Area Health Authority and the DHSS* [1985]). Interestingly, it is not the case that parental consent is

Box 9.9   ANCILLARY MEASURES

Power	Condition	Effect	Social work role
Drug treatment and testing: s. 279, Sched. 24 Criminal Justice Act 2003	Ancillary to action plan or supervision order Consent of child if 14 or over YOT member recommends Suitable arrangements are available		Possible contribution to assessment and supervision
Intensive supervision and surveillance	Ancillary to youth community order, bail or second part of detention and training order	At least 25 hours of purposeful activity must be provided each week	Possible contribution to assessment, provision and supervision
	Maximum duration six months	Electronic tagging and voice verification technology may be used	
Sex offender ss. 2, 3 Crime and Disorder Act 1998	Additional to any sentence passed on conviction for a sexual offence	Restrictions as deemed necessary by the court to protect the public from serious harm, for period at the discretion of the court	
Parenting order ss. 8, 9, 10 Crime and Disorder Act 1998, Pt. 3 Anti-social Behaviour 2003, Act Sched. 34 Criminal Justice Act 2003	Presumption that this order will be made ancillary to any child safety order, ASBO or sex offender order in respect of 10–18-year-old and any conviction of a child under 16	Parent required to comply with specified requirements including attending guidance and counselling sessions Failure to comply is an offence punishable with a fine	May be 'responsible officer'

Power	Condition	Effect	Social work role
Binding over (parent/ guardian)	Consent of parent/guardian (but if unreasonably withheld, court can fine up to £1,000) Maximum duration three years	Parent/guardian enters into recognisance (bond) for up to £1,000 to take care of and exercise control over the child	

required before the imposition of such an order on a child under 14. The implication is that if parental consent is not forthcoming, the treatment and testing may be imposed on children deemed too young to consent for themselves. Outside of this specific context, such a situation would normally require an application to the High Court in the exercise of its inherent jurisdiction to decide whether treatment is in the best interests of the child. The issue may not arise frequently, but if and when it does, it appears that the fact of offending thus puts the question of medical consent on a different footing, and it is not clear why this should be so.

Process, purpose and proportionality

Case Studies A and B below illustrate some of the issues that may arise in social work practice with children involved with the criminal justice system, focusing on the key notions of process, purpose and proportionality.

CASE STUDY A

A single mother of five children living on a council housing estate has been in receipt of services under s. 17 Children Act 1989 because of multiple difficulties she and the children experience. The two oldest boys, aged 13 and 11, both of whom have learning difficulties, are truanting from school and are alleged to be part of a gang on the estate which is responsible for various acts of harassment, verbal abuse and vandalism. The mother has admitted to her social worker that she is struggling to control their behaviour and finds it easier to cope with the younger children when the older boys are out. The local authority housing department and the police are now collecting evidence with a view to obtaining an ASBO against the two oldest boys and possibly prosecuting them for criminal damage.

Process

In Case Study A, since there has already been intervention under the Children Act 1989, the CAF will have been completed as well as any specialist assessments of the children's needs. When the problems manifest as criminal justice issues, the separate set of statutory responsibilities under the Crime and Disorder Act 1998 come into play, and the same local authority is obliged to consider using measures to reduce the impact on others of the older children's behaviour. Onset (above) ought to be used to address prevention of offending or further offending, drawing on information from CAF and other previous assessments. Preventive schemes may be available for the older boys. An acceptable behaviour contract might be considered. Underpinning these actions will be the clear threat of an ASBO application if the boys' behaviour does not improve.

At the same time, further need for support and services may be identified. The local authority needs to guard against a potential conflict of interest. In **R M (a child) v Sheffield Magistrates Court [2004]** the court had to deal with the case of a child in the care of a local authority which was also applying for an ASBO against the same child. In this situation, the court said that the local authority must still fulfil its duty to the public (as reflected in s. 22(6) Children Act 1989) but that particular care must be taken to ensure the rights of such children are not breached. Formal measures would include that a social worker handling the care of the child (or, as in Case Study A, the provision of support or services to the child and family) should prepare a report as information for the authority on behalf of the child. The authority's ASBO panel should ensure this is taken into account before making a decision to apply for an ASBO. The child care social worker should not be otherwise involved in the preparation of the ASBO application and in particular should not participate in the decision to apply for an order. The court should ensure that someone from social services can speak for the child at the hearing.

Purpose

Social workers, like any other persons 'having functions in relation to the youth justice system' are required under s. 37 Crime and Disorder Act 1998 to have regard to the principal aim of the youth justice system, to 'prevent offending by children and young persons'. They must have regard to this aim 'in addition to any other duty to which they are subject'. The social worker who has been dealing with the family in Case Study A must therefore reconcile the statutory duties under the Children Act 1989 with his duty under s. 37 Crime and Disorder Act 1998. This presents an interpretative and ethical challenge which goes to the heart of the tension between the aims of 'welfare' and of 'justice'.

The official line is that the statutory provisions governing child welfare and those governing youth justice are wholly complementary. After all, Sched. 2 Children Act 1989 requires the local authority to take steps to encourage children within their area not to commit criminal offences and to reduce the need to bring criminal proceedings against such children. This seems consistent with the youth justice system's principal aim of preventing offending by children and young persons. The action being considered by the police and local authority housing department would no doubt serve that aim. But it is questionable whether it would really 'safeguard and promote the welfare' of the boys and their siblings and promote their upbringing by their family, as required by s. 17 Children Act 1989. There is an inescapable tension here between the purposes of child welfare and public protection. As explained below, a rights-based analysis offers the best conceptual basis for reconciling the two purposes.

Proportionality

The principle of proportionality requires that any interference with the rights of the children and other family members must be only such as is necessary to achieve a legitimate aim. The effect of an ASBO, restricting the boys' freedom to associate outside the home, may be to increase the pressure on their mother to the extent that she would no longer be able to cope at all. First, there will be a public court hearing in the magistrates' court. Then, although an ASBO is not a criminal sanction, any breach of it would be a criminal offence for which the boys could be prosecuted just as they might be prosecuted for the offence of causing criminal damage. Whether or not the order is breached, there may be targeted but quite widespread publicity about the boys and their ASBOs. This action may send a clear message to others who behave in an anti-social manner, thereby contributing to the aim of preventing offending by children and young people in general, but at the cost of stigmatising two children who are known to be 'in need'.

A rights-based analysis

The dilemma can be reformulated in terms of a balancing of rights. Clearly an order restricting the boys' freedom of movement and association and which seeks to regulate their personal behaviour engages their rights under Articles 8, 10 and 11 ECHR and Articles 15 and 16 UNCRC. So far as the ECHR is concerned, interference with their rights must be justified and must be proportionate to the end to be achieved. On the other hand, the Article 8 ECHR rights of members of the local neighbourhood are also engaged. The ECtHR has held, as shown in Box 9.10, that the State may be required to take

---

Box 9.10   *SURUGIU V ROMANIA* [2004]

S complained of more or less constant interferences by M, S' neighbour, with the enjoyment of his home over a period of more than 5 years. This included numerous instances of trespass and disruptive activity by M which at one point forced S to move out temporarily. S argued that the State authorities' failure to use their powers effectively to protect S from M's actions violated the Article 8 right of S to respect for his home and private life. The ECtHR agreed.

---

positive action to protect people against nuisance behaviour by their neigh-bours. The case concerns adults rather than children behaving in an anti- social manner, but the reasoning is readily transferable, as has been recognised in the courts in England and Wales when dealing with legal issues arising from ASBO applications against youths: see Box 9.11. Criticism of the youth justice system tends to focus on potential violations of children's rights, but it should not be forgotten that the rights of other members of the community must also be respected and that a failure by the relevant authorities to exercise powers in a way that could help protect those rights may also constitute a violation of the UK's international human rights obligations.

Box 9.11 *STANLEY, MARSHALL AND KELLY V COMMISSIONER OF POLICE FOR THE METROPOLIS AND CHIEF EXECUTIVE OF BRENT COUNCIL [2004]*

On an estate in the London borough of Brent a group of youths was causing trou-ble, throwing stones and rubbish or spitting from balconies, damaging other people's property by graffiti, deliberately starting fires, smoking drugs in public, shouting and playing loud music, abusing and threatening residents. The local police together with the local council decided to apply for anti-social behaviour orders (ASBOs) and in September 2003 Brent Magistrates Courts granted ASBOs against seven youths. The police and local authority then decided to use publicity as a means of backing up the ASBOs. They published leaflets giving the names, ages and photographs of the youths and details of the restrictions contained in their ASBOs. These leaflets were distributed to local residents and similar information was published in the Council's newsletter and on the Council's website.

Three of the youths, aged 15, 16 and 18, complained that this publicity vio-lated their rights under Article 8 of the ECHR. The Court held that their Article 8 rights were indeed engaged, but so were the Article 8 rights (and also Article 10, 11 and 17 rights) of others. The State (in the form of the police and the Council) could be found to be under a positive obligation to protect the rights of past and potential victims of anti-social behaviour. It was necessary to balance the rights of individuals against those of the community as a whole. Publicity in this kind of case would be lawful provided it was necessary and proportionate to the legitimate aim, and in this case the Court found that the methods used by the Council were both necessary and proportionate so that the interference with the youths' Article 8 rights was justified.

This balancing of rights resonates with the Key Roles of social workers set out in the NOSCCPQ, in particular Key Role 4 (risk assessment and risk manage-ment) and Key Role 5 (support for people to represent their needs, views and circumstances) and with the requirement in the social work Codes of Practice to 'respect the rights of service-users whilst seeking to ensure that their behaviour does not harm themselves or other people' (Care Council for Wales, 2002; General Social Care Council, 2002). Specifically, child care social workers must have an understanding of the 'rationale of strategies for reducing crime and disorder in their area and the impact of offending behaviour on victims of juvenile crime as a means of challenging behaviour' (Sector Skills Council, 2005: Unit D).

In the balance between the rights of children who offend and the rights of other members of the community who may be affected by their offending behaviour, the key question is the weight to be attached to the child's welfare or 'best interests'. Article 3 of the UNCRC is clear: it must always be a 'primary consideration'. This is binding on child and family social workers as a matter of their professional standards. Children's interests include their interest in receiving their entitlement as envisaged by the UNCRC, so it would be right to consider the support given to the family in exercising its primary responsibility for the nurture of the children (Article 18.2) and the State's obligation to ensure their development (Article 6), to the maximum extent of available resources (Article 4). As 'a primary' not 'the paramount' consideration, the welfare interest of the child must compete with other interests. The advantage of a rights-based analysis is that it tends to prevent suppression of the child's welfare interest and articulates it in terms of entitlement to support as well as correction.

CASE STUDY B

Natalie was 14 when she participated in a serious attack on a man in the street. The other three defendants were Rhys, aged 19, Dan, 18, and Paul, 17. All four were convicted in the Crown Court of inflicting grievous bodily harm contrary to s. 20 Offences Against the Person Act 1861. Pre-sentence reports revealed their backgrounds. They had graduated from playing truant to roaming the streets wearing hoods to cover their faces and using mobile phone cameras to record their acts of violence. Natalie's parents had been addicted to heroin. When very young she was found wandering alone in the streets and was taken in by a relative, but when this did not work out she was taken into care at the age of seven. Since then she had had five placements and six changes of school and was due to move again at the time of her arrest. Rhys, Dan and Paul had all experienced multiple difficulties in their childhood and had several previous convictions. Natalie had been given a warning in the past for criminal damage in which the co-defendants had also been involved. At the trial for the assault, Natalie pleaded not guilty but did not give evidence. By the time she was convicted she was 15 and her sentence was an 18 month detention and training order.

Process
Both the UNCRC and the Beijing Rules require States Parties to establish laws, procedures, authorities and institutions specifically applicable to children alleged

to have or recognised as having infringed the penal law (Art. 40.3 UNCRC; Beijing Rules, Rule 2.3). These should be designed to meet the needs of children and safeguard their rights as well as to 'meet the needs of society' (Beijing Rules, Rule 2.3). Separate treatment of children in this way is deemed necessary in order to protect them and to enable them to participate effectively in the process.

In England and Wales, at the investigation stage, special treatment takes the form of the requirements of the Codes issued under the Police and Criminal Evidence Act 1984. Code C deals with detention, treatment and questioning of persons by police officers and this would require the custody officer at the police station to which Natalie was taken following her arrest to ensure the attendance of an 'appropriate adult'. As she was in care this might have been her foster carer, her social worker or some other person representing the local authority. Failing all of these, it could be any responsible adult not employed by the police. The extent to which this provides effective protection in practice is the subject of some doubt (for example, Parry, 2006). Natalie would be allowed to consult privately with a solicitor in the absence of the appropriate adult if she wished. Code C also requires she should not be placed in a police cell unless no other secure accommodation is available. After being charged, if she was held in custody rather than bailed to appear at court, she would be held in local authority accommodation rather than police custody – unless it was impracticable to arrange this.

The decision to prosecute Natalie would have been taken by the Crown Prosecution Service (CPS). The exercise of this discretion is subject to the Crown Prosecutor's Code issued under s. 10 Prosecution of Offences Act 1985. The Code lays down a two part test: the first part comprises a consideration of the evidence to assess whether there is a 'realistic prospect of conviction', and the second part is the question whether prosecution is needed in the public interest.

The Code recognises the need to have regard to the interests of children in applying the public interest test, but states that Crown Prosecutors should not avoid prosecuting simply because of the defendant's age. The seriousness of the offence, and the child's past behaviour are very important, and the Code states that cases will normally only be referred for a decision whether to prosecute when previously a reprimand or final warning (see above) has been administered. Subject to this, a prosecution will usually occur unless there are clear public interest factors against it. In practice, at this stage in the criminal process there is little difference in treatment of adults and children. It has been suggested that the CPS should be given a discretion to refer young offenders who commit minor offences but who have received a previous Final Warning to a youth offender panel without the need for a court hearing (Audit Commission, 2004). Given the seriousness of the offence in which Natalie was involved, these options would anyway be unlikely to be applicable to her.

When it came to the trial, Natalie was of an age where she might expect to be tried in the Youth Court, which is normally closed to the public, has a less formal procedure, layout and atmosphere than an adult criminal court, is run by specially trained magistrates and has a range of special measures available on conviction. These special features mean that, on the whole, the process in the Youth Court will be compliant with the UNCRC, Beijing Rules and the ECHR. However, some 5,000 children are also committed for trial in the Crown Court each year. This includes children charged with murder and other grave crimes and children charged jointly with adult co-defendants where it is judged that the interests of justice require them to be tried together. Hence, children as young as 10 can be tried in the Crown Court, where far fewer adjustments can in practice be made to take account of their age. Because Natalie was charged jointly with older defendants, it is likely that her trial would take place with them at the Crown Court in front of a jury: that is, it would be a trial on indictment as opposed to a summary trial in the Youth Court. Her social worker would have an important role to play, making representations on Natalie's behalf to the magistrates' court early in the process when that court would have had to decide:

(a) whether her case could be 'severed' from that of the older defendants; and
(b) whether it was appropriate for her to be tried on indictment or by summary trial (this question arises because the offence under s. 20 Offences Against the Person Act 1861 is 'triable either way', meaning that the magistrates can decide to try the case summarily or can commit the defendant to the Crown Court for trial).

Assuming she was committed for trial with the other defendants, she would then be in a situation that has been recognised as problematic in terms of the ECHR, UNCRC and the Beijing Rules. The leading case is *V and T v United Kingdom* **[1999]**, where the ECtHR found breaches of Article 6 in that, despite modifications as to the duration of the court's sittings and efforts by the judge to ensure the child defendants could understand what was going on, the formality and ritual of the trial was incomprehensible and intimidating and, given evidence about their disturbed emotional state, they were unable to participate effectively in the trial. A minority of the Court thought that the conditions were sufficient also to breach Article 3.

The UN Committee has made it clear that compliance with the UNCRC requires that 'no child can be tried as an adult, irrespective of the circumstances or the gravity of his/her offence', and that 'the privacy of all children in conflict with the law is fully protected' (UN, 2002: para. 62). Continued use of adult courts, albeit in a minority of cases, is in conflict with this position.

Following the ECtHR's decision in *V and T v United Kingdom*, a Practice Note was issued for the courts, aimed at avoiding any future violation of the rights of a child defendant tried in the Crown Court. The Practice Note specified considerations to be taken into account before, during and after the trial, including further adjustments to the physical court room environment aimed at reducing the sense of formality and intimidation. It emphasised the need to

CHILDREN IN THE YOUTH JUSTICE SYSTEM

have regard to the welfare of the young defendant in accordance with s. 44 Children and Young Persons Act 1933. Despite this, potential for incompatibility with Article 6 ECHR remains: in *S.C. v United Kingdom* **[2004]** (Box 9. 12) the ECtHR found the UK to have violated a child's Article 6 rights despite full compliance with the Practice Direction. This case provides a good example of the difficulties presented both for the child and for the child's social worker when a child is tried in an adult court.

Box 9.12   *S.C. V UK* (2004)

S.C., aged 11, along with a 14-year-old co-defendant, was tried and convicted for attempted robbery in the Crown Court. S.C. had a low IQ and a mental age of around 8 or lower but the judge thought S.C. was 'streetwise': S.C. had a history of offending despite his young age, and had an 'appalling' family background. He was sentenced to two and a half years' detention. At the trial the Practice Note had been followed meticulously. His social worker was allowed to be with him to explain what was going on, he was not required to sit in the dock, the court took frequent breaks and dispensed with wigs and gowns. The hearing took only one day, evidence being given by two eye witnesses, S.C. himself (who said he had acted under duress from the older boy) and S.C.'s social worker. The social worker said that despite her efforts to explain, S.C. had had little idea of what was happening throughout the trial and afterwards. She felt that his frequent turning to her, confusion and short attention span gave a misleading impression to the jury that 'he couldn't care less'. His appeal against conviction and sentence was refused. The ECtHR found that there had been a violation of Article 6 ECHR. S.C. had not been able to participate effectively in the trial, despite the efforts to facilitate this. 'Effective participation' in this context, the ECtHR said, presupposed that the accused has a broad understanding of the nature of the trial process and of what is at stake for him or her, including the significance of any penalty which may be imposed. S.C. had little comprehension of the role of the jury or of the importance of making a good impression on them and had not grasped the fact that he was at risk of a custodial sentence. Even after sentence had been passed, the social worker had been unable to get him to understand that he was not going home to his foster father.

The position of child defendants in criminal trials can be contrasted with that of child witnesses. The Youth Justice and Criminal Evidence Act 1999 introduced 'special measures' for vulnerable witnesses in criminal trials (whether in the Youth Court, magistrates court or Crown Court). These may be applied in the case of witnesses under 17 at the time of the hearing. They include using screens behind which the witness can give oral evidence, evidence by live video link or video recording and examination of witness through an intermediary. These do not apply to defendants, whether or not under 17. Perhaps they should. It is easy to imagine that in Case Study B there might be questions about the extent to which Natalie was led or pressured into participating in the offence by the older defendants, and that she might be reluctant to give evidence about this in front of them. A similar situation was considered in **R (S) v Waltham Forest Youth Court and others** [2004] (Box 9.13).

After Natalie's conviction the court would have considered the pre-sentence report prepared by the YOT using ASSET. The YJB's National Standards prescribe standards for detention and training orders. These require the YOT to allocate a supervising officer and to ensure that regular planning and review meetings are held throughout the custodial and community parts of the sentence.

Box 9.13   *R (S) V WALTHAM FOREST YOUTH COURT AND OTHERS*

S, aged 13, was tried and convicted of robbery in the Youth Court, together with three older girls who were co-defendants. The two victims, who were also young girls, gave their evidence by video link following a special measures direction by the judge. It was argued on S' behalf that she too was intimidated by the older girls to the extent that she would not give evidence (which would include evidence against them) in their physical presence. The trial judge held that there was no power either under the Youth Justice and Criminal Evidence Act 1999 or inherent in the court to apply special measures to enable S to give evidence by video link. The Court of Appeal confirmed this and also considered that withholding special measures from a defendant in the position of S would not in itself violate Article 6 ECHR.

Purpose and proportionality

Natalie's sentence had combined aims. It was supposed to help prevent her from further offending but the custodial part also served the purpose of recognising the seriousness of the offence, condemning it, exacting retribution and deterring her and others from similar behaviour in the future.

None of this necessarily creates any conflict with the ECHR. Detention of a child pursuant to a sentence passed by a court will not, without more, constitute a violation of the ECHR: the action can be justified under Article 5 (right to liberty and security) as 'the lawful detention of a person after conviction by a competent court'. Nor will it, without more, constitute a breach of Article 3 (inhuman or degrading treatment). Even the application of reasonable force to maintain order or prevent worse harm to a child would be acceptable, though corporal punishment would not: *Tyrer v UK* **[1978]**. However, the ECtHR has recognised that there may be circumstances where the conditions of detention are such as to amount to a breach of Article 3 or Article 8: ***Lukanov v Bulgaria* [1997]**; ***D.G. v Ireland* [2002]** – if, for example, they had a serious adverse impact on the prisoner's mental or physical health or if they prevented contact with family members and could not be justified as a proportionate response to a security consideration.

Nor is there necessarily any conflict with the standards set by the UNCRC. Article 37 requires measures to promote recovery and social reintegration of a child victim of any form of neglect (which Natalie is, as well as being a young offender). Article 40 requires treatment under the penal law to be directed at promoting her reintegration and helping her assume a constructive role in society. A detention and training order is not in principle in conflict with these provisions, nor is there necessarily any conflict with specific requirements such as familial contact (Article 9.3) and respect for privacy (Article 16). However, the UN Committee has expressed concern at the very young age at which children can be given custodial sentences in the UK and at the conditions of their detention in practice – in particular, their lack of access to education, health and child protection on an equal footing to children not in custody (UN, 2002a para. 48, 62). The ***Howard League*** judgment reinforced the need to improve provision of support for children in custody and this is the target at which the efforts of both the YOT supervising officer and Natalie's local authority social worker, working collaboratively, must be aimed. A failure to deliver in practice services directed at the purpose of effective resettlement may ultimately cast doubt on the proportionality of the measures in relation to their aims.

Another aspect of Case Study B which potentially engages the issue of proportionality is that of Natalie's right to protection of her privacy. We have already noted the special case of juveniles recognised in Article 6 ECHR. Article 16 UNCRC similarly requires protection for children's privacy, 'honour and reputation', and Article 40.2(b)(vii) UNCRC requires a child's privacy to be respected at all stages of criminal proceedings. The Beijing Rules recognise the particular harm to children caused by 'undue publicity and labelling' and lay down the general principle that child defendants should not be identified (Rule 8). In England and Wales, the degree of protection afforded to children in criminal proceedings varies between the different courts (Box 9. 14).

It can be seen that it is only in the Youth Court that automatic restrictions apply, and that these can be lifted. Current government policy is to try to open up Youth Court proceedings to enable the general public to become better aware of what goes on and how young offenders are dealt with. Accordingly, government guidance suggests that lifting restrictions might be particularly appropriate where the nature of a young person's offending is persistent or serious or has impacted on a number of people or his local community in general, or where alerting others to his behaviour would help prevent further offending (Home Office, 2006b).

Box 9.14 RESTRICTIONS ON PUBLICITY ABOUT CHILD DEFENDANTS

	Youth Court	Magistrates court	Crown Court
Attendance	Members and officers of the court, parties, legal representatives, witnesses and other persons directly concerned in the case, bona fide representatives of a news gathering or reporting organisation, such other persons as the court may specially authorise to be present: s. 47 Children and Young Persons Act 1933	Open to the public	Open to the public
Reporting restrictions	Automatic bar on reporting child's name, address, school, or details likely to lead to the child's identification. Applies to child defendants and child witnesses alike. Court has discretion to lift some or all of these restrictions: s. 49 Children and Young Persons Act 1933	None, except as specified by the court in exercise of discretion conferred by s. 45 Youth Justice and Criminal Evidence Act 1999	None, except as specified by the court in exercise of discretion conferred by s. 45 Youth Justice and Criminal Evidence Act 1999

Where no automatic restrictions apply, the courts have held that there would have to be good reason, aside from age alone, to prevent the identification of any child or young person concerned in the proceedings (*R v Lee* [1993] applied by the Divisional Court in *R v Central Criminal Court ex p W, B and C* [2001]). In weighing the balance between the public interest in disclosure and protection of children's rights to privacy, current law and policy both tend to favour disclosure.

This certainly appears at odds with UN standards, which suggest that this degree of exposure of children to adverse publicity is not regarded as justified by the ostensible aim of improving public confidence and deterrence. Once again, the position of the child defendant can be contrasted with that of the child witness. The Youth Justice and Criminal Evidence Act 1999 provides for revised restrictions on the reporting of the identity of young persons involved in criminal proceedings and a new power to restrict reporting in respect of certain adult witnesses. Current law and policy thus protects child witnesses and vulnerable adult witnesses substantially more than child defendants.

Conclusion

The youth justice system has undergone extensive change since 1997, both in the organisation of services and in the formulation of powers available to the courts and other agencies. The Audit Commission's Report, *Youth Justice 2004*, sought to evaluate the impact so far, reflecting back on its 1996 Report, *Misspent Youth*, which had been a major driving force behind the changes. They found some positive developments:

- young offenders were being dealt with earlier and more quickly;
- they were more likely to make amends for their wrong-doing;
- magistrates were on the whole very satisfied with the service given by the YOTs;
- some of the new orders and programmes appeared to be having a positive impact on preventing re-offending;
- the role of the YOT, enabling joint working between criminal justice, health and local government services, was critical to effective performance;

and some less positive:

- public confidence in the system remained low;
- too much time was taken up in court by relatively minor offences;
- there were still too many remands in custody, especially of black and mixed race children;
- there was a greater than ever disproportion between the use of custodial sentences for black and ethnic offenders and other groups;
- there was insufficient focus as yet on the wider needs of offenders and on prevention;
- there was still too little involvement of schools and other mainstream agencies.

Positive appraisal of the role and working of the YOTs suggests that the highly managed and structured approach has gone some way towards addressing some of the difficulties in inter-agency co-operation identified in earlier research (e.g. Ball and Connolly (2000) in relation to education and youth justice professionals). The Youth Justice Board, which itself represents a broad range of expertise from different professions and from the wider community, is promoting greater integration in training and development, for example by means of introducing training in youth justice in the Post Qualifying Framework for Social Work. Successful synthesis in practice of expertise in child welfare and development on the one hand and crime reduction and community safety on the other, ought to result in progress towards the realisation of the dual aims of serving the interests of children and promoting community safety or, to repeat the populist slogan, being both 'tough on crime' and 'tough on the causes of crime'.

Complex as it is, the range of powers and duties now contained in youth justice legislation does supply a rich menu of responses which can be seen in principle to serve both aims, and these should be read together with continuing statutory duties under the Children Act 1989 and initiatives such as Sure Start within the wider social inclusion agenda. However, from the standpoint of the children who are the subject of youth justice interventions, the acid test is in the outcome – the extent to which State intervention empowers and enables them to overcome the multiple disadvantages that exist in many cases and to participate in the social and economic opportunities that are available in society as a whole. A key continuing concern is the way in which children are treated within the system, especially in court and in custody. It is unsurprising that this has been a particular focus for challenges under the ECHR and for criticism by the UN Committee. Social workers, whether working in social services departments, YOTs or in other agencies, applying their professional judgement based on sound knowledge and values, will continue to play a critical part in determining the result, in individual cases, of the acid test of outcomes.

Further Reading

J. Muncie and B. Goldson's *Comparative Youth Justice* (Sage, 2006) provides critique and analysis both of different systems and of global trends in the subject. It provides ample material to explore further some of the underlying policy themes and contradictions which it has been possible to do no more than introduce in this chapter. B. Goldson's *The New Youth Justice* (Russell House Publishing, 2000) remains an excellent, critical introduction to current law policy in England and Wales.

For an internal UK comparison, C. Mcdiarmid's book *Childhood and Crime* (Dundee University Press, 2007) presents insight into the Scottish system of children's hearings. The book also contains thoughtful discussion of the wider issues of developmental capacity, criminal responsibility and the 'justice' and 'welfare' approaches.

Detailed, frequently updated, information about offences, the court process and sentencing in England and Wales can be accessed in *Stone's Justices Manual* (Butterworths) (magistrates and Youth Court), *Blackstones' Criminal Practice* (Oxford University Press) or *Archbold's Criminal Pleadings Evidence and Practice* (Sweet & Maxwell). These are standard references for lawyers practising in criminal law.

END NOTE

Throughout this book it has been emphasised that a rights-based approach to social work practice with children is both a legal and professional requirement. Rights-based thinking is required in order to give effect to the values set out in the NOSCCPQ, the Codes of Practice and the social work Code of Ethics. It helps to refocus attention on children's services users as rights bearers rather than on the services themselves and their organisational context. It helps to promote an approach which is child-centred but which also places the child clearly in a wider community of other rights bearers of all ages, as a citizen in relation to government: as a 'being' rather than a 'becoming'. Based on the assumption of universal entitlement, it necessarily tends to support non-discriminatory practice and to promote a broad notion of equality. It provides an assertive rather than plaintive language in which to advocate on behalf of children denied access to this universal entitlement, and a conceptual system within which conflicts between competing claims and policy objectives can be resolved.

It has been suggested in this book that social workers should acquire legal knowledge to assist them in developing a rights-based approach. Court judgments demonstrate the way in which specific statutory powers and duties bear additional meaning when construed in accordance with the principles set out in the ECHR and UNCRC. Case-law examples have shown how this impacts on the way in which local authorities exercise the discretion given to them by statute, whether in identifying and supporting children in need and their families, in taking compulsory measures to safeguard children, in supporting looked after children or in dealing with children within the criminal justice system. However, it would be wrong to leave matters there, with an impression that social workers must simply become ever-more adept at receiving and applying messages from the courts about human rights compliance. The child care social worker can and should have a much more active role in developing rights-based thinking and practice than that would imply.

It has been seen that social work functions are 'executive' functions within a constitutional democracy. A constitutional separation of governmental powers allocates to the elected legislature the role of law-making and political scrutiny; to the executive, the role of policy development, administration and law enforcement; to the judiciary, the role of conferring lawful authority on enforcement measures in individual cases and of dispute resolution. Section 6 Human Rights Act 1998 gives 'further effect' to the ECHR by requiring both executive and judicial functions to be carried out in a way which is compatible with the Convention rights, subject only to deference to the UK Parliament as supreme law-maker in the British constitution. Section 6 necessitates for both the legal and the social work profession a careful and ongoing examination of the way in which their practice respects and promotes human rights. In doing this both the lawyer and the social worker will be mindful not only of the ECHR but also of other human rights texts, notably the UNCRC, which can be used as an aid to interpretation of the rights of children under the ECHR.

There are two ways of approaching the requirement to act compatibly. These apply both to lawyers and to social workers. The first is a narrow approach which regards human rights obligations as a compulsory adjunct to domestic powers and duties – an additional check to be made having first applied traditional reasoning to a decision.

The second (and preferable) way is to strive to develop a new approach drawing on human rights principles, recognising synergies and disparities with pre-existing traditions. This may result in a conception of individual rights which ranges more widely than the ECHR or any other particular international text – a conception which, whilst compliant with the internationally agreed standards, is developed and owned by the individual State, reflecting its own social and legal characteristics. There is evidence of a tendency towards each of these approaches by the judiciary in England and Wales post-Human Rights Act 1998 (Masterman, 2005). But whatever approach is taken by the judges, they adjudicate upon only a small part of the decision-making that affects children, and hence the need for a pro-active approach by child care social workers.

The majority of decisions concerning children are not taken by judges in court but by adults operating in other spheres. The most obvious is the private sphere of the family which is protected from external scrutiny unless a certain threshold of need or risk is reached. At that point, positive obligations arise, requiring State intervention to support or protect the child. In the course of carrying out those obligations, many administrative decisions fall to be made, very few of which are ever scrutinised by the courts. Decisions made in the course of social work assessment, about provision of services, placement and treatment of looked after children, are all such administrative decisions.

Law provides systems of accountability for these administrative decisions. Some are judicial, involving an application to court: notably judicial review, negligence claims and freestanding human rights claims. Others are administrative, involving an administrative authority such as an audit or inspection body external to the decision-making authority, or involving internal complaints and review systems such as complaints under s. 26 Children Act 1989 and review of looked after children by an independent reviewing officer. There are limits to the reach of any of these systems and in particular there are limits to their ability to effect a change to rights-based thinking and practice.

Judicial mechanisms are limited by a number of factors. First, legislation confers substantial discretion on the local authority as an administrative body and it is well established that the courts will not interfere with decisions made within that discretion but will limit themselves to review of the way in which a decision is made. Second, statutory duties relating to support and provision of services are normally owed not to any individual but to the public at large, and therefore do not readily lend themselves to individual litigation. Third, even where an individual duty is owed (for example to looked after children under s. 22 Children Act 1989), because of the limitations of legislative incorporation the courts have only restricted powers (that is, those set out in the Human Rights Act 1998) to redefine it as a human rights issue in terms of the ECHR and even less power to deal with it as a children's rights issue in terms of the UNCRC. Fourth, there is the issue of accessibility to legal services. This means not just the availability of legal aid but also acknowledging the emotional, mental and physical effort involved in pursuing a claim for people who, because of their personal and social circumstances, may be amongst the least well equipped to sustain it. Fifth, individual claims are often not the best way to seek review of broad policy decisions: even where an individual claim succeeds, there is no guarantee that it will lead to a change in policy.

This last point is equally true of administrative complaints in individual cases. In fact the position is even worse, because not only is there no guarantee that a successful complaint will lead to a change in policy, it may not even lead to redress in the individual case. Audit and inspection may be better mechanisms than individual complaints for examining broad policy decisions, especially those decisions about the allocation and management of resources which are so crucial to implementation of the social and economic rights of children and with which the courts are least likely to interfere. Audit and inspection operate within a statutory remit and measure performance against pre-ordained criteria. In England and Wales these are not as yet couched in terms of fulfilment of children's rights but the Audit Commission has demonstrated the potential for use of general powers of investigation to embrace inquiring into and reporting on the extent to which administrative decision-making properly reflects human rights principles (Audit Commission, 2004). The Children's Commissioners offer a further opportunity to promote rights-based practice and there is evidence of this being put to good use in the early years of operation of all four of the UK's Children's Commissioners, despite the weak formal connection between the English Commissioner and the UNCRC. Common to all these administrative mechanisms, however, is that their decisions and recommendations are not legally enforceable so that their impact is very largely dependent on political will.

Social work decisions, assessments and judgements made in day to day child care practice are based on the values held by the individual practitioner in her professional capacity. The limitations on the reach of judicial and administrative accountability mean that the way in which social workers operationalise their rights-based professional values is in practice of far more significance to far more people than the decisions made either by the courts or in the course of administrative processes for accountability.

It has been suggested here that constant attention to process, purpose and proportionality, combined with a thorough understanding of what the ECHR and UNCRC require, will help keep decision-making compliant with human rights obligations in individual case-work. No doubt the well-trained, qualified child care social worker will acquire the necessary understanding and be able to see how individual case-work can be conducted from a position which puts first the child's entitlement to protection, provision and participation. Yet the social worker will encounter barriers to fulfilment of this aspiration. The barriers may be cultural (for example, a rights-averse 'child view'), structural (for example, organisational or geographical barriers to integrated service delivery) or simply a question of capacity (put crudely, insufficient numbers of people like her to deal with increasing case-loads). Such were amongst the barriers explored by Morris (2000), in discussion with a wide range of participants including looked after children and key service personnel having responsibilities in relation to their care. She concluded that the relationship of social worker and child was critical to the realisation of the children's entitlement within a rights-based perspective, but she also recognised that other matters, in particular the organisation and funding of services and the training and recruitment of staff, were equally important.

In a rights-based perspective, the effective provision of adequate resources is properly to be seen as an aspect of the State's positive obligation to deliver the universal entitlement. It is not one which is likely to be achieved solely by doing individual case-work better. As Masson (2006) has argued, the tendency in major inquiries and reviews to concentrate on failings in individual case-work serves to obscure the underlying policy problems for which responsibility lies at a collective, political level rather than with individual practitioners. The adequate supply and effective direction of resource should properly be seen as UNCRC-compliance issues. The question then arises what mechanism, if any, can be employed to effect the necessary change, given the limitations of the systems for accountability referred to above. The most obvious answer lies in the monitoring and reporting process provided in Article 42 UNCRC itself. This is a legal process in the sense that it is contained in an instrument of international law, but is in practice essentially a political process, in which arguments about policy and about the allocation of resources (directly addressed in Article 4 UNCRC) sit more comfortably than in any judicial process and fall to be determined unequivocally by reference to children's rights. The publication of this book will coincide with the final part of the conflated third and fourth reporting periods for the UK within this process.

The UN process provides an opportunity to promote the changes necessary to fulfil the positive obligations of the State. A key role may be played by those statutory bodies and non-statutory alliances which prepare independent reports for the UN Committee (in practice, in both England and Wales, the Children's Commissioners and alliances of non-governmental organisations). Through their networks these bodies and alliances are able to identify short-falls in provision and to consider aspects of policy and practice which need to change. When they submit their report to the UN Committee, they are com-municating messages to a supra-national body, to which the UK Government must account. Child care social workers can engage with this process, whether as individuals or collectively, contributing their expertise to the task of influ-encing policy development and legislative change. This would be consistent both with professional standards and ethics and also with the self-executing ordinance of s. 6 Human Rights Act 1998. It would accord with the pleas of senior family judiciary, some of which have been referred to in this book, for greater absorption of human rights principles into practice. Accordingly, the last message here is an optimistic and exhortatory one, to commend consider-ation by all practitioners of the potential of the UN process, in conjunction with governmental and non-governmental organisations, to further the devel-opment of rights-based policy and practice at national and sub-national levels of government, as well as in their individual case-work with children and their families.

REFERENCES

AASW (2002) *Australian Association of Social Workers Code of Ethics*, 2nd edition. Available online at www.aasw.asn.au (accessed November 2007).

Addis, R. (2004) 'Professional Perceptions of Twin Track Planning for Looked After Children', *Social Work Monographs*, University of East Anglia.

Alston, P., Parker, S. and Seymour, J. (eds) (1992) *Children, Rights and the Law*. Oxford, Clarendon Press.

ANAS (1994) *Code de Deontologie de l'Association Nationale des Assistants de Service Social*, available on line at www.anasinfo.ifrance.com/code.doc (accessed November 2007).

Audit Commission (1996) *Misspent Youth*. London, The Audit Commission.

Audit Commission (2003) *Human Rights, Improving Public Service Delivery*. London, The Audit Commission.

Audit Commission (2004) *Youth Justice (2004) A Review of the Reformed Youth Justice System*. London, The Audit Commission.

Ball, C. (2004) 'Youth Justice? Half a Century of Responses to Youth Offending', *Criminal Law Review*, pp. 167–80.

Ball, C. and Connolly, J. (2000) 'Educationally Disaffected Young Offenders: Youth Court and Agency Responses to Truancy and School Exclusion', *British Journal of Criminology*, pp. 594–616.

BASW (2003) *Code of Ethics for Social Work*. British Association of Social Workers, Birmingham, Venture Press.

Beckett, C. and McKeigue, B. (2003) 'Children in Limbo: Cases Where Care Proceedings Have Taken 2 Years or More', *Adoption and Fostering*, 27 (3), pp. 31–40.

Beijing Rules (1985) *United Nations Standard Minimum Rules for the Administration of Juvenile Justice*, adopted by General Assembly resolution 40/33 of 29 November 1985.

Bichard, M. (Lord) (2004) *The Bichard Inquiry Report*. HC 653. London HMSO.

Brophy, J. (2006) *Care Proceedings under the Children Act 1989: A Research Review*. London, Department for Constitutional Affairs.

Care Council for Wales (2002) *Code of Practice for Social Care Workers*. Cardiff, Care Council for Wales.

CCfW (2003) *Telling Concerns: Report of the Children's Commissioner for Wales' Review of the operation of Complaints and Representations and Whistleblowing procedures and arrangements for the provision of Children's Advocacy Services*. Swansea/Colwyn Bay, Children's Commissioner for Wales.

CCfW (2004) *Clywch: Report of the Examination of the Children's Commissioner for Wales into Allegations of Sexual Abuse in a School Setting*. Swansea/Colwyn Bay, Children's Commissioner for Wales.

CCfW (2006) *Annual Report of the Children's Commissioner for Wales, 2005–6*. Swansea/Colwyn Bay, Children's Commissioner for Wales.

Cobley, C. (2004) 'Working Together? Admissions of Abuse in Child Protection

Proceedings and Criminal Prosecutions', *Child and Family Law Quarterly*, 16, pp. 175.

Council of Europe 1998: *European Strategy for Children*. Recommendation 1286/1996, formally adopted by the Council of Ministers on 15 December 1998.

CPS (2004) *Code for Crown Prosecutors*. London, Crown Prosecution Service.

Curtis Report (1946) *Report of the Care of Children Committee*. London, HMSO.

DCA (2006) *Legal Aid Reform: The Way Ahead*. London, Department for Constitutional Affairs.

Defra (2000) *Preparing Community Strategies: Guidance to Local Authorities*. London, Department for Environment, Food and Rural Affairs.

DfES (1998). *Quality Protects*. London, Department for Education and Skills.

DfES (2004) *The Finch Report on Delay in Public Law Children Act Proceedings*. London, Department for Education and Skills.

DfES (2005) *Every Child Matters: Change for Children, An Overview of Cross Government Guidance*. London, Department for Education and Skills.

DfES (2006a) *Every Child Matters: Change for Children, Practitioner's Guide to Information Sharing*. London, Department for Education and Skills.

DfES (2006b) *The Common Assessment Framework, A Practitioner's Guide*. London, Department for Education and Skills.

DfES/DCA/WAG 2006: *Review of the Child Care Proceedings System in England and Wales*. London, Department for Education and Skills, Department for Constitutional Affairs, Cardiff, Welsh Assembly Government.

DfES (2005)/WAG (2006) *National Minimum Standards for Private Fostering*. London, Department for Education and Skills; Cardiff, Welsh Assembly Government.

DfES (2006)/WAG (2006) *Working Together to Safeguard Children: A Guide to Inter-agency Working Together to Safeguard and Promote the Welfare of Children*. London, Department for Education and Skills; Cardiff, Welsh Assembly Government.

DoH (1991) *The Children Act (1989) Guidance and Regulations, Vol. 2: Family Support, Day Care and Educational Provision for Young Children*. London, The Stationery Office.

DoH (1995) *Child Protection, Messages from Research*. London, Department of Health.

DoH (2000) *Adoption, A New Approach*. Cm 5017. London Department of Health.

DoH (2003) *Confidentiality: NHS Code of Practice (England)*. London, Department of Health.

DoH (2006) *Bearing Good Witness – Proposals for Reforming the Delivery of Medical Expert Evidence in Family Law Cases. A Report by the Chief Medical Officer*. London, Department of Health.

DoH (2000)/NAW (2001) *Framework for the Assessment of Children in Need and Their Families*. London, Department of Health; Cardiff, National Assembly for Wales.

Dickens, J. (2004) 'Risks and Responsibilities – The Role of the Local Authority Lawyer in Child Care Cases', *Child and Family Law Quarterly*, 16, pp. 17–30.

DWP (2006) *Working Together: United Kingdom National Action Plan on Social Inclusion 2006–08*. London, Department for Work and Pensions.

Eddon, G. (2007) 'Special Guardianship – Imaginative Use?', *Family Law*, pp. 169–70.

EU (1976) Council Directive 1976/207/EEC.

EU (1995) EC Directive 95/46/EC on the protection of individuals with regard to the processing of personal data and on the free movement of such data.

EU (2000a) Council Directive 2000/78/EC.

EU (2000b) Council Directive 2000/43/EC.

Eekelaar, J. (2002) 'Beyond the Welfare Principle', *Child and Family Law Quarterly*, 14, p. 237.

Evans, R. and Puech, K. (2001) 'Reprimands and Warnings: Populist Punitiveness or Restorative Justice?', *Criminal Law Review*, pp. 794–805.

FJC (2005) *Mapping an Inclusive Curriculum for Continuing Professional Development of Family Justice Professionals.* Family Justice Council. Available online at www.family-justice-council.org.uk/paper–continuing–profdev.htm (accessed November 2007).

FJC (2006) Terms of reference of the Family Justice Council. Available online at www.family-justice-council.org.uk/ourwork.htm (accessed November 2007).

FJC (2007) *Linked Care and Placement Order Proceedings.* Family Justice Council, London, 1 January 2007.

Fortin, J. (2003) *Children's Rights and the Developing Law*, 2nd edition. London, LexisNexis Butterworths.

Fortin, J. (2006) 'Accommodating Children's Rights in a Post-Human Rights Act Era', *Modern Law Review*, 69, 299.

General Social Care Council (2002) *Code of Practice for Social Care Workers.* London, GSCC.

Goldson, B. (ed.) (2000) *The New Youth Justice.* Lyme Regis, Russell House Publishing.

Hart, D. (2006) *Tell Them Not to Forget about Us. A Guide to Practice with Looked After Children in Custody.* London, National Children's Bureau.

Hayes, M. (2004) 'Uncertain Evidence and Risk Taking in Child Protection Cases', *Child and Family Law Quarterly*, 16, 63–86.

Hendrick, H. (2003) *Child Welfare. Historical Dimensions, Contemporary Debate.* Bristol, Policy Press.

Henricson, C. and Bainham, A. (2005) *The Child and Family Policy Divide.* York, Joseph Rowntree Foundation.

HMCS (2003) *Protocol for Judicial Case Management in Public Law Children Act Cases.* Her Majesty's Courts Service. Available online at www.hmcourts-service.gov.uk/docs/protocol-complete.pdf (accessed November 2007).

HM Treasury (2003) *Every Child Matters.* Cm 5860. London, The Stationery Office.

HM Treasury (2004) *Child Poverty Review.* London, The Stationery Office.

Home Office (1997) *No More Excuses. A New Approach to Tackling Youth Crime in England and Wales.* Cm 3809. London, The Stationery Office.

Home Office (2002) *Updated Drug Strategy.* London, Home Office.

Home Office (2003) *Respect and Responsibility – Taking a Stand Against Anti-Social Behaviour.* Cm 5778. London, The Stationery Office.

Home Office (2006a) *Respect Action Plan.* London Respect Task Force/Home Office.

Home Office (2006b) *A Guide to Anti-Social Behaviour Orders.* London, The Home Office.

Hudson, B., Hardy, B., Henwood, M. and Wistow, G. (1999) 'In Pursuit of Inter-agency Collaboration – What Is the Contribution of Theory and Research?', *Public Management: An International Journal of Research and Theory*, 1 (2): 235–60.

Hunt, J. (2001) *Family and Friends Carers: A Scoping Paper prepared for the Department of Health.* November 2001, London, Department of Health.

James, A., James, A. and Macnamee, S. (2004) 'Turn Down the Volume? – Not Hearing the Children in Family Proceedings', *Child and Family Law Quarterly*, 16, pp. 189–202.

James, A., Jenks, C. and Prout, A. (1998) *Theorizing Childhood.* Cambridge, Polity Press.

Jordan, Bill (2004) 'Emancipatory Social Work? Opportunity or Oxymoron', *British Journal of Social Work*, 34, pp. 5–19.

JRT (2005) *Thematic Review of the Protocol for Judicial Case Management in Public Law Children Act Proceedings.* London, Judicial Review Team. Available online at www.judiciary.gov.uk/docs/judicial_reform_team_final_report_141205.pdf (accessed November 2007).

King, M. and Piper, C. (1995) *How the Law Thinks About Children*, 2nd edn. Aldershot: Arena.

Labour Party (1995) *A Quiet Life: Tough Action on Criminal Neighbours*. London, The Labour Party.

Labour Party (1996) *Tackling Youth Crime, Reforming Youth Justice: A Consultation Paper on an Agenda for Change*. London, The Labour Party.

Laming (Lord) (2003) *The Victoria Climbié Inquiry: Report of an Inquiry by Lord Laming*. Cm. 5730. London, The Stationery Office.

LCD (1996) *Delay in Public Law Children Act Proceedings* (by Dame Margaret Booth). London, Lord Chancellor's Department.

LCD (2002a) *Promoting Inter-Agency Working in the Family Justice System: A Consultation Paper*. London, Lord Chancellor's Department.

LCD (2002b) *Scoping Study on Delay in Children Act Cases, Findings and Actions Taken*. London, Lord Chancellor's Department.

LCD (2002c) *The Report of the Working Party to Consider Delay in Family Proceedings Courts under the Children Act 1989*. London, Lord Chancellor's Department.

Levitas, R., Pantazis, C., Fahmy, E., Gordon, D., Lloyd, E. and Patsios, D. (2007) *The Multi-Dimensional Analysis of Social Exclusion*. London, Cabinet Office.

Macdonald, A. (2007) 'Legal Aid Reform – Beyond "No More Money"', *Family Law*, pp. 130–34.

Macdonald, S. and Telford, M. (2007) 'The Use of ASBOs against Young People in England and Wales: Lessons from Scotland', *Legal Studies*, pp. 604–29.

Marshall, K. (1997) *Children's Rights in the Balance: The Participation–Protection Debate*. Edinburgh, The Stationery Office.

Masson, J. (2006) 'The Climbié Inquiry – Context and Critique', *Journal of Law and Society*, 33 (2), pp. 221–43.

Masson, J. and Winn Oakley, M. (1999) *Out of Hearing*. Chichester, Wiley.

Masterman, R. (2005) 'Taking the Strasbourg Jurisprudence into Account: Developing a "Municipal Law of Human Rights" under the Human Rights Act', *International and Comparative Law Quarterly*, 54, pp. 907–32.

Millar, M. and Corby, B. (2006) 'The *Framework for the Assessment of Children in Need and Their Families* – A basis for a Therapeutic Encounter?', *British Journal of Social Work*, 36 (3), 887–99.

Mnookin, R. 1975: 'Child Custody Adjudication: Judicial Functions in the Face of Indeterminacy', *Law and Contemporary Problems*, 39, p. 236.

Morris, J. (2000) *'Having Someone Who Cares?' Barriers to Change in the Social Care System*. Joseph Rowntree Foundation National Children's Bureau.

Munby J (2004) '"Making Sure the Child Is Heard": Part 2 – Representation', *Family Law*, pp. 427–35.

Murphy, J. (2004) 'Children in Need: the Limits of Local Authority Accountability' *Legal Studies*, 23, pp. 103–34.

NAW, (2000) *Tackling Substance Misuse in Wales: A Partnership Approach*. Cardiff, National Assembly for Wales.

NAW (2001) *Preparing Community Strategies: Guidance to Local Authorities from the National Assembly for Wales*. Cardiff, National Assembly for Wales.

NAW (2002) *Too Serious a Thing: The Review of Safeguards for Children and Young People Treated and Cared for by the NHS in Wales*. Cardiff, National Assembly for Wales.

NE Lincs (2004) North East Lincolnshire Serious Case Review, Ian Huntley, 2004. Available online at www.nelincs.gov.uk/socialcare/childprotection/serious-case-review.htm (accessed November 2007).

Ofsted (2005a) *Every Child Matters: The Framework for the Inspection of Children's Services*. London. Ofsted.

Ofsted (2005b) *Every Child Matters: Joint Area Reviews of Children's Services*. London, Ofsted.

O'Halloran, K. (1999) *The Welfare of the Child: The Principle and the Law*. Aldershot, Ashgate.

Palmer, E. (2003) 'Courts, Resources and the HRA: Reading section 17 of the Children Act 1989 Compatibly with Article 8 ECHR', *European Human Right Law Review*, 3, pp. 308–24.

Parry, R. Gwyned. (2006) 'Protecting the Juvenile Suspect: What Exactly is the Appropriate Adult Supposed to Do?', *Child and Family Law Quarterly*, 18, pp. 373–96.

Reichert, E. (2003) *Social Work and Human Rights*. New York, Columbia University Press.

Robinson, A. (2004) *Evaluation of Multi-Agency Risk Assessment Conferences for Very High Risk Victims*. Cardiff, Women's Safety Unit.

Ruegger, M. (2001) *Hearing the Voice of the Child: The Representation of Children's Interests in Public Law Proceedings*. Lyme Regis, Russell House Publishing.

Sector Skills Council (2005) *National Occupational Standards for Child Care at Post Qualifying Level*. Sector Skills Council, Skills for Care and Development (also available from the Care Council for Wales and Skills for Care, England).

Spicer, D. (2006) 'Whose Care Plan Is it Anyway?', in *Durable Solutions: The Collected Papers of the Dartington Hall Conference (2005)*. Bristol, Jordan Publishing.

SSIW, WAO (2005) *Joint Review in Wales*. Wales Audit Office and Social Services Inspectorate for Wales.

Statham, J., Cameron, C., Jones, E. and Rivers, K. (2004) *Getting Help: A Survey of Reception and Initial Contact Arrangements in Social Services Departments*. London, Thomas Coram Research Institute.

Stuart, M. and Baines, C. (2004) *Progress on Safeguards for Children Living Away from Home. A Review of Actions since the People Like Us Report*. York, Joseph Rowntree Foundation.

TSO (1996) *Childhood Matters: Report of the National Commission of Inquiry into the Prevention of Child Abuse: Volume 1: The Report*. London: The Stationery Office.

TSO (1997) *People Like Us: Report of the Review of Safeguards for Children Living Away from Home* (by Sir William Utting). London, The Stationery Office.

TSO (1998a) *Tackling Drugs to Build a Better Britain*. Cm. 3945. London, The Stationery Office.

TSO (1998b) *Modernising Social Services: Promoting Independence, Improving Protection, Raising Standards*. Cm 4169. London, The Stationery Office.

TSO (2000) *Lost in Care: The Report of the Tribunal of Inquiry into the Abuse of Children in Care in the Former County Council Areas of Gwynedd and Clwyd since 1974*. HC 201, 2000. London, The Stationery Office.

TSO (2003) *Safety and Justice: The Government's Proposals on Domestic Violence*. Cm. 5847. London, The Stationery Office.

UN (1986) *Declaration on Social and Legal Principles relating to the Protection and Welfare of Children with Special Reference to Foster Placement and Adoption Nationally and Internationally*. New York, United Nations.

UN (1995a) *Report of Day of Discussion on Juvenile Justice*, 13 November 1995. Geneva, UN Committee on the Rights of the Child.

UN (1995b) *Concluding Observations of the UN Committee on the Rights of the Child on the UK's Initial Report*. CRC/15/Add. 34. Geneva, United Nations Committee on the Rights of the Child.

UN (2002a) *Concluding Observations on the UK's Second Periodic Report*. CRC/15/Add. 188. Geneva, United Nations Committee on the Rights of the Child.

REFERENCES

UN (2002b) *General Comment on the Role of National Human Rights Institutions.* CRC/GC/2002/2. Geneva, UN Committee on the Rights of the Child.

UN (2003a) *General Comment on General Measures of Implementation.* CRC/GC/2003/5. Geneva, UN Committee on the Rights of the Child.

UN (2003b) *General Comment on Adolescent Health and Development.* CRC/GC/2003/4. Geneva, UN Committee on the Rights of the Child.

UN (2005) *General Comment on Treatment of Unaccompanied and Separated Children Outside their Country of Origin.* CRC/GC/2005/6. Geneva, UN Committee on the Rights of the Child.

UN (2006) *General Comment on Implementing Rights in Early Childhood.* CRC/C/GC/7/Rev 1. Geneva, UN Committee on the Rights of the Child.

UN (2007) *General Comment on Juvenile Justice.* CRC/C/GC/10. Geneva, UN Committee on the Rights of the Child.

WAG (2004a) *Rights to Action.* Cardiff, Welsh Assembly Government.

WAG (2004b) *A Fair Future for Our Children. The Strategy of the Welsh Assembly for Tackling Child Poverty.* Welsh Assembly Government, 2004.

WAG (2005a) *Statutory Guidance on Making Arrangements under Section 28 Children Act 2004.* Cardiff, Welsh Assembly Government.

WAG (2005b) *Tackling Domestic Abuse: The All Wales Domestic Violence Strategy.* Cardiff, Welsh Assembly Government.

WAG, (2005c) *Confidentiality: Code of Practice for Health and Social Care in Wales.* Cardiff, Welsh Assembly Government.

WAG (2006a) *The Wales Accord on the Sharing of Personal Information for People Involved in the Health and Social Well Being of People in Wales.* Cardiff, Welsh Assembly Government.

WAG (2006b) *Towards a Stable Life and a Brighter Future.* Cardiff, Welsh Assembly Government.

WAG (2007) Common Assessment Framework in Wales. Available online at www.cafwales.co.uk.

WAG/YJB (2004) *All Wales Youth Offending Strategy.* Cardiff, Welsh Assembly Government and Youth Justice Board for England and Wales.

Ward, H., Munro, E., Dearden, C. and Nicholson, D. (2003) *Outcomes for Looked After Children: Life Pathways and Decision Taking for Very Young Children in Care or Accommodation – a Study of 242 Children Looked After by Six Local Authorities between 1996–1997.* Loughborough University, Centre for Child and Family Research.

Welsh Office (1999) *The Children First Programme: Transforming Children's Services in Wales.* Welsh Office Circular 20/99.

WEU (2004) *The Cost of Domestic Violence,* report by Sylvia Walby for the Women and Equality Unit. London, Department for Trade and Industry.

Williams, Jane (2007) 'Incorporating Children's Rights: the Divergence in Law and Policy', *Legal Studies,* 27, pp. 261–87.

Williams, John (2004) 'Social Work, Liberty and Law', *British Journal of Social Work,* 34, pp. 37–52.

Wylie, Tom (2004) 'How Connexions Came to Terms with Youth Work', *Youth and Policy.* Leicester, National Youth Agency.

YJB (2003) *Application of the Children Act (1989) to Children in Young Offender Institutions.* Report by the Association of Directors of Social Services, Local Government Association and the Youth Justice Board, September 2003. Available online at www.yjb.gov.uk.

YJB (2006) *The Common Assessment Framework, Asset and Onset. Guidance for Youth Justice Practitioners.* Youth Justice Board (England only; separate Welsh guidance pending at time of writing).

INDEX